Teaching Low-Achieving Children
Reading, Spelling and Handwriting

Teaching
LOW-ACHIEVING CHILDREN
Reading, Spelling and Handwriting

DEVELOPING PERCEPTUAL SKILLS WITH THE GRAPHIC SYMBOLS OF LANGUAGE

By

ANNABELLE MOST MARKOFF, Ph.D.

Department of Special Education
San Francisco State University
San Francisco, California

CHARLES C THOMAS · PUBLISHER
Springfield · Illinois · U.S.A.

Published and Distributed Throughout the World by
CHARLES C THOMAS • PUBLISHER
Bannerstone House
301-327 East Lawrence Avenue, Springfield, Illinois, U.S.A.

With THOMAS BOOKS *careful attention is given to all details of
manufacturing and design. It is Publisher's desire to present books
that are satisfactory as to their physical qualities and artistic possibilities
and appropriate for their particular use.* THOMAS BOOKS *will be true
to those laws of quality that assure a good name and good will.*

Printed in the United States of America
W-11

Library of Congress Cataloging in Publication Data

Markoff, Annabelle Most.
    Teaching low-achieving children reading, spelling,
and handwriting.

    Bibliography: p.
    Includes index.
    1. Lnaguage arts.   2.   Slow learning children.
I.   Title.
LB1575.8.M37   371.9'26   75-17727
ISBN 0-398-03483-4

for Mortimer, John, Ellen and Joan

PREFACE

THIS VOLUME STARTED as a series of teaching suggestions—one or two pages in length—which were written for students at San Francisco State University in the Counseling and Special Education Departments and for use in consultation and in-service education with both special education and regular classroom teachers. While the suggestions proved valuable to those using them, there was no organization to the information provided and no rationale for their use. The book was written to explain in greater detail why some of the suggestions being made might be successful strategies with low-achieving children and to amplify the information provided for the teacher. The intent was not another "how to do it" book, but a discussion of some research findings in the areas of reading, spelling and handwriting, some theoretical background and, finally, a summary which included specific suggestions. The idea was to discuss the curriculum areas in a manner that would free the teacher from dependence on the "methods" approach to teaching. The book represents an attempt to foster a more analytical and independent role for teachers working with children whose academic achievement depends, in large measure, on the teacher's skill in matching need to appropriate teaching strategy.

The basic research reading and the first draft were completed in the summer of 1973 and the chapters used with the students in the curriculum classes working for master's degrees in the various areas of Special Education. The final drafts were completed in the summer and fall of 1974.

The comments, criticisms and suggestions of the students were extremely gratifying and helpful as they read the chapters and experimented with the teaching suggestions. I wish to express gratitude also to Gail Marshall who typed the preliminary draft and to Lois Robinson who drew many of the illustrations.

Two teachers, Mary Bulf and Nancy Kostyshak, read and criticized several chapters and took time to discuss their comments with me. Steven Most read the manuscript and provided very specific criticism and helpful suggestions on the form of several chapters. The final draft was read and typed by Thirza Hibner and her attention to the many details involved and the suggestions she made were invaluable. Bonnie Wilkins provided some of the illustrations in the final draft and her skill and speed were greatly appreciated. Finally, to my husband and children, who patiently listened to the typewriter for many, many hours without complaint, I express my deepest gratitude.

ANNABELLE M. MARKOFF

INTRODUCTION

T HIS BOOK WAS written to provide a rationale for shifting the emphasis in perceptual training from the predominant use of geometric form to consistent use of the basic language forms, sounds, letters and words. It was also written to suggest some teaching techniques for use with low-achieving children when teaching reading, spelling and handwriting. It is intended to reduce the amount of "ditto sheet" teaching which is current practice in the education of this group, and to provide a means for integrated perceptual training in the teaching of the subjects themselves.

The results of the research in perceptual motor training demonstrate very confused relationships between the training usually given and reading improvement (Keogh, 1974). There is no doubt that a relationship between reading skill and visual perceptual skill exists. We know from analyzing the errors children make in all areas of graphic language function that children do indeed demonstrate visual perceptual difficulties. But visual errors are not the only relevant ones in reading performance, at least in initial reading experiences. Auditory perceptual skill and general verbal competence are also required. These should be viewed in relationship to each other as well as in the developmental sequence in which general language skill is acquired when training programs are designed and when research is conducted. The research results may be confused in part because reading is usually not regarded in proper perspective in the total communication process or in the developmental sequence in which language is acquired and reading occurs.

One of the problems may rest in the fact that much of the research and training reported in the literature is based on the work of Kephart (1960, Frostig, 1964, and Kirk (ITPA), 1968), the theoretical leaders of the 1960's, whose ideas provided the base for interventions which were spurred by governmental interest in the education of various low-achieving groups. These theoreticians suggested direct relationships between gross-motor training, sensory-motor training involving object manipulation, geometric-form discrimination and academic success. The ITPA, a language test widely used to design teaching programs, is based on highly abstracted and complex processes of language function. All assumed generalization and transfer of the training suggested to successful school performance.

Kephart and Frostig were probably correct in their developmental approach, but overemphasized the directness of relationships between generalized gross-motor and sensory-motor training and its possible effect on academic performance. This occurred in part because they ignored the very direct relationship between language function and school success.

Kirk, on the other hand, did relate language function to academic success, but ignored the developmental relationships in language acquisition and language function. Much of the teaching generated by these approaches tends to be disassociated. Children are trained on a wide variety of skills presumed to be supportive, but which are not directly and developmentally related to the learning tasks at hand. The low-achieving group has a greater, not lesser, need for integrated and meaningful learning experience, and this basic educational fact seems to be ignored in the enthusiasm for training skills.

The suggestions made here favor a direct analysis of the errors made by children in a developemntal appraisal of language fucntion. Verbal language skill should be observed first, including a perceptual analysis at this level, and then an appraisal of the child's perceptual skill with graphic language symbols should follow. The analysis should be made using samples of the child's actual performance rather than depending solely on clinical and abstract tests. When training is provided, it should involve the exact symbols and processes of the various forms of communication skills, no matter what other supportive teaching in the Kephart or Frostig frame of reference is provided, and the personal interest of the child should always be considered. The teacher must know a great deal about developing perceptual skills, but skill training should never be the child's total educational program. While this book focuses on skill training, it attempts to relate that training directly to the subjects being taught. It does not cover in any depth the need for balance between skill training and personally meaningful learning. This is equally important and every child who is having learning problems should receive this teaching attention. Motivation is always a factor in learning and may be even more important for the low achiever because of the depressing effect of repeated failure.

The present emphasis on education by ditto master is reducing the time available for experience-based learning. While teaching materials which are carefully sequenced in infinitely minute steps are invaluable in the teaching of the low achiever, it is their use as a total education program which is ultimately limiting. This book attempts to provide explicit training procedures within the framework of the subject matter of the language arts, rather than attempting to rely on transfer of skills from the training of general form perception. This should make available more time for individualized social studies, science or personal interest projects which offer a medium for the integration of perceptual and conceptual learning.

The title of the book, *Teaching Low -Achieving Children,* was selected in response to another practice which is common in American education and has not proved beneficial for children. When special teaching is provided for children who are encountering learning difficulties in school, the children are first labeled "inadequate" by the descriptive terms applied to their needs and then they are given help. This practice can only further limit the child's ability to learn. When children are called "disabled," retarded, "disadvantaged" or "handicapped," an inadequate and negative connotation is implied and the children are always stigmatized by such appellations. These labels are not seen by the children themselves as designations involving honors. The inadequacy is always seen as inherent in the child. The intent in the use of the term "low-achieving" is not to deny possible or actual deficits in children, but to reduce the burden of stigma which the categorization usually places on a group least able to defend against its results. It also allows for the possibility that the child may not be essentially inadequate but that his education may have been. If there is a deficit, it may well reside in the teaching-learning process to which the child has been exposed and in the environmental limitations where it occurred. If, as has been suggested in theory, perceptual skills are basic to learning and are in themselves learned, then teachers should know something about how to teach them.

Each of the four chapters in the book deals with developing the perceptual skills required to function in the area under discussion. In the chapter on teaching reading, six areas of teaching concern are discussed. The main point being made is that all six must be considered by the teacher when a child fails to learn to read. Because so much of the teaching practice for low-achieving children has been influenced by the decoding-comprehension dichotomy emanating from linguistic theory, many children are being subjected to very meagre and limited reading experiences. Teaching decoding as a first step may well raise test scores, but it will not turn children into readers if that is the total reading program.

The six areas discussed are perceptual skill, decoding, vocabulary development, comprehension, fluency and motivation. Each requires observation of individual differences in the children who are not learning and decisions about what and how to teach are based on the observations. An emphasis is placed on the experience story as a means of relating verbal and graphic language and to provide a vehicle for making reading meaningful and interesting to children. Its use is not limited to "creative writing" but is exploited as a means of motivation, integration and the possible teaching of the structural elements in verbal language.

In the chapter on teaching spelling, very specific guides are given on how to observe and interpret errors that children make and suggested teaching methods are related to the most common error patterns. Word knowledge, which has been related to proficient spelling, is elaborated so that it can be deliberately taught. Word knowledge is divided into subareas and each is discussed in turn. These are word selection, word meaning, word structure, word perception, word production and learning management. In the *15 Suggestions in Teaching Spelling* which serves as the conclusion to the chapter, teachers are given a guide for covering all of the aspects discussed in the chapter, and the section entitled Teaching Spelling in Groups provides some suggestions on how to manage the teaching when groups of children are involved.

The *Reading-Spelling Inversion* was written to explain the perceptual relationships between reading and spelling and to discuss some of the processes used; an effort is made to relate this to perceptual theory. The chapter closes with a discussion of the relationship between reading and spelling and verbal language. Developmental relationships are emphasized and a great deal of stress is placed on the necessity of observing listening and verbal skills when teaching either reading or spelling. While some children may rely predominantly on visual skill, others do not; teachers can pick up cues through children's mistakes and relate teaching to these.

The chapter on handwriting sets forth very clear procedures for visual motor training using the letters of the alphabet. If, as theory suggests, the letters of the alphabet are the basic form to be discriminated in graphic language, then some attention should be paid to this task when children have difficulty in naming or writing the letters or associating them with sounds. Teaching letter-form discrimination explicitly is certainly not common practice at this time. Training procedures outlined in this chapter are suggested for early learning but are suitable for remedial or compensatory education as well. Many other issues related to the teaching of handwriting are discussed so that teachers will have information on which to design teaching programs.

None of the chapters are intended as absolute teaching methods but rather as discussions of the variables, approaches, techniques or strategies which can be used when children fail to learn to read, spell or write.

CONTENTS

Teaching Low-Achieving Children
Reading, Spelling and Handwriting

CHAPTER 1

THE READING-SPELLING
INVERSION

READING AND SPELLING are usually considered by teachers as separate activities in a language arts program. They recognize commonalities in the use of identical symbols but usually do not consider the processes and how they may be related or the skills which they require in the children. Understanding the relationships can explain a puzzling pattern which is common in almost every classroom: the good-reader/poor-speller syndrome. It could also help in understanding some ignored factors basic to successful reading.

While understanding these processes will be of assistance in the teaching of all children, for the low achievers—those who neither read nor spell well—it is essential because of the critical role the teacher plays in adapting instruction to meet their needs and create their successes. In fact, if those teachers who introduce reading and spelling to children in the primary grades were given some inkling about the perceptual demands of the processes, more individualization could occur early and many a good reader in later years might not need to proclaim with dubious pride his inadequacy in spelling as if it were a lesser accomplishment. Reading itself would be viewed from a different perspective, and its relation to verbal language would be clarified. The value of teaching "phonics" would be explained and justified, and the number of nonreaders might be reduced.

Reading and spelling are inverse processes. While the symbols are the same, they demand different perceptual approaches, one visual, the other auditory. As schools usually teach reading first, this will be the first process discussed. Interestingly enough, even though reading is taught first and spelling second, both rely on graphic symbols and similar verbal skills are extraordinarily important to initial success in either subject. Most teachers assume that these skills function equally in all children and are not directly related in their minds to teaching reading and spelling. As this chapter unfolds, these relationships will be explored.

The Reading Process

When a child reads, he translates a message from visual cues which are external; that is, letters and words on a page. He has no control over the symbols, their arrangement or the content of the message. The message in the text is from someone else who is not present. In silent reading he translates the visual information to verbal language and the process involves self-communication.

When the child reads orally, he utilizes the same processes but an external response is added; spoken words and communication becomes dual, for himself and others. The child is the medium in receiving or transmitting another person's message.

In the beginning the whole process is usually slow because the child may not remember all of the whole words or read from context—he must "sound out" many words. He is identifying and associating the elements of the reading process and a good deal of his time is spent in learning words and becoming familiar with the rules by which letters combine. The message or meaning in reading frequently is pushed aside in the mechanical aspects of "decoding." Once this initial period is past, teaching shifts its emphasis to the cognitive process of generalization, inference and interpretation and the larger ideas of the message become the main reading objective.

For the reader the objective is always meaning and comprehension. People read only to get the message or content. For the teacher of reading the objectives are frequently more diversified, especially for teaching the low-achieving child. While the end-point objectives and goals involve comprehension, the enroute objectives may be concerned with the detailed skills of the process. The teacher herself must have an overview so that inadvertently her enroute objectives do not become a total program and limit the children.

If the child falters at the beginning, the teacher must be able to observe perceptual-cognitive function and make an approximate match to the structure of instruction. While our knowledge of what is critical to be determined in curriculum structure— teacher behavior and child performance and their relationships— is still relatively primitive, attempting to make the match will be better for the children than the current practice of labeling them inadequate and systematically reinforcing that condition. If the teacher knows something about teaching the mechanics of reading, more time will be available for getting information and reading for pleasure.

The Spelling Process

Spelling is a skill involved in recording thoughts and messages. Because of the writing involved, spelling is not usually thought of as a response to an auditory-visual cue. Most often, the cue is not overt or spoken and heard (except in a spelling test or in dictation or if the child whispers or subvocalizes) but occurs in internal language or thinking. Spelling reqiures the recognition of the auditory cue and the recall and writing of graphic symbols.

When a child spells, he says the word to himself and writes what he hears in order. He must be able to think of the sounds individually and order them in the word and then recall the letters and their order and direct the motor activities of the writing. These are the mechanical skills, the parallels to decoding in reading. Three skills, at least, must be operative: (1) *auditory sequencing* or hearing sounds in order included in this skill is auditory memory and discrimination of sound, (2) *visual memory* or recalling letter form, including discrimination of detail, orientation, expected sequence and size; and (3) *visual motor integration*—the use of the eye and the hand. All this becomes automatic with fluency, and the child probably responds to cues from auditory, visual and motor patterns rather than details; his attention is focused on meaning and intent to record or communicate.

As a content subject, demands in spelling involve single words, uniquely differentiating it from reading. This is the case in spelling tests, which is the way spelling proficiency is measured. When the child writes in other school activities—such as reports, letters or creative writing—he must also maintain the total thought or sequence of thoughts, include punctuation, know grammatical structure, and use language creatively to express meaning. This kind of spontaneous spelling is closer to the total reading process. Spelling is constrained by the rules which govern the combination of letters in a word as well as by the auditory sequence or phonemic rules.

Horn (1969) makes the point that teaching the meaning of words in spelling is not necessary; the child knows what he wants to record. Instead, the problems lie in the encoding process of spelling. It is true that the child may know the meaning if he is spelling spontaneously, but if he is working from a spelling book this cannot be taken for granted. With words like *to, two,* and *too,* and *hear* and *here,* only meaning within context will provide the information for choosing correct form.

The spelling process can be viewed as having similar characteristics to the two-step process Carroll (1964) hypothesizes for reading: decoding and comprehension. In the case of spelling, encoding takes the place of the decoding step in reading. The research literature always notes strong correlations between "word knowledge" and spelling proficiency. While word knowledge will be explored extensively in the chapter on spelling, at this point two very important factors can be stressed. One is the fact that the word must be familiar and, especially if the spelling pattern deviates from the sound sequence, it must have been seen. Secondly, the speller should know what it means. Correct spelling of the word is dependent on both factors. For the low-achieving child, where memory, attention and motivation may not be sufficient, quite a few exposures and definitions may be necessary and then may still be insufficient without the use of other support strategies.

The communication process differs from that in reading; the speller is the communicator, initiating the message, and the organization of meaning in the message must be maintained as the speller functions. The problem is not just one of encoding, but of coordinating two very separate functions, a two-step cognitive one (the intraword and general meaning sequence) and a two-step motor one (the possible internal verbalization and the external motor expression or writing). In reading only the eye movement is involved; in spelling, eye and hand movement makes for more motor complexity. Motor proficiency may depend on the clarity and efficiency of the perceptions, or may facilitate them. According to Gibson (1969) theoretical positions differ on this point. Thus kinesthetic factors will be an important aspect of the learning support strategies to be discussed. The reading and spelling processes are compared in Figure 1.

In this diagram the perceptual cognitive processes used in both reading and spelling are differentiated and listed as comparison, identification, labelling, association categorization and generalization in the perceptual processes involved in the decoding-encoding aspects of reading and spelling, and evaluation, interpretation and inference in the cognitive processes. Of course, this is an artificial separation, as in actual function, perceptual and cognitive processes occur simultaneously.

In order to focus teaching effort, the dissection of process is presented because many children cannot identify symbols. Identification, as used here, indicates awareness of attributes, characteristics or salient features of sounds and letters. Children with these identification problems would have difficulty in articulating sounds and in recognizing and matching letters. Labelling, as a perceptual process, would be demonstrated in isolating sounds and naming letters; association would be evident when childern could give letters for sounds or sounds for letters. Categorization could be viewed as the ability to detect groupings of sound sequences and their association with letter sequences. Generalization could be seen when the child transferred these associations to new words. These processes are considered as ascendant in the decoding and encoding efforts in early and foundation learning in both reading and spelling. They must function in order to support cognitive process. The cognitive process of evaluation interpretation and inference is seen as

READING

MODE	STIMULUS	PROCESS			RESPONSE		PRODUCT
		Operations					
		Perceptual	Motor	Cognitive	Silent	Oral	
R E C E P T I V E	External Graphic Symbols Spatially Sequenced	Discrimination Matching Identification Labelling — Memory Recognition Visual Recall Auditory	Eye Lip Throat Ear Movements	Association Categorization Generalization Evaluation Interpretation Inference	Internal Verbal Symbols Temporally Sequenced	Oral — External Verbal Symbols	M E A N I N G

SYMBOLS – – – – – – – – – – – – – – – – – MEANING

1 spelling pattern – – – – – 1 sound

Constrained by the context in which it occurs and auditory recall ability when initial stimulus is visual

SPELLING

MODE	STIMULUS	PROCESS			RESPONSE		PRODUCT
E X P R E S S I V E	Internal Verbal Symbols	Discrimination Memory	Eye Hand Movements	Association Categorization Generalization Evaluation Interpretation Inference	External Written Graphic Symbols Spatial Sequence		W R I T I N G

MEANING – – – – – – – – – – – – – – – – – SYMBOLS

1 sound – – – – – Several possible spelling patterns

Multiple choice in encoding process constrained by visual recall ability when initial stimulus is visual

Figure 1. Reading and spelling compared.

related to the message content, and as a consequence of the mechanics of reading and spelling.

In the diagram, not only is the inversion presented but the two-stage matching process is mentioned to direct attention to the fact that children must be able to manipulate oral language symbols before they can be expected to associate manipulations of graphic symbols.

The two-level amalgamation process is set forth so that decoding activities can be viewed in hierarchical relationship to comprehension.

In Figure 1 some of the perceptual skills are listed as comparison, identification and labelling; in Figure 2 the whole decoding process is placed in the perceptual sphere. As there is actually no distinction in function, the placement is purely arbitrary for purposes of clarity, or as in Figure 1 to severely limit what is considered perceptual and then to expand it as in Figure 2.

INVERSE, BUT NOT NECESSARILY
REVERSIBLE, PROCESSES

While reading and spelling are roughly inverse processes, they are not necessarily reversible. Motor involvements are different, as are the qualities of the initial stimulus conditions. Reading involves responding to a stimulus which is independent of the learner. Spelling, on the other hand, involves a stimulus which is supplied by the performer or learner (except in dictation situations). This means that the parameters of spelling proficiency are circumscribed uniquely by the skills, inadequacies or desires of the child. It is not unusual to find exceptionally good readers who are also exceptionally poor spellers. Usually this is not simply a matter of carelessness, although it may be a factor and have special perceptual results as we shall see when we discuss attention behavior. Analysis of the errors (Chapter 3) can yield an individualized picture of the perceptual skills which are functional or nonfunctioanl in a particular case. The inversion is presented in Figure 2.

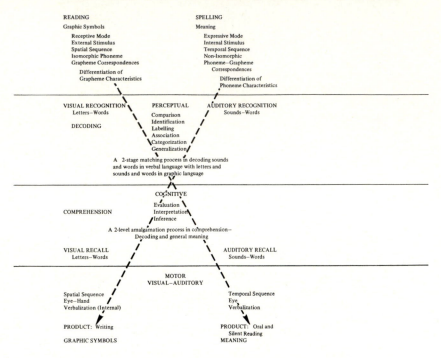

The Major Differences

Seven major differences in reading and spelling become apparent from this diagram:

1. The nature of the process—receptive for reading, expressive for spelling.
2. The nature of the stimulus—external for reading and internal for spelling.
3. The direction of the process—visual to auditory for reading and auditory to visual for spelling.
4. The kind of motor involvement—eye movement only for silent reading and eye-hand movement for spelling. (Both reading and spelling use lip, throat and inner ear movements in relation to vocalization.)
5. The nature of the paired or dual sequencing—the integration of temporal and spatial for spelling and the inverse for reading.
6. The relationship and directionality of symbol and meaning:

in reading, graphic symbols to meaning and, in spelling, meaning to graphic symbols.

7. The last one may be the difference which is critical in differentiating the individual who is a good reader and has difficulty in spelling. In reading each letter or spelling pattern has only one possible sound in the word in which it occurs; in spelling the process is not isomorphic and many sounds can be represented by more than one grapheme.

This last problem is like a multiple choice situation. Visual memory becomes very important, especially absolute recall. Good visual memory may be reflected in the fact that the speller has noticed all of the details in the word, such as small differences between look-alike letters, the orientation or the turn of a letter such as *b* or *d,* the spatial sequence of the letters such as *ia* or *ie.* It may also reflect knowledge of the meaning of inflectional endings such as *s, es* and *ed.* Some of these characteristics are relatively constant in various words and reflect the rules of orthography. Good spellers note and remember common spelling patterns and generalize their use to other words. The poor speller does not notice or remember the details clearly enough to determine the invariant or relatively constant patterns; therefore, structure is not available and each word must be learned as if it were unique.

Common Performance Patterns

The "poor-reader/poor-speller" is a common performance pattern. Even the "good-reader/poor-speller" is frequently encountered. It is not usual to find a "good-speller/poor-reader" except among deaf children. This is often puzzling to teachers as there is a tendency to think of reading as a more demanding and higher-order skill and to be perplexed by the inadequate performance of a very able reader who fails in spelling activities. Visual and auditory perception are common factors in both reading and spelling. Visual perception is basic to the use of visual symbols just as auditory perception is basic to the use of verbal ones. The hierarchical arrangement of these skills and the developmental sequence in their acquisition may be one of the keys to the dilemma. The exact differences in the inversion may also be helpful in gaining an understanding of the problems for a particular learner.

Children learn to speak without ever visually perceiving the symbols they use. Spoken words are not visible. The visual demands in early childhood are related to perceiving objects, relationships and events which words represent. Children do not learn to read without having mastered verbal language at all levels.

In the use of the graphic code, the visual demands become quite refined. The "poor-reader/poor-speller" may be a child with poor auditory, visual or motor skills. His problem may involve more generalized perceptual- or language-dysfunction, or inadequacy in any one of the subskills may inhibit performance once motivation is ruled out.

The "good-reader/poor-speller" may have problems in saying the word to himself and keeping the sounds in order. Frequently, he omits sounds. Or there may be difficulties in recalling the spelling patterns or letter sequences where sounds are not available clues (*tion* is a good example) but where visual recall of the pattern must serve. With young children and those just learning to spell, the act of writing itself often distracts the speller from the perceptual-cognitive aspects of the task and errors are made. He may be able to say the letters in the word in correct order but will make a mistake as he writes them.

As spelling is so clearly related to word knowledge, it is very likely that when errors occur clear discriminations in the initial learning may not have been made. Overlearning may be necessary.

A case could also be made for a psycho-dynamic explanation relating the need to make choices in ambiguous situations and personality traits in poor spellers. This is also true in reading and quite familiar to remedial teachers. The child knows the element but hesitates because he is not sure he is right and does not want to fail. With support from the teacher, "You know that," or "Go ahead and try it," or with a supportive whisper of a sound, the correct response is forthcoming. The stored information is adequate for the recognition needed in reading but the child lacks confidence. For the recall required in spelling it is necessary to know the relationships so well that no hesitation occurs.

We know from the performance of deaf children that it is possible, in spelling, to rely entirely on visual skills. Some deaf children can learn the spelling patterns of words and are better "decoders" and spellers than readers. They can say and spell the words but meaning may elude them because of the difficulty in developing concepts. However, children who do hear use auditory information in spelling. They often say the word and write the letter equivalents as they go along. The visual channel, not having to carry the whole information-processing load, may not be as highly developed as it must be in deaf children. But for teaching purposes, perhaps the performance of deaf children may point to a weakness in teaching methodology with low achievers. We simply do not emphasize enough the visual perception of words for some poor spellers. We assume they "see" the details they will later have to recall. The fact that they didn't notice well enough is demonstrated by the performance of many poor spellers.

Broadening the Definition of Comprehension

When limited to single words, meaning and spelling proficiency are easily related. Schools usually teach and test spelling this way. It is not as usual to test it by having children write compositions which would make the spelling process more clearly related to the process used in reading.

Reading comprehension can be categorized in various ways: in relation to the message of the text itself and in association with the reservoir of knowledge in the mind of the reader. As the reader gets meaning from the page, he links the ideas with others already stored, or he may reorganize them on the basis of the new information he is receiving. This is what is commonly meant by "comprehension." In reading, his ability to do this is based on his proficiency to "decode."

Decoding is usually viewed as nonmeaningful. In actuality, in the decoding phase of either reading or spelling, meaning is an important cue as children decipher the word elements. It is simply more limited. Gibson (1969) relates the child's detection of structure in orthography to learning syntax in spoken language. Decoding, even though less meaningful, serves as the foundation for larger comprehension demands.

> How children pick up the spelling pattern is a problem of great importance. They must perceive recurrent clusters so as to treat them as units; they must detect positional constraints; and they must abstract the patterns from varying contexts. It seems as though a kind of learning to notice and abstract spelling regularities develops in the young reader, and, at some stage, permits transcendence of rote learning of individual words and transfer of regularities found in them to the perceiving of new words (p. 440).

Provisions for teaching decoding in both reading and spelling are legitimate teaching activities to enhance comprehension. For low-achieving children it facilitates the need "to notice and abstract" which Gibson mentions. Cronbach and Snow (1969) have provided some support for this position in their conclusion that "cue training" is beneficial for low-achieving children. "Cue training" means pointing out details and simple relationships. They compared a structured phonics program in beginning reading with a more conventional whole word approach and found that the instruction produced results for low "ability" children while the whole word treatment appeared best for high "ability" children. The fact that high "ability" children achieved more when taught a whole word approach might be an indication of their ability to abstract and generalize the sound-symbol relationships without direct instruction. They "perceive" the relationships. Low-achieving or low "ability" children need to have them pointed uot. This particular characteristic has been pointed to as a distinguishing factor in the behavior of low- and high-achieving children and suggestions for teaching approaches based on this hypothesis favor inductive methods for the low achiever. [In this text the term "achiever" also substitutes for the term "ability" as the designation is applied as a result of tests which measure achievement.] In order to clarify the perceptual-cognitive differentiation of skills which was made earlier, some examples and definitions are in order.

Comparison

If this perceptual process is used for training visual perception, a directly relevant exercise might look like this:

The direction given to the child is: "Find one like this one." No cue or associated label is provided. The child must scan the figures and find one which is the same. In training auditory skills teachers frequently present two words and ask children to use auditory analysis to determine if the words are the same or different. Here again, comparison is the perceptual process used.

Identification

When this process is used, a cue will be singled out and the child's attention directed toward that cue as a means of differentiation and selection. The cues will be characteristics of the form; as examples, size, orientation or color. The teacher might say: "Find the one which is largest."

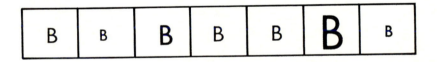

In an auditory discrimination exercise, several words might be given and the child asked to identify on the place of articulation, the number of syllables, or the number of sounds. As an example, using place of articulation as a cue, the teacher would say to the children: "I am going to say some words. Which word do I say which begins with my lips pressed together—*list,*

put, have?" Using the number of syllables as a cue, the teacher might say: "I am going to say some words. Pick out the word that has three syllables—*Dad, baby, grandfather."*

Labeling

In perceptual activities in which a name or a label is used as the provided cue, the child might be asked to find a letter or a word in a group. "Find all the A's in this sentence, either in capital form or lower case letters." [The teacher provides the label and the child finds the form which he has already associated with it. This is a recognition activity.]

An apple has a great deal of flavor.

The teacher might also say, "What is the name of this letter, this letter or this letter [pointing to different ones in the sentence]?" In this case the teacher points to form and the child supplies the label. This is a direct recall activity and is more difficult.

For auditory training, the teacher might label the position of a sound as a cue and ask the child to retrieve the sound. "Tell me the 'first sound' in this word." Or the teacher might say, "This word has the sound *m* in it. Where is the sound, at the beginning, middle or end?" In the first case the teacher labels position and the child labels sound; in the second the teacher labels sound and the child labels position.

Association

The activities which have been described involve an association process, but when we talk about association in reading and spelling we usually mean establishing the association between vision and sound, between letters and phonemes. This associative process involves being able to respond to a sound with a letter and a letter or group of letters with a sound. It is the basic task in decoding activities.

Categorization

This involves the process where the child realizes that there are many words that contain sound and spelling patterns in some recurrent order and that these sound-symbol associations are not entirely chaotic or arbitrary. In teaching activities when support is provided, these may be patterned for the child; lists of words will be presented where there are isomorphic relationships with identical correspondences at the verbal level. Then those patterns which contain nonisomorphic correspondences— such as *ai* and *ie*—may be presented. Here there is a sound relationship which is relatively constant and one of the letters represents a sound which it ordinarily might represent. Finally, lists are presented where there is no sound relationship between the letters and the sound, such as *tion* or *ough*, but there may be other meaningful relationships. Most children abstract these categories for themselves. Low-achieving children do not, and the relationships need to be ordered for them. When this is provided, they can usually learn them.

Generalization

If the child has had enough experience with categorized learning, generalization usually follows and the child can read or spell words when they are encountered in diverse school activities.

Evaluation, Interpretation and Inference

These activties, related as they are to comprehension, will be discussed later under the comprehension aspects of Reading, Writing and Thinking.

If we accept the idea of "cue training" as it has been defined and described here, the question then arises: To which cues shall we direct children's attention? Should all low-achieving children receive the same treatment? Are there individual differences in low achievers which might serve as a guide for selecting appropriate methods? Are there skills in the perceptual process which should be trained?

PERCEPTUAL THEORY

Cue training or directing children's attention to the elements in a learning situation is based on the idea of hierarchies in both the abilities in the learner and in the structure of instruction. While our theories and research are in their infancy, we still can look at some characteristics in the learner and try to make some match in the teaching strategies to be used. Admittedly, our matches will be crude, but the results should be better than the situation which only allows and reinforces failure. In any discussion of cue training, an implicit factor is a focusing of the attention of the learner.

Gibson's (1969) theory of perception, Differentiation Theory, postulates a hierarchy of perceptual development which isolates attention behavior as one of its mechanisms. Keogh (1973) also discusses attention but focuses on some different characteristics of attention behavior. Attention is a basic mechanism of perception but abstraction and filtering are also involved.

According to Gibson, the learner in a complex learning situation improves by noticing differences between the stimuli presented. He may actually form some sort of mental image which makes possible noting differerences which can be used to compare absent items. The clarity of this image may play a role in the quality of any production. Gibson (1969) states unequivocally that learning should improve when distinctive feature differences are emphasized in training. In this respect, support is offered for the idea that "perception" is learned. She also points out that contrasting items should be helpful in isolating critical characteristics. This means that for teaching purposes not only is it valuable to point out details but also to contrast and compare stimuli to demonstrate and highlight differences and similarities.

In discussing the mechanisms involved in perceptual learning according to this theoretical approach, Abstraction is presented first.

Abstraction

Gibson (1969) states that "abstraction ocurs when an invariant relation is discovered over a number of varying objects or events."

> Phoneme discrimination must progress in some such way, for the essential contrasts come to be detected despite differences in pitch, loudness, speed, and other vocal attributes. Similarly, in the discrimination of letters written by different hands, one man's tilt may be another man's upright, but the tilt-upright contrast is rela-

tional and invariant with respect to the other features and must
be detected as such if the letters are to be read (p. 110).

The other mechanism which may play a definitive role in the
perceptual process is filtering. Filtering involves the disregard
of irrelevant stimuli. This seems to be reciprocal with abstraction.
What makes this possible is not clearly known, but other theorists
speculate about neural and inhibitory mechanisms. Gibson feels
that it is an important area for research, since the ability to ignore
irrelevant stimuli is such an important developmental aspect of
perceptual function. The teacher involved in cue training may
facilitate filtering by actively directing attention and emphasizing
the relevant stimuli.

The last mechanism involves attention conceived as a central
process which selects and rejects from stimuli which are presented.
Exploratory activity is characteristic of all sensory systems and
is active, not passive. Common activities which illustrate this
are seen in eye movements as they stop and move across a page
or as a child's head turns toward a sound to hear better. Even
in touching something, the fingers move and the whole hand
touches the object and learns more about it than if the touching
is "motionless." Gibson feels that this selective, exploratory
activity of attention may be practiced so that noticing very
important details can be facilitated.

Keogh (1973) has elaborated on other aspects of attention
behavior that teachers might find of value. These are impulsive
reflective attention, scanning behavior and the span or duration
of attention.

Impulsivity vs. Reflexivity

When attention behavior is regarded as impulsive or reflective, differences can be observed in the child who does not look
or listen carefully or reach out to pick up information or perceive
selectively. The impulsive child seems impetuous. Any answer
will do and, characteristically, he may not compare all items
before he makes a choice, or he may not compare all aspects
of the items. The reflective child takes more time and is more
deliberate in his behavior. Pick (1974) suggests that tendencies
toward impulsivity are antecedents of a nonalytic style of cogni-

tive processing. In order to notice details or perceive, some deliberation or reflectivity must occur.

With this in mind, teachers can focus on deliberation in perceptual function as an objective in teaching. As a characteristic in children's behavior that depresses their performance, teachers are usually aware of this but tend to overlook it in planning instruction, not giving it the importance it deserves. While impulsivity or reflectivity may be a part of a child's personality pattern and quite difficult to modify, direct teaching attention to this aspect of learning may make major differences in the performance of some low-achieving children. Teachers usually talk about a "short attention span" relating to the quantitative aspects of behavior; the impulsive-reflective dimension relates to a qualitative aspect of the same behavior.

Scanning

Several kinds of scanning behavior must function in reading and spelling. The child must be able to analyze a word at the verbal level. Scanning of words may be for general form or for detail. The details may include identifying or naming sound or position, or sequence. If the task is scanning lines in reading on a page, then phrase form, sentence form and idea form are involved. Any one of them may present problems to individual children especially if they have had a "decoding" emphasis with no compensatory teaching for the single word emphasis. There is also the problem of visual shift in this type of scanning which may present another set of problems to some children. Children who fail in reading and spelling may not have developed this scanning ability either at the verbal level or the graphic level. Training in listening for sounds in words, for position of sounds and for their sequence could prove helpful to many children. Watching for letters in words, defining position and noting which letters come first and those that follow, could be helpful to others. Extending phrase and sentence reading could be valuable. Separating the auditory verbal aspects of this scanning skill and teaching auditory skill first may prove enabling to many low-achieving children. Scanning is usually incidental learning and the separation of auditory and visual skill is not a usual teaching procedure. However, teaching children to hear sounds in order in words in verbal langauge may be a fundamental skill for both reading and spelling. Very little deliberate teaching attention is given to this skill in the primary grades. Instruction is usually given in visual and auditory terms simultaneously.

Attention Span or Duration

In any perceptual learning behavior, the duration of attention is a very important aspect. Many low-achieving children have not learned to "pay attention" consistently and simply do not take in the available information. The amount of time of attention behavior is a factor. They are not perceptually inadequate in the sense that the modalities do not function; when they attend consistently, they learn. This is a particular problem involving motivation. Incentives and reinforcements usually suffice to extend the child's atteniton span. As far as teaching techniques are concerned, a combination of the use of reinforcements—"behavior modification" techniques and changes in the content of the lessons so that they are inherently interesting—will usually be all that is necessary. For another group of low-achieving children, however, these techniques will need to be paired with assessments of preferential learning modes of reception. Some children will only learn visual information when it is paired with kinesthetic supports such as tracing and manipulation. Others will only learn the auditory skills when it is paired with proprioceptive supports, the awareness of the sensations in the productions of the sounds. The short attention span may have quite different characteristics in individual children and this difference should be kept clearly in mind in any assessment. Low-achieving children are not a homogeneous group and success in teaching will be based on how well the teacher differentiates the behavior and need of each child and uses methods and materials appropriate to him. Keogh (1973) analyzes attention from a different perspective touching on some characteristics which Gibson has not emphasized.

Returning to the perception of language symbols themselves, let us see what Gibson (1969) states:

Learning enters into the perception of symbols in three important ways. First, the symbols themselves, such as speech sounds and letters must be perceptually differentiated from one another. Second, invariants of mapping from the symbol set to the set symbolized must be learned. This may be a matter of paired associate learning of a code, but it is also possible that the correspondences are abstracted from the stimulus flux. A letter sound correspondence, for instance, may be induced from a larger context where a recurrent regularity can be detected. Third, a set of symbols has rules for how they may be put together in a sequence. These rules constitute structure and man must learn to perceive the structural constraints in the sequence for the information in even the simplest sentence to be transmitted (p. 442).

According to Gibson (1969), the three critical dimensions of perception are (1) *differentiation,* which includes attention and involves noticing characteristics of the symbols, both letters and sounds, (2) *noting invariants,* which in the case of verbal and graphic symbols includes the ideas of segmentation and sequence. *Segmentation* means that both verbal and graphic words are made up of pieces—sounds and letters. *Sequence* means that they occur in order in both systems. (3) The last dimension is *structure,* which means that there are rules which govern the way sounds and letters are ordered, and how words are used in phrases and sentences to yield meaning. These three dimensions are considered hierarchical, with differentiations yielding invariants which in turn yield structure and, finally, meaning.

Differentiation

In the teaching of reading and spelling and handwriting, there is a great deal, according to Gibson's (1969) view, which can serve as a guide for teaching and instruction. First, the teacher needs to determine that the child can discriminate and articulate all of the sounds well, and second, that the child can identify, name and write all of the letters well. Using the differentiation idea as the first step in an hierarchy involves making certain that the characteristics of the basic elements which are necessary in reading and spelling—sounds and letters—are clearly perceived by the child. They should be observed separately. Discussions on how to teach the perception of sounds and letters using kinesthetic and proprioceptive supports will be covered in later chapters. The child must also be able to write the letters when presented with the sounds in spelling and say the sounds when presented with the letters in reading. This skill could be regarded as part of the awareness of the segmented nature of verbal and graphic langague and is the first cross-modal step. Suggestions about comparison, identification, labeling, and categorizing can provide some structure in the sequence of activities used to teach differentiation of the basic forms—sounds and letters.

Invariants

While there may be other invariants which hold between verbal and graphic language, the most obvious are *segmentation* and *sequence*. This is the second area of perceptual instruction in a teaching program for the low achiever. If these two characteristics are not clearly differentiated by children—especially in verbal language—direct instruction may be beneficial. The poor reader or poor speller simply may not be aware that the words he says have parts (segmentation) which occur in order (sequence). The word is used and perceived only in its entirety. The same situation may hold for reading words. The child may not be aware that the words he looks at are made of parts which can be assembled in various ways. Teachers show this to children by writing or reading different words with the same letters. Infrequently do they tell the children what they are doing as they recombine the elements or deliberately show the children the transformations. Almost never are comparisons made with sequences which are *not* used in the English language so that children are made aware very early that the combinations are not arbitrary.

In reviewing the relationship between a variety of auditory skills and later reading success, Hammill (1974) comes to the conclusion that significant relationships are not demonstrated in the research. Yet he reports there are consistent but very low correlations between two of the tested skills—sound blending and auditory discrimination. These two skills could be interpreted as representing an awareness of segmentation and sequence at the verbal level which were previously singled out as the most basic invariants between the two systems. Perhaps with advanced tests and research methods more positive correlations will appear. It is worth teaching attention on an individual basis. A very decisive differentiation should be made between sound blending which uses letters on a page as a stimulus condition and sound blending which is tested at an verbal-auditory level only in order to clearly differentiate skill in the verbal and graphic systems.

Structure

When the word *structure* is used in relation to verbal language, what is meant is that the child has detected the regularities and order from the patterns of language that he hears and understands; which sounds combine and word order in sentences are examples. When a child acquires reading skill, structure or regularities and order must also be perceived. According to Gibson (1969), first the skill of learning to speak a language must be developed; second, discrimination of letters of the alphabet must be learned; third, decoding must be learned, and the last step is learning to read in "chunks" including words, phrases and sentences. Not only does the child need to develop a sense of regularity and order from the patterns in verbal language; he must match these to the graphic system. These are different kinds of codes. While the child learns to speak without formal instruction, a great deal of instruction is provided in learning to read in schools. He is barraged with language for all of his waking hours, but very little time in the total day is given to reading. Predetermining the hierarchical arrangement of the structure becomes important to successful teaching. Increasing the time spent in reading activities is also in order, and the chapter on reading will discuss perceptual skill, decoding, vocabulary development, comprehension and fluency. Basically, the point of view adopted in this discussion is that perceiving the structure in graphic language is the end product of the adequate function of the subskills of letter perception and decoding skills and that their mastery will yield comprehension. This is not as simple as it sounds, since structure in graphic language always relates to structure in verbal language and the teaching must deal with the intricacies of perceiving the structure of the two symbol-systems. The fact that a single phoneme can be graphically represented in different ways complicates the problem. Perception itself involves two major modalities, not just one.

Cross-modal, Association, Equivalence and Transfer

While it might be quite possible to train the child to perceive the structure of verbal langauge by itself, another problem exists in reading and spelling. Cross-modal information processing between the hearing of verbal langauge and the visual input from reading graphic language is involved. This area of research interest investigates three dimensions. The first is *association,* which is what occurs when children pair sound symbol relationships. The second, *equivalence,* is concerned with the issue of *redundancy* (or receiving the same information) in information reception between the senses. Sight and touch can pick up some of the same information. As has been pointed out, there is some redundancy between hearing and vision; at least segmentation and sequence are invariants in the two processes. The last dimension involves the actual transfer of information between the senses, where input in one channel is actually used by another (which may or may not be functioning).

There is a great deal of support for the equivalence of information used by vision and touch. Association of information in the two senses is also well supported. However, there is little available in the literature which is helpful in the facilitation of either equivalence or transfer between vision and hearing which we can directly apply to the reading and spelling tasks.

In summarizing some recent studies in cross-modal integration, Bryan (1974) suggests that most of the studies failed to establish at the outset if differences did exist in intramodality function— that is, in the visual or auditory function. Generally, the studies indicate that poor readers and aphasic subjects were inferior to comparison groups in visual-auditory stimulus integration. However, there are indications that one of the major difficulties may lie in the child's ability to mediate the responses verbally, to attach verbal labels to visual stimuli. Bryan further suggests that auditory and visual processing skills be examined separately before claims are made about inadequate integration function. This supports the position taken in this discussion.

The same conclusion was reached by Pick (1963) over ten years earlier:

> If the child is impelled to organize stimuli for himself, then it is obvious that mediating responses—and linguistic labels in particular— are the most important and effective means of doing so. While orienting reflexes and relevant attending responses are important, they can account for only a fraction of the power that generic labels and semantic mediations provide as he uses language to order his world (p. 192).

Pick is saying that attention behavior and perceptual discrimination are important, but that the kind of verbal mediation used is especially important. This is echoed by Bryan in discussing cross-modal issues.

For teaching purposes, the conclusions which might be drawn are that the factors which might serve as facilitators in learning involve improving selective attention through cue training, stressing the invariants between the two systems—segmentation and sequence—and teaching children some techniques of verbal mediation to facilitate necessary cross-modal associations.

Recognition and Recall

Our discussion, in large part, has related to problems of discrimination which involve recognition. But memory has two distinct aspects—recognition and recall. *Recognition* requires only enough information about the stimulus to allow us to distinguish it from other stimuli that would be possible in the particular context in which it occurs (Simon and Simon, 1973, p. 119). *Recall,* on the other hand, requires complete information. Recognition inherently presumes that we are distinguishing something from a previously presented stimulus. A time lapse is inferred, implying that discrimination has taken place, associations have been made, and an analysis of the form and content has occurred so that the distinctive properties have been noted. Some internalized form of representation is necessary which can be used for comparison. Its quality may depend on the thoroughness of the discriminations of the distinctive features, as has been stated.

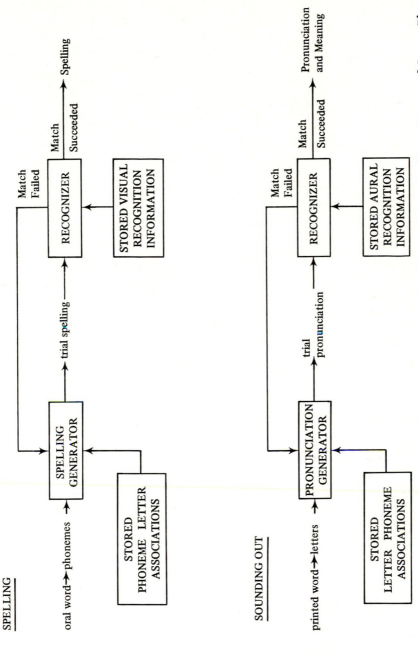

Figure 2. Spelling (above) and reading (below) by means of a generator-test process. (From Simon and Simon, Phonemic Information in Spelling, Review of Educational Research. 43:118, 1973. Used with permission.)

Reading is initially a recognition task and its recall aspect, as we have noted in the inversion section, is for auditory information. Spelling is a total recall task. (It could be argued that when the word is verbalized it is recognized, but it has to be recalled in the first place as the referent which stands for objects, events and relationships in experience.)

The reader recognizes visual patterns of whole words, going to details (if necessary) to differentiate highly similar words or to decode unfamiliar ones. The speller, on the other hand, must recall visual detail and construct the correct form. The reader moves from the whole to the detail; the speller from the detail to the whole. Pattern recognition is initially important in reading and of final importance in spelling. Probably in ambiguous situations both the reader and the speller move back and forth from whole to detail and from detail to whole pattern. Very few teaching approaches emphasize this perceptual aspect of the process. The teaching tasks which might be supportive for the low achiever involve making certain the initial discriminations are made in an attempt to expose the invariants and the structure so that they are more readily recognized and recalled. Teaching total pattern awareness might also be helpful.

The Simon and Simon Model

A diagram of the reading and spelling decoding process which clarifies several relationships was presented by Simon and Simon in 1973. From a theoretical point of view, it is based on both a sequential discrimination process and matching a stored representation against an image. The model is designed for a computer program which looks at the ways in which phonemic information is used in spelling.

Calling this model a "generator-test-process," they hypothesize a two-level matching process which occurs as the speller and reader proceeds through the decoding activities. In spelling, sound-letter associations are made enroute and trial spellings based on sored visual information of the whole words are matched and accepted or rejected. A visual pattern of the whole word helps correct for the alternatives which are possible for some of the ambiguous spelling of words.

In the spelling process the Simons describe, "the word must be decoded phoneme by phoneme, recoded letter by letter, but recognized at the level of the whole word" (p. 118). It is quite common to find that words can be recognized—or correct form chosen from alternatives—when the same word cannot be directly recalled in spelling. A word can even be pronounced correctly at the phoneme-by-phoneme level and not constructed into a known whole in reading. The former is probably related to the amount of information in the stored visual representation but the latter may be related to the speed of pronunciation which distorts the stress and inflection which are part of the recognition information sored at the verbal level, or to the fact that a decoding emphasis tends to focus on single words and may reduce the use of context clues or intonational patterns.

In discussing typical errors in spelling, the Simons regard phonetic irregularity as the source of the main type of error made. A spelling can be so classified if it is ambiguous; that is, one or more of its phonemes can be represented by several different letter combinations or if it is nonphonetic (as the k in *knife*), having what teachers call "silent letters." Consonants can be slurred and vowels completely changed, such as "family" being pronounced "famoly" and spelled correctly according to pronunciation.

A reader gradually accumulates word-recognition information and uses it to produce spellings close to the correct ones which, according to this model, enables him to retrieve information about form. A sorting process takes place and the information in the image can only be retrieved when an appropriate visual stimulus is presented; that is, the word not quite correctly spelled. The reader may also store direct associations from the spoken word and its meaning, the sequence of letters, and possibly some verbalized rules.

Most errors are made in the middle of words. The letters in the middle are vowels which are ambiguous in the spelling pattern and can involve small phonemic differences.

This Simons' model reinforces the idea of placing teaching emphasis on developing some particular methods of improving word recognition information. The initial word study period becomes quite important. Phonemic information or information about sounds and letters and visual information need some method of differentiation and teaching emphasis. Pattern recognition also becomes very important in reading and spelling as the model suggests.

Developmental Sequences

The exchange of information between the senses develops after intrasystem development. The sequence is, very roughly, an emphasis on tactual, kinesthetic perception in early infancy and then refinements in auditory and visual perception. This occurs as children learn to explore the world with their eyes and ears more than with their hands and bodies. There is evidence to suggest that the development of intersensory relationships is age-related, that there is an active and rapid growth period between the ages of five and seven in both auditory and visual integration (Birch and Belmont, 1965). Children are also required to perform in reading and spelling activities between these ages. Developmentally, this occurs after the period of oral language development with its emphasis and reliance on auditory skills. It is commonly assumed that reading and spelling place the greatest demands on visual skills because of the nature of the symbols. When children fail in reading, great emphasis is placed on visual perception training. While this may be necessary and valuable, at the same time it may be insufficient.

Which Skills Require Early Emphasis

In a study which investigated the ability of primary school children to deal with auditory-visual associations, the results indicated that matching visual pairs was easy for most children and that matching auditory pairs was most difficult. The visual matching skill was not related to successful prediction of reading achievement, but matching abilities between visual-auditory, auditory-auditory, and auditory-visual was significant (Muehl and Kremenak, 1966). Visual perception alone is not sufficient for successful reading. The interesting aspect of this study, and its difference from Hammill's study in 1974 is that it attempted to look at cross-modal perceptual function. In assessment, probably auditory and visual skills should be assessed separately, but cross-modal integration should also be determined. Even then the problem is not resolved, for all of us are familiar with the child who has good auditory-visual associational skills and can be trained to give rapid responses upon the presentation of the letter or the sound, but cannot blend them. The child's auditory-sequencing skills have not been analyzed sufficiently to provide clues for appropriate teaching approaches. Such clues are cross-modal, requiring auditory-visual integrations, and involve the speed of response among other factors.

Interestingly, auditory discrimination skills as a group were not found by Dykstra (1966) to be a significant predictor of reading success. However, he did find that discrimination of beginning sounds was the best of the auditory predictors. This discrimination is part of the ability to scan the word auditorially and indicates an awareness of temporal position and sequence. This may explain why it is a good predictor. In this respect, it may be similar to the class of abilities involving the skill in differentating the visual-spatial pattern which is functioning when the child can name the letters of the alphabet.

Naming the letters of the alphabet is also used as a predictor of reading success. When a child has not learned to name the letters of the alphabet and the teacher has used the traditional repetition and exploited motivational techniques, it certainly would be in order to explore the child's discrimination abilities as related to this task—in this instance his ability to distinguish characteristics of letter form. Single skills are not enough for reliable prediction of school success. However, when children are not achieving, an analysis of perceptual function and non-function—as best as can be done at the time—can be helpful in providing clues for areas of possible instruction. We know that there is a relationship between verbal language and reading and spelling. Until the research is more definitive about auditory perceptual function, teachers will have to make do with developmental guides and attempts to analyze process. Individual children may fail because of difficulties which are ruled out as related to group failure, and while auditory skills do not show up as significant factors in research studies, they may be very important for a single child. Predicting failure and determining teaching goals are two very different uses of this information. First, a look at the whole communication process is in order so that skill teaching may be placed in a developmental as well as a logical hierarchy.

THE COMMUNICATION SYSTEM AS A HIERARCHY AND A DEVELOPMENTAL SEQUENCE

This hierarchy describes the normal developmental process in language learning. There are, of course, many factors which may interrupt its development and cause difficulties. Language is a socially agreed upon symbol system which represents human experience. It is used to share and record knowledge and feelings. If the experiences are meager, the use of the symbol system will reflect the insufficiency. If learning is interrupted by trauma—physical or emotional—this too will take its toll in performance. These factors need to be considered when planning for individual children. Even when meager or interrupted, language acquisition follows this general pattern.

THE COMMUNICATION SYSTEM HIERARCHY

THE PRIMARY SYMBOL SYSTEM—VERBAL LANGUAGE
(Spoken Words)

Age	Activity	Major Skills
Acquired by Age 5	Listening Speaking	Auditory Perception Focused on verbal symbols, sound segments, sequences. (Visual perception at this age is related to objects, events and relationships represented by spoken words.)

THE SECONDARY SYMBOL SYSTEM— GRAPHIC LANGUAGE
(Written Words)

Presented for Learning at Age 5-7	Reading Writing Spelling	Visual Perception Focused on graphic symbols and letter sequences. (Auditory perception presumed to be mastered and required in recall.) Visual perception—related to symbols of symbols.

The Problem of Second-order Symbolism

Graphic language entails the use of symbols for symbols. A refinement in the use of the representative function in learning is involved as well as the operation of the perceptual systems. With the presentation of reading and writing activities, children are required to command a new set of symbols; these stand for a set of symbols which are learned earlier and may not have been completely mastered.

The Developmental Importance of Auditory Perceptual Skill

In a Primary Language System in which listening and speaking are the main activities, auditory perceptual skills are critical for success. In the *Secondary System,* graphic language involving reading and spelling is dominant. While these processes represent verbal or spoken language, visual perception now takes precedence but does not substitute for auditory perception. It is added to and associated with it. The nature of the representation changes and the visual performance requirements of the child become quite demanding. The symbols are not only second-order ones, but they are quite small, difficult to discriminate, and ordered in sequences which are not exactly isomorphic with the sound sequences they represent but with which they must be accurately associated.

Proficiency with graphic symbols rests on the bedrock of well-developed verbal symbols. Visual perception for symbols is not necessary for learning spoken language; auditory perception is. But as reading and spelling involve learning symbols for symbols, the perceptual base for the first set must be operating before another set can be attached if we expect the final product to be "meaningful." Without well developed auditory-verbal skill, cross-modal associations will not be possible. This point will be explored further because so much teaching in compensatory or remedial education is spent on phonics, using decoding materials. The teacher may need to move back a step and make certain the auditory skills are functioning without using graphic language symbols.

Which Auditory Skills Should Be Taught?

Frequently children who have difficulty learning to read and write are tested by specialists to attempt to determine the reasons for their failures. They administer tests which have the children tell them whether a word is the same or different (Wepman, 1973). The child is presented with two whole words which he must compare. This is an analytic task which he must solve as whole words are given to him. He must possess stored information about the words which he compares, but he is working from total form which is supplied. The words contain comparisons which involve initial, medial and final sounds. Implicitly, the skill of scanning words must be functioning at some level for the child to be able to perform on this test. But a child may be able to analyze the word and not be able to synthesize it or construct it from its segments—sounds and syllables. It is this skill which must function in decoding in reading. The Lindamoods (1971) have developed a test which looks at the child's abiilty to manipulate the sounds in words and gives some valuable information about the function of this skill. Probably, one of the skills which needs to be observed is that involved with the sequencing exactly as it is required in the reading and spelling process.

In reading, the recall skill involves synthesizing the sounds which are retrieved without prior knowledge of the whole word. The child doesn't have a model which is available, but the construction process makes it available and when he retrieves it he can recognize it. Very few, if any, teaching approaches build this training into their materials. The child may need practice in stringing sounds together to arrive at a whole form. In words which he has in his speaking vocabulary where knowledge of meaning and concepts of the words are already well developed, this would be a verbal-auditory exercise with no graphic symbols involved. Sound blending is usually taught with the printed page as stimulus.

In spelling the child starts from the whole-word form, and segments and synthesizes as he adds sounds. He also may need to practice the exact skills required for this task at an auditory-verbal level. Teaching suggestions for these problems will be discussed in their respective chapters.

These skills are very specific ones. In assessing auditory skill, teachers will find that children will vary in the skills they possess and/or lack and they may need to develop a particular one. The discrimination of sound and the memory of sound may also be problems. With these difficulties, the most basic skills necessary for improvement are considered to be segmentation and sequence.

Listening-Language Skills

In the following tables, Chalfant and Scheffelin (1969) provide a guide for general receptive language skills. If the auditory problems of the child are more extensive than the perceptual ones related to the use of graphic language, this task analysis can serve as a frame of reference for the teaching activities. Listening skills are essentially thinking skills and in the early years, or in compensatory or remedial teaching, they should not be left to implicit learning. The use of a task analysis can provide a framework for diversity in teaching which is not haphazard or arbitrary but possesses some organization.

Acquiring Auditory Receptive Language:
A Task Analysis*

I. Attention: Attend to vocally produced auditory sound units, i.e. noises, speech sounds, words, phrases, sentences.
II. Discrimination: Discriminate between auditory-vocal sound units.
III. Establishing correspondences: Establish reciprocal associations between the auditory-vocal sound units and objects or events:
   A. Store and identify auditory-vocal sound unites as meaningful auditory-language signals: Substitute auditory-language signals for actual objects and/or events.
   B. Establish word order sequences and sentence patterns.
IV. Automatic auditory-vocal decoding:
   A. Improve interpretation by analyzing increasingly more complex auditory-language signals.
   B. Increase the speed and accuracy of the reception of

auditory-language signals through variation, practice, and repetition to the point of automatic interpretation.

C. Shift attention from the auditory-language signals to the total meaning that is carried by the signal sequence.

V. Terminal behavior: Respond appropriately to verbal commands, instructions, explanations, questions, and statements.

Receptive Task Analysis[*]

This task analysis is rather formal. In teaching reading and spelling a task analysis which may be more specifically related and more easily used would differentiate between perceptual skills and comprehension and thinking skills. In using a task analysis in the adaptive form of teaching suggested for low-achieving children, the task analysis needs to be brief and succinct so the teacher can keep it in mind and use it during the teaching act itself for diagnosis in analyzing the errors that are made.

A Task Analysis—A "Stripped Down" Model

This task analysis is not a definitive one, but contains the barest essentials for diagnostic purposes in observation of behavior and error analysis and classification purposes in teaching. It can be remembered, for one thing, and can serve as a framework for more elaborate task breakdowns necessary for more extensive teaching. In brief, the auditory perceptual skills which are crucial for language function are:

DISCRIMINATION

	Attention
	Attributes of letters
	Characteristics of phoneme production
PERCEPTUAL SKILLS	Segmentation
	Orientation of letter form
	Localization of phonemes
	Sequence

---

[*] From Chalfant and Scheffelin: *Central Processing Dysfunctions in Children: A Review of Research,* 1969, p. 77. Used with permission.

MEMORY

Recognition

Recall

Short-term
Long-term

In a sense, these two skills are hierarchical. Discrimination precedes memory, and the quality of its representation, its characteristics, invariants and structure will depend on the quality of the initial or repeated perceptions and the amount of information that was picked up by the senses which are involved. If memory is regarded as the result of the perceptual process rather than as a distinct skill, it may help the teacher understand why the child's attention should be directed to the characteristics and dimensions, invariants and structure. The child will remember the difference between short vowel sounds if they have been sufficiently differentiated. "Sufficiently" will differ from child to child.

The emphasis in this chapter is on perceptual processes as the foundation skills for learning. Just as auditory perception is basic to any possible cross-modal associations in reading or spelling, so auditory comprehension of verbal language is basic to the comprehension required for both. Children have to be able to understand what they are being directed to do. With low-achieving children, where language development may be inadequate, or possibly where foreign language may be a factor, it may be useful to look briefly at comprehension skills in the same manner and relate some of the processes to those used in perception.

LITERAL THINKING

	Word knowledge
	Recognition or recall of Detail
COMPREHENSION	Recognition or recall of Sequence
	Simple inference; if . . . then

NONLITERAL THINKING

Evaluative

Inductive-deductive
Convergent-divergent

Appreciative

Aesthetic

Affective

At this point it might be valuable to emphasize the starting point of comprehension. It rests on word knowledge. Here the emphasis is on the meaning of words, the concepts they represent. No amount of training of perceptual skill will make up for a deficiency in vocabulary development.

Minskoff (1974) suggests a differentiation of recognition and recall questions dealing with literal comprehension. In recognition questions the child is provided support in that both correct and incorrect responses are provided and the child chooses from the alternatives. ("Did Columbus or Washington discover America?" [p. 16]). Receptive processes are involved and expressive ones are minimal. In recall questions, expressive processes are required and the amount and length of response becomes a factor. Open-ended questions can be asked ("Who discovered America?", *ibid.*) requiring one word or questions where the child adds or completes information. ("Besides the *Nina*, what were the names of Columbus' ships?", *ibid.*) The most difficult recall question is that requiring recall of a larger amount of information ("What were all the things that happened to Columbus on his voyage?", *ibid.*). The recognition questions provide structure for performance and the recall requires spontaneous performance which is structured by the child.

Minskoff uses Guilford's model of those psychological processes used in thinking: *cognition; memory; convergent, divergent* and *evaluative* thinking. The cognitive-memory questions relate to literal comprehension and involve:

1. Recapitulation or review ("What did we do on our trip to the fire station?")
2. Giving facts, labels or definitions ("What is a submarine?")

3. Detailing or describing ("What are all the things that happened to Bill when he got lost in the desert?") [Minskoff, 1974, p. 17]

These questions don't require going beyond simple memory and understanding. They reflect the fact that the information was processed and stored.

The three other kinds of questions—convergent, divergent and evaluative—call for analysis, reasoning and integration of information. *Convergent* questions require the child to arrive at a predetermined or conventionally acceptable answer. Minskoff (p. 17) gives examples:

1. Make relationships ("How are a guitar and a piano alike?" or "What's the opposite of fast?")
2. Give explanations ("Why can't people fly?")
3. Reason ("If Bill had six tokens and he lost two, then he earned three more, how many tokens did Bill have?")
4. Arrive at conclusions, principles or inferences ("If people continue to use their cars at the same rate, what will happen to the energy supply?")

Divergent questions involve thinking where the responses are not exact or predetermined but involve a variety of possible answers. According to Minskoff (*ibid.*), they may require the child to:

1. Create new ideas ("What would be another title for *Moby Dick?*")
2. Generate a number of varied responses ("What are all the words that end in *tion?*")
3. Arrive at novel responses through reasoning or inference ("What would happen if there was no more rain?")

Evaluative thinking questions might include:
1. Judgments based on specified criteria ("What's the best way to go from New York to California if you have five dollars?")
2. Judgments based on unspecified criteria ("Which one doesn't fit—apple, pear, bread, grapes?")
3. Giving opinions ("Do you like Picasso's work?")

Inductive and deductive questioning might also be valuable. An inductive question might give specifics and ask the child to supply a generalization. With a deductive question, the child goes from a generalization which is given to an isolation of aspects, incidents or details which support the generalization. "Picasso is considered a great artist. Why?" (Deductive) "Picasso's artistic expression was exemplified in painting, drawing, sculpture, ceramics. How did this contribute to his position in the field of art?" (Inductive)

The last category of questions is one which deserves some amplification. In the Minskoff suggestions there is little mention of personal feeling in relationship to the information which is being received and processed. Affective considerations are also important in determining what and how information will be stored, processed and retrieved. Questions which deal with feelings can be prefaced with such words as "How did you feel when . . .", "Did you sense . . .", "Were you afraid . . .?", or "What mood was created by . . .?" These questions allow the child to personalize the information and to integrate it more readily. They are important in learning and should be included in all questioning activities.

Whenever comprehension is discussed, whether it is in relation to listening, to reading or in creative writing, the same issues in thinking are involved. No matter what other kind of training is provided in workbooks or in programmed instruction, according to Minskoff (p. 17), "the teacher-pupil verbal interaction must be the major training vehicle." Initially the teacher may focus on literal comprehension and finally on nonliteral.

It is not difficult to see that when we talk about listening comprehension we are discussing thinking. We will see that the comprehension skills required in reading are essentially the same ones listed here. They will be discussed later in greater detail, but for the low-achieving child it could be very helpful if the teacher abstracted some such classification for teaching purposes. Teachers do lead verbal discussions with children, but their emphasis is usually on content, not process. Process orientations can be helpful in teaching this group of children because it enables the teacher to individualize the kinds of questions asked, either to establish a set for what to attend to in the information being received, to retrieve information, or to interpret, evaluate and appreciate information.

The perceptual and comprehension skills function concomitantly in the child. They are separated in order to focus teaching and to provide more teaching options. In the classification of skills just presented, perception and comprehension are presented as a sequence. This is done for clarity. It is not suggested that in teaching, attention to comprehension await the development of perceptual skill. Rather, it is suggested that the teaching consider both aspects of auditory performance for individualized instruction at a verbal level only without reading, writing or spelling as complicating factors.

Individualized instruction involves verbal exchanges between teachers and children with clear teaching objectives, goals and strategies. Many of the children in the low-achieving group have had insufficient adult-child verbal interactions. The goals should not be ones which only use language to direct the behavior of children, but use it to elicit language behavior from the child, so that teachers can guide them in understanding, comprehending, thinking and becoming aware of the value of their feelings.

Getting the Information "In"

Turning from the issues regarding the use of information received by the child, let us consider another area covered extensively in the research literature, one that is worth discussion as a possible teaching technique: verbal mediation. Rudel (1963), Pick (19..) and Bryan (1974) all suggest that language may be involved in cross-modal association and transfer. Children attach labels and use language covertly in most learning situations. The question is whether or not language can be exploited deliberately to enhance the processing and reception or "perception" of information.

Jensen and Rohwer (1963) explored the issue of verbal mediation in paired associate and serial learning. They found that children with poor academic achievements and those from lower socio-economic groups or deprived backgrounds did not employ "mnemonic elaboration." They suggest that middle class children use, among other learning techniques, verbalization. When verbalization was required of a group who had been labeled "mentally retarded" in the lower socio-economic class, some astonishing results occurred. Some continued in poor perform-ance, but others equalled the performance of gifted middle-class children. Gibson (1969, p. 229) feels verbalization may increase cross-modal transfer but that it is not essential, and that in transfer situations mediation responses may not be as important as higher order relational properties. Even though there are some un-resolved questions, verbal mediation does seem to have some effect on focusing attention and learning and may be worth using systematically as a support strategy in teaching.

Teaching Children to "Talk" to Themselves

In teaching all aspects of the language arts, the technique of verbalizing cognitive and perceptual function can become a strategy for learning. Successful perceptual function may par-tially depend on consistent attention. In a teaching situation it can be directed and guided by language. It also may be facilitated by "self" communication. Children can "talk what they are doing," actually labeling or describing actions as a means of fixing atten-tion. This "talk" can be whispers or murmurs or be entirely internal. Verbalization is suggested as a strategy for developing visual perceptual skills in the chapter on teaching handwriting, but if teachers see this technique as an attention-directing aid, and children are encouraged to use it themselves in directing their own attention; it may foster more active participation in the whole learning process.

The Word as a Manipulative Cognitive Object

In a more specific description of the lack of verbal facility, Bereiter and Englemann (1966) have suggested that children—especially "culturally deprived" children—have difficulty treating words as units. While these authors relate this lack to cultural and socio-economic factors, another explanation might be related to the amount of verbal exchange between adults and children in early childhood. This is not a characteristic which should be attributed only to children who come from poor or culturally different backgrounds. Many other children whose social class and cultural background is harmonious with that of the school exhibit this difficulty. Rather than using concepts such as "cultural deprivation" which is so heavily loaded with connotations of inferiority, teachers would better serve the adaptive function in education being stressed here, if the children were not viewed as inadquate but only as having not learned that particular skill. In the particular language behavior which Bereiter and Engelmann describe, the word is not a unit singled out from the sentence for children also have difficulty with the ideas of beginning, middle or end in relation to the word. For some children, the word is not a "thing" to be observed by the "mind's eye." There seems to be no model, no structure, no representation to call upon. The meaning base for language may be limited experientially, and many of the children often behave as if the words were motor responses which were automatic. They do not use or manipulate language in the same way that achieving children do. Teaching children to manipulate words, to scan them, is difficult but it is not impossible.

Frequently as young children are asked to tell if a word is the same or different, or to compare beginning and ending sounds, their eyes will shift as they contemplate the word, sometimes they say it softly to themselves. They appear to be looking inward. This is an indication that the child can examine the word and think about it as a "cognitive object" which has a form with a beginning, middle and ending which can be contrasted with other words. Gibson (1969, p. 467) has stated that detecting similarities is basic to finding structure. When children are not aware of words or cannot compare them, very specific teaching is in order. The first step is to establish the boundaries of individual words and then to specify beginning and ending. As teaching begins, this can be elusive for the child; he may simply not understand what is expected of him. In this case several teaching strategies can be helpful. Among these are the use of gesture, objects, modeling and imitation.

The Use of Gesture to Convey the Concept of Segmentation

Some children will be helped to get the idea of the word as an object which has parts that can be distinguished and sequenced if the teacher taps at the same time that the word is said. The gesture and the sound of tapping, paired with the word, may give the child the idea of what to attend to that his experience has not developed and which language has failed to impart. Tapping can then be removed to see if the concept has been grasped. Either sounds or syllables can be taught in this way. Syllables as larger units are probably easier in initial teaching. As perceptual teaching, this is an attempt to teach the concept of segmentation at a verbal level only.

Other hand signals can give the child a visual cue to position and sequence of sounds when they are paired with verbalization. Gesture can also serve to denote beginning, duration and ending of the sound sequences that occur in whole words. These gestures are used successfully in Distar's instruction system (Bereiter and Englemann, 1966). Upbeats, sweeps, the turn of the hand, and downbeat gestures can serve to convey these ideas as they are paired economically with the verbalization. The index finger can be used effectively to show beginning, middle and ends of words. The right index finger points to the position of each sound as it occurs verbally on the left index finger. Usually this is done by the teacher while the child watches. The "self-communication" and mediation function would be better served if the child performed these acts as well.

Object Cues

Another method which may be helpful in directing the child's attention in following the sequence of sounds, is to make use of objects such as blocks, discs, beads, beans or any other set of discrete objects which can be paired and ordered visually and manipulatively with the sounds as they occur in sequence in words. The Lindamood *Auditory Conceptualization Test* (1971) uses this strategy. The value in this pairing is that it helps the child become aware of the distinctiveness of the units of sound which make up the word and their sequence. It externalizes a perceptual-cognitive process and demonstrates the segmentation, position and order of phonemic units in words. If the child were asked to manipulate the objects, matching position with sound as he verbalized, there might be added value.

Imitation and Modeling as a Teaching Technique

In the use of all techniques which involve teaching auditory discrimination or sequencing, the teacher demonstrates the exact verbal behavior which will be required of the child. Seeing the sounds produced can often be a support condition for perceiving difference or similarity. Usually vision is restricted in observing or teaching auditory skills. Watching the formation of sounds can provide redundant information. The child is asked to watch the teacher's lips as the words are said. If the child is having difficulty hearing the difference, he can see it. He then is asked to say it himself. The sequence can go like this: "Watch my lips—*Mary*—*Mary*. Did I say the same word two times or did I say two different words? Now you say it—*Mary*—*Mary*. Did you say the same word or two different words?" In the use of this technique the teaching calls on the observation of the formation of the sound as a visual cue to help establish the similarity or difference of the auditory pattern. The modeling establishes some of the proprioceptive cues (sensations from the body itself) which the child learns to attend to in support of auditory function. This is discussed in the chapter on teaching reading. Most teaching of awareness of similarity and then difference in words restricts the use of visual cues in an attempt to focus on auditory analysis. In the initial period of teaching this is probably a mistake, for it can be a valuable support condition when analysis does not function naturally.

Matching Temporal and Spatial Sequence—The Second Step

While the pairing of sounds and letters is the cross-modal associational skill which needs to be taught eventually, it is the second step in the process. Teachers frequently have difficulty in deciding what to teach when children have great difficulty with reading and spelling. The assumption is usually made that the verbal-auditory skills are functioning. This may not be the case. If the child is reading, he will go from the visual back to the auditory. If he is spelling, he will go from the auditory to the visual. Visual skill is not first, either developmentally or in terms of curriculum demands, and therefore the auditory skills must be observed firmly and established in the teaching of graphic language.

Sound Spelling

Another technique which limits the perceptual demands and teaches the auditory sequencing skills is *Sound Spelling* (Markoff, 1973) which will be discussed in teaching spelling. This is a remedial technique which limits motor involvement by having children recall and verbalize visual equivalents, or spelling patterns, without reading or writing. The child thinks and verbalizes.

In this procedure, the child says the word, says the sound in the word, and names the letter for each sound in order as he proceeds. The sound-letter relationships are controlled so that each sound is represented by one letter. No graphic symbols are used and no writing is involved. The intent is to force the child to recall the written letter—or letters—for the sound so that it is brought to the level of consciousness. The problem of ambiguity is purposely avoided because the skill being taught is only segmentation and sequence in a dual relationship. Several reading methods use writing as a means of introducing reading. The *Initial Teaching Alphabet* (Downing, 1966) teaches this skill directly by controlling the sound-symbol relationships; here the initial process involves going from verbal-auditory to visual-graphic representations controlled by the child.

"VAKT"

In sound spelling, motor involvement is restricted in an attempt to clarify and stabilize perceptual-cognitive function. The perceptual aspects are regarded as primary with good motor performance regarded as the result. Theorists differ on the role of motor involvement in perception. The usual belief is that the VAKT (combined visual, auditory, kinesthetic, tactual inputs) reinforce each other in the pick-up of information. Most special education texts support an undifferentiated use of this approach when teaching symbol perception. Sound spelling departs from this procedure deliberately in an attempt to provide a systematic teaching alternative. VAKT may not always be the best support strategy in teaching for all children, and if there is either poor auditory function and/or difficulties in writing, this separation in teaching may be valuable.

SUMMARY

The emphasis in this chapter has been on the exploration of the processes of reading and spelling in their developmental and cross-modal aspects. Auditory perception is relied upon in the use of the primary symbol system as verbal language skills are acquired. When the child faces reading, he must be able to link the symbols to sounds. The sound system must be clearly differentiated in his mind in order for this to occur. The word must be something which has meaning and which he can manipulate. If he cannot do this, he may not be able to take the next step which involves the association of the sound and the symbol.

When the child is required to spell, which is usually a year after he begins to read, again he must be able to think the individual sounds in order, link them to ambiguous graphic symbols, sequence those symbols and maintain an idea in a sentence or possibly a set of ideas in a paragraph or composition.

Auditory skills are the foundation for all areas of language function and deserve more readiness training in early learning and much more attention in remedial and compensatory education. It is not simply "phonics" or "decoding" which must be taught. In teaching these, the differentiations, invariants and structure of words may be clarified for the child. Both of these approaches teach dual relationships. For early training and for the child who has failed, teaching auditory perception alone and gradually pairing differentiated visual symbols may provide a base for perceiving structural relationships between verbal language and orthography. The research on auditory perception and its unclear relation to reading proficiency as well as the fact that deaf children can perceive all of the visual information in words and still not read well, warns us that the meaning base of language is critically important. Training a skill not rooted in personally meaningful language will not develop good readers and spellers. Whenever perceptual skills are taught, the relationship to conceptual ones is also important; this also explains the emphasis in this chapter on comprehension.

REFERENCES

1. Bereiter, C., and Engelmann, S.: *Teaching Disadvantaged Children in the Preschool.* Englewood Cliffs, Prentice, 1966.
2. Birch, H. G., and Belmont, L.: Auditory visual integration, intelligence and reading ability in school children. *Percept Motor Skills, 20:* 295-305, 1965.
3. Bryan, T. H.: Learning disabilities: a new stereotype. *J Learn Disab,* 7(5), 1974.
4. Carroll, J.: The analysis of reading instruction: prospectives from psychology and linguistics. In Hilgard, E. R. (Ed.): *Theories of Learning and Instruction,* 63rd Yearbook, Pt[1] NSSE. Chicago, U of Chi Pr, 1964.
5. Chalfant, J. C., and Scheffelin, M. A.: *Central Processing Dysfunctions in Children: A Review of Research.* Urbana, Institute for Research on Exceptional Children, U of Ill Pr. 1969.
6. Cronbach, L. J., and Snow, R. E.: *Individual Differences in Learning Ability as a Function of Instructional Variables. Final Report.* Stanford University School of Education. Washington, Office of Education (DHEW), 1969. Eric Reports, ED 029001.
7. *Distar Instructional System. Beginning Programs in Reading, Language and Arithmetic.* Chicago, Science Research Associates, 1972.
8. Downing, J. A.: *The Initial Teaching Alphabet.* New York, MacMillan, 1966.
9. Dykstra, R.: Auditory discrimination abilities and beginning reading achievement. *Read Resh Quart, 1:*5-34, 1966.
10. Flavell, J. H.: *The Developmental Psychology of Jean Piaget.* Princeton, Van Nostrand, 1963.
11. Fries, C. C.: *Linguistics and Reading.* New York, H R & W, 1962.
12. Frostig, M., and Horne, D.: *The Frostig Program for the Development of Visual Perception, A Teacher's Guide.* Chicago, Follett, 1964.
13. Gagne, R.: *The Conditions of Learning.* New York, H R & W, 1965.
14. Gibson, E. J.: *Principles of Perceptual Learning and Development.* New York, Appleton, 1969.

15. Hammill, D. D., and Larsen, S. C.: The relationships of selected auditory perceptual skills and reading ability. *J Learn Disab,* 7(7):429-436, 1974.

16. Horn, T. D.: *Spelling, Encyclopedia of Educational Research.* 4th ed. London, MacMillan, 1969.

17. Jensen, A. R., and Rohwer, W. D., Jr.: Verbal mediation in paired associate and serial learning. *J Verbal Learn & Verbal Behav,* 1:346-353, 1963.

18. Keogh, B. K.: *Attentional Characteristics of Children with Learning Disabilities.* Invited Paper, Int. Symposium on Learning Disabilities, San Diego, November, 1973.

19. Lindamood, C. H., and Lindamood, P. C.: *Auditory Conceptualization Test.* New York, Teaching Resources, 1971.

20. Markoff, Annabelle M.: *Sound Spelling.* Palo Alto, Urban Education Press, 1971.

21. Minskoff, E. H.: Remediating auditory-verbal learning disabilities: The role of questions in teacher-pupil interaction. *J Learn Disab,* 7(7), Aug-Sept, 1974.

22. Muehl, S., and Kremenak, S.: Ability to match information within and between auditory and visual sense modalities and subsequent reading achievement. *J Ed Psychol,* 57:230-238, 1966.

23. Pick, H.: Some Soviet research on learning and perception in children. *Research in Child Develop.,* Monograph 28, No. 2, Vol. 28, No. 2, 1963.

24. Pick, A. D.: Some basic perceptual processes in reading. *Young Children,* 25:162-181, 1970.

25. Reudel, R. G.: *Cross-modal transfer effects in children and adults psycho-physiological laboratory, Massachusetts Institute Technology, Cambridge.* Paper given at APA meeting, Philadelphia, 1963.

26. Simon, D. P., and Simon, H. A.: Alternative uses of phonemic information. *Spelling Rev Ed Resh,* 43(1), 1973.

27. Vygotsky, L.: *Thought and Language.* Cambridge, MIT Pr, 1962

28. Wepman, J.: *The Auditory Discrimination Test.* Rev. ed. Chicago Language Research Associates, 1973.

CHAPTER 2

TEACHING READING

IN THE LAST CHAPTER, the perceptual demands of the reading and spelling processes were related to the total communication process, in a developmental hierarchy. This was linked to the perceptual process hierarchy suggested by Gibson (1969) of differentiation, invariants and structure. Throughout this book, an attempt will be made to provide an analysis of the skills needed to function in the reading-spelling-writing process. These will be provided in hierarchies wherever possible but, in large part, they will be sequences or classifications of skills because their complexity precludes setting them in hierarchies at this time. However, as this kind of discussion dissects the reading process, and in a sense disassociate it from its purpose, which is to obtain meaning, it is time to look at the whole reading process and put perceptual function in its proper perspective.

A Larger View

Teachers will frequently say, when questioned about teaching a child who is a near nonreader: I am only going to teach decoding, because that is *the* basic skill." In justification of this they add: "He won't be able to read at all until he can decode, and can put the sounds and symbols together." They see decoding in a hierarchical position. This may very well be true about the perceptual process and about the reading process, but it is not necessarily true about the teaching-learning process.

Teaching decoding, sound-symbol associations, or word attack skills is indeed valuable and necessary. It enables the child to discern structure and leads to the higher levels of comprehension that yield the message of the text. But because our knowledge of the development of the perceptual process and how motivation, meaning and perception interrelate to foster understanding in reading is quite limited at this time, it is not safe to teach decoding alone or to overemphasize it.

The teacher would serve better the guidance function of education if decoding and all skill teaching were kept in their proper perspective in the teaching of reading. Teachers are always faced with the "whole child" in a school situation and they must attempt to provide compensatory education to make up for some characteristic lacking in the child. These could be such factors as poor achievement motivation or anxiety. Remedial education must also be provided for learning missed skills in a task hierarchy related to the subject matter. Also necessary is preferential education, which adapts instruction to take advantage of some strength the child possesses or a mode in which he learns best. Aptitudes and treatments interact and while research in this field is in its infancy (Salomon, 1971; Cronbach and Snow, 1969), teachers can get some "hunches" about preferred modes of information processing, motivations or special abilities and use them in planning instruction.

The low achiever needs an education with structure and an emphasis on individualized teaching. However, he needs these in addition to an education which is concerned with the relevance of content, the issue of the amount of teacher direction and child choice, the need of the child to develop independence, fostering creativity and initiative, not instead of these. "Instead of" is what the low-achieving child frequently gets. Skill teaching can be very boring no matter how much external reinforcement is provided and, in the long run, boredom can defeat any instructional effort.

The teacher stands between the child and the educational program and can make modifications which lean in one direction or another, attempting to provide balance between skill teaching or meaningful teaching. This depends on the view the teacher holds about what education should be for low achievers and the amount of skill and motivation teachers themselves may have to function in this adaptive role.

Programs, as they stand, may tend to foster the idea that more skill teaching is all that is needed to "cure" the child. Tutorial, "pull-out" programs, where children receive special help in one area of one subject, are based on this notion. No one plans systematically for the total instructional needs of the low achiever.

As it functions in schools, skill teaching tends both to lend itself to or perhaps be fostered by an interest in raising test scores. The pressure of higher test scores frequently means teaching children in order to meet teacher and institutional goals. A teacher who understands where skill teaching fits into a larger curriculum design will be less likely to teach in a manner which may ultimately limit the child, and will enhance the possibilities of developing readers, not decoders. Raised test scores, as an incidental benefit, will accrue.

In some ways, skill teaching in reading can be likened to practicing a backhand in tennis. Playing the game must be included in the program of instruction. In fact, the player must play tennis all of the time to determine if the practice helps his game. He might be able to return every ball in the structured and limited practice session and fail in a game wtih its freer and more diversified demands. The low achievers frequently do not progress to reading for recreational value or even for gathering information because they are always practicing a skill. They are not encouraged to "play the game" of reading sufficiently in most school programs.

A "Succinct" Task Analysis of Reading

Earlier the point was made that in relating individual differences in children to subject matter, it was useful to deal with essentials, with succinct task analysis, rather than complicated elaborations of skills. Simply, this makes it possible for teachers to remember an overall picture or the structure of the major areas that might require attention in teaching, and prevents an overemphasis on isolated "skill" teaching.

The reading curriculum areas suggested to serve that function are classified but not arranged in hierarchical order. They are simply a list of areas of instruction which should be given careful attention when a reading program is individualized. They are:

1. Perceptual Skills
   Visual and visual motor
   Auditory
2. Decoding
   Phoneme grapheme relationships
3. Vocabulary
   "Basic Sight Vocabularies"
   Developing word meaning
4. Comprehension
   The experience story revisited
   Some common problems
5. Fluency
   Intonation
   Speed
6. Motivation
   Achievement motivation
   Incentive reading

Obviously, this is not intended as an exhaustive task analysis of the reading process from a theoretical point of view. It is, instead, a teaching approach addressing itself to some of the common problems found in the performance of low achieving children. One of the dilemmas in teaching children in this group is that they benefit from cue training. Teaching which attends to the details of any perceptual field is very time consuming. It tends to become the only content of instruction and, because of its inherent limitations, will be self-defeating. In part, this overemphasis occurs because of the time factor, but is also dependent on the teacher's awareness of its pitfalls.

In using the classification system of areas of instruction the teacher may emphasize any one, depending on individualized need, but all are considered and instruction is provided in each one. The areas listed above will be covered in order in this chapter. The emphasis will be on exploring the dimensions of the problems which occur in the teaching of this group of children and some teaching suggestions will be provided with a rationale for the choice of the described techniques.

DEVELOPING PERCEPTUAL SKILLS

Earlier, in the discussion of the reading-spelling process, the conclusion was reached that there were enroute and whole word differentiations to be made in the decoding process. In reading this would mean that the visual stimuli would have to be discriminated, ordered and the pattern of the whole word noted. These are three distinct teaching objectives in visual perception. To make children aware of these characteristics of words, there are various approaches which might be exploited. One is to verbalize them and in this way direct the child's attention. Another is to provide repetition. Both techniques are commonly used to help children remember words. However, kinesthetic teaching is one of the very best techniques as it is useful for any visual or visual motor task.

Kinesthetic Teaching

As suggested here, kinesthetic teaching has a restricted meaning: tracing the letters of the alphabet or words with two fingers of the preferred hand while saying the sound, letter or word. An adaptation and fusion of Montessori and Fernald techniques, its use is supported by the results of experiments in perceptual psychology (Pick, 1963; Reudel, 1963; Reudel and Teuber, 1963) and it is designed so that these techniques can be more widely used by teachers. It does not concern itself with training the larger motions of the body as suggested by the work of Kephart (1960), or with training in geometric form perception as suggested by Frostig (1964) but proposes the *systematic* use of the finer movements of the fingers, hand and arm, the small movements of the jaw, throat, lips and tongue, the vibratory movements of the ear and the movements of the eye, *simultaneously*, for graphic language form perception. Tracing as well as verbalization are being proposed as additional ways to process the information in the letters and words and to involve the child, and as mediators and reinforcers of simultaneously presented visual and auditory information.

Perception and Motion

As background to the understanding of why kinesthetic teaching is helpful to children, it may be of value to examine perception and its relation to motion. Perception and motion are innately inseparable. We tend to think of motor behavior that is visible as the only sign of activity in the learning process. But in vision and hearing, and in any cognitive perceptual activity, much of the activity of the central nervous system is not visible, and in addition the motion of the eyes in vision or the movements of speech or the vibrations of the apparatus of the ear is not usually even considered by us to be motion. We think of motion in terms of grosser movements. Developmentally, the motor system is the first to function, and with growth and maturation it differentiates its functions and generalizes its activities, and develops the underlying structure of the burgeoning perceptual-cognitive systems.

> When we analyze the course of development in the individual, we see that the first movements to appear are the more generalized postural movements, following by transport movements and finally manipulative movements. The development of the more specific perceptual activities follows this same course; from general to specific adjustments and from gross to fine discrimination. It is our belief that motion and perception are inseparably related. The development of perception in the child is the development of motion and the only valid understanding of perception at any level is in terms of the movements that define it. The so-called perceptual activities of detection and discrimination involve the adaptive movements of orientation and differential response whether these movements are large, easily seen, overt responses or minimal, implicit responses. The organization and stability of the perceptual field depends on movements of orientation, location, and differential manipulation that have become established in the motion patterns of the individual (Smith and Smith, 1962, p. 7).

Here the translation of the earlier physical contacts is extended to all perception. The tracing used in kinesthetic teaching is an attempt to use motion to enhance visual perception and to aid the eye in active scanning behavior as well as providing redundant information through touch.

Educators and Activity

Historically, many great educators have understood the importance of activity on the part of students. Dewey (1960) called for learning "by doing." Piaget's (1952) central theme of equilibration makes activity, movement and change its core concept. Montessori (1964) advocated it as a cardinal part of her teaching throughout her writing, and Fernald (1943) focused it into a method of teaching reading. While each interpreted the function of activity differently and used it for different purposes, they all underscored its value. The work of Montessori and Fernald is particularly germane to this discussion, because they were concerned with low-achieving children.

Montessori

In *The Secret of Childhood* (1962), Montessori first emphasizes the general need to move and explore the world and then specifically discusses the hand and brain in their relation to the two developments that have special meaning in man's evolution— walking and speech. She points out that the motor activity which has special meaning in man's development, as distinctive from other animals, is his use of his hand.

> The hand is the delicate and structurally complicated organ that allows the mind not only to manifest itself but to enter into special relations with its environment. Man, we may say, takes possession of his environment by his hand and transforms it as his mind directs, thus fulfilling his mission on the great stage of the universe (*ibid.*, p. 85).

Man's walking liberated the hand to do other work and in the child the hand is used to know the world through touch and movement.

Montessori's teaching emphasizes the use of the hand early in tracing the letters. It is an important aspect of the acquisition of the graphic symbols of language in both writing and reading in her teaching. In explaining the recognition of form by touch, she states:

> To recognize the form of an object by feeling it all over, or rather touching it with the fingertips (as the blind do) means something more than exercising the tactile sense. The fact is that through touch, one perceives only the superficial qualities of smoothness and roughness. But whilst the hand (and the arm) is moving all around the object, there is added to the tactile impression that of the movement carried out. Such an impression is attributed to a special (a sixth) sense which is called the muscular sense, and, which permits many impressions to be stored up in a "muscular memory" or a memory of movements accomplished. It is possible for us to move without touching anything and to be able to respond and remember the movement made, with regard to its direction, the limits of extension, etc. (a pre consequence of muscular sensations). But when we touch something as we move, two sensations are mixed up together—tactile and muscular—giving rise to that sense which the psychologists call the "stereognostic sense." In this case there is acquired not only an impression of movement accomplished, but knowledge of an external object. This knowledge may be integrated with that gained through vision, thus giving a more concrete exactness to the perception of the object. (p. 163)

Montessori understood the importance of movement in school life and the neglect which schools accord its importance in cognitive development.

> . . . movement has great importance in mental development itself, provided that the action that occurs is connected with the mental activity going on (1961, p. 142). The wonderful thing is that man's movements are not fixed and limited like those of animals, he can decide upon and choose those he will learn . . . But such versatility depends on work. They cost him the effort of much repetition of "practicing" because the nervous interconnections have an unconscious way of finding the needed harmony giving an initiative provided by the will. . . . Without this companionship of movement the brain develops on its own account, as if estranged from the results of its work (*ibid.*, pp. 144-145).

While Montessori is more poetic than modern experimental psychologists, she understood and was able to translate to successful action a host of ideas which are still being explored in psychological laboratories today. What she suggested for the education of the poor and the retarded of Rome, is still extremely relevant for all children. Perhaps more to the point, it was clearly formulated in educational terms and procedures.

In her discussion of teaching reading and writing, she describes in detail how she used touching to teach the letters without writing:

> Tracing the letter, in the fashion of writing, begins the muscular education which prepares for writing the child who looks, recognizes and touches the letters in the manner of writing prepares himself simultaneously for reading and writing. Touching the letters and looking at them at the same time, fixes the image more quickly through the cooperation of the senses. Later, the two facts separate; looking becomes reading; touching becomes writing. According to the type of the individual, some learn to read first, others to write (1964, p. 266).

She continues, in a description of reading and writing activities:

> I have noticed, also in normal children, that the muscular sense is most easily developed in infancy, and this makes writing exceedingly easy for children. It is not so with reading, which requires a much longer course of instruction and calls for a superior intellectual development, since it treats of the interpretation of signs and of the modulation of accents of the voice in order that the word may be understood. And all of this is a purely mental task, while in writing, the child, under dictation, materially translates sounds into signs, and moves, a thing which is always pleasant for him. Writing develops in the little child with facility of the spoken language— which is a motor translation of audible sounds (*ibid.*).

Relevance to Kinesthetic Teaching

Montessori's teaching methods and ideas have special relevance to the subject of kinesthetic teaching. She speaks of establishing the visual-muscular image of the alphabetical signs and of the movements necessary to writing and she does this in three stages: First, by the association of the visual and muscular tactile sensation with the letter sound (not the name of the letter). She is calling on visual, tactile and muscular sensation to fix the image of the graphic sign and she states that it is fixed in a much shorter time than when it is presented only visually. She emphasizes the direction of the stroke and the sound.

The second stage involves comparison and recognition when the sound is presented and the third stage involves recall of the sound from the visual symbol alone. These are three different tasks. The first involves identification. The second involves recognition, and the third involves recall. This is very important in teaching and our previous discusion sets forth some of the different perceptual-cognitive issues involved in each of these activities and the fact that for some children they may need separate teaching emphasis.

It is interesting to note that Montessori suggests a period when it is advantageous to teach through "muscular memory" and that this corresponds to the sensory-motor stages of early development which Piaget discusses. The teaching of letter form perception and sound equivalents, reinforced kinesthetically, might be more easily learned early. This might be of great benefit to those children we can now identify as potential low achievers. It bears investigation for the kindergarten year.

Montessori was an inspiring educator. The teaching she advocated took into account stages or sequences of development, the need for activity and movement on the child's part, the importance of self-selection and choice, and the necessity for variety in experiences. She takes her place beside Dewey and Piaget, and provides educational substance to educational theory.

Fernald

Another woman was active at the same time as Montessori and adapted these ideas specifically to teaching reading. While she did not range over the whole gamut of learning as did Montessori, her kinesthetic method of teaching reading reflects the same understanding. She successfully taught hundreds of students to read and teachers to teach reading. Her name was Grace Fernald (1943) and her perceptual method was based on tracing words.

It was an individual method of teaching reading and was never successfully adapted to group teaching. It had many unique qualities and it was successful partly because it tapped the existing language structure of the child. It was an "organic" approach and by its very nature depended on establishing and clarifying the relationships of the individual's communication system. It used the tracing of words, not letters, as its basic tenet. Dr. Fernald understood the reading process and the learning process and she neatly tied them into one bundle that became her "method." She dealt effectively with problems of motivation, meaning and the need for training perceptual skill.

The child begins by transcribing his own language, whatever that may be. (This immediately establishes the stage or hierarchy of skill.) He writes a story based on an interest (allowing self-selection and choice). The child uses his own language as his reading material, controlling conceptual and contextual problems that may arise with the use of other materials. The relationships between the divisions of the communication process are established naturally and implicitly. It provides for repetition based directly on the child's need. It teaches the association between sound and symbol in its natural setting, the word, through assured visual and auditory pairing. It supports this association by direct kinesthetic tactile experience with the material to be learned (using a dynamic interaction involving increased body motion of the child). It allows for self-selection in terms of perceptual need. This is extremely difficult to assess because of the inherently inseparable nature of the perceptual processes. In spite of all the tests available, the ITPA (1968), the Frostig (1964), the Wepman (1973), the Bender (1938) and others, it is very difficult to determine the exact modal preference of children because the tests attempt to test in terms of isolating factors and the problem occurs in terms of complex inter-relationships, many of which are not accessible for observation and must be inferred. This makes it very difficult to translate the results of these tests to any kind of meaningful teaching. In fact, they tend to generate teaching strategies which involve practice of the skills tested and may not be truly germane to the problems of the child.

Fernald's Explanation of Modal Preference

Fernald explains why this difficulty exists in her discussion of individual differences in imagery:

> One difficulty with any such tests is that the sensory type of image changes from time to time in the case of most individuals and varies in type according to the class of objects recalled. Most individuals are able to recall objects in what is often called a mixed type of imagery; that is, they think the object in terms of two or three sensory types. For examples, a person who is recalling music may visualize the music as it is written, at the same time that he hears it as it is played or sung, and is conscious of the movements of singing or producing it on some instrument. In the case of a word, a person may picture the word and at the same time say it or feel himself writing it. As a matter of fact, the image is usually in at least two of these terms (1943, p. 319).

Fernald gets around this problem by allowing the child to select modality preference. The teachers are taught to be responsive to the child's behavior and not to require tracing if it is not necessary and to leave it as soon as the child is able. Many other problems basic to learning are considered. Within the framework of her method, problems of attention, of recognition, of discrimination, sequencing and immediate and delayed recall are all treated with the tracing and saying of words. The reading and rereading of words and stories, which grow out of something which interests the child or about which he is curious, provides both motivation and practice.

Her approach meets many of the criteria for "good" education. It is meaningful to the child for no other reason than interest. It is naturally organized around the stage of development of the child, with the child as the determiner of the stage. It does not subject him to a theoretical framework of graded skills which is arbitrarily imposed and often is not a good fit, or which forces the fragmentation of the communication process. It follows him in terms of learning speed, a factor which is usually not attended to at all for the low achiever and is probably the basic way in which we serve to handicap the children we teach. The child can take as many trials as he needs to learn words. He studies and repeats the words until mastery, no matter how long it takes. He learns the alphabet incidentally in the alphabetizing activities, but he is always dealing with the sound-symbol relationships within context of word and sentence meaning. The constant visual-auditory pairing is probably as important as the kinesthetic tactile factors in the success of this method.

The Kinesthetic Mystique

While Fernald was a psychologist, her explanation of why her method was successful was very inadequate. Her book is an exposition of a teaching method, not a report in the tradition of experimental psychology. Teachers who were trained by her know very little about why the method works, except for its uniqueness in terms of a total approach to the problems of teaching language arts or communication skills to children. There is little in her book that specifies what cognitive or perceptual behavior is being dealt with in terms which are familiar to us today. This is an added reason why the method has not been used for greater numbers of children. There has been something of a "mystique" about using tracing to learn to read and, as it is a clumsy method, it fell into obscurity. With the interest in Special Education increasing in the last few years, it has been resurrected, in desperation, by teachers who struggled to work with the "learning disability" population.

Fernald, herself, used the technique primarily with children of normal or superior intelligence and there was a considerable fee connected with attending her clinic, making the population she taught quite select in terms of social-cultural economic background. She was quite successful in teaching this group to read and to go on to academic success.

Admittedly, this sounds like an exceptional method with much to commend it. If this is so, why has it not been more widely used? First, it requires one-to-one teaching, something which has been rare in public schools, and is only now making its appearance to any degree. Second, it is a very slow and time-consuming method of teaching, as it follows the child's interest and his individual learning patterns in terms of amount and speed of learning. This makes its discouraging to teachers who have the concept of "everyone up to grade level immediately" or who have not had much experience with the learning behavior of low achievers. He retains just as well once learning occurs (Zeaman and House, 1963) but he takes longer to learn. Teachers are not prepared to support the children in terms of the expectations about the length of time learning will take and the changes which occur as they "learn to learn." Also, just what the tracing accomplishes has not been clarified, and teachers approach it with skepticism. Feeling uncertain about it themselves, they cannot transmit their commitment to the method to the children. Lastly, they usually use it in a haphazard, unsystematic approach, and it loses its potency. When tracing is used effectively, it is used as vision and hearing are used in learning—constantly—to perceive what is being presented. The need for doing this falls away as the child learns to differentiate the stimuli, to use his eyes in place of his hand to take in details, and to move back and forth between vision and hearing.

What Occurs in "Tracing and Saying?"

When the kinesthetic tactile modalities are used systematically to support the visual-auditory learning of written language, a variety of skills are being developed:

1. The attention of the child is focused on the material to be perceived. He must attend in order to guide his hand over the model. This provides added opportunity for the perception to be made and to insure that the experience gets internalized or "gets in." More of the central nervous system is involved in the learning task, there is a physical "rehearsal" of the perception, and there is motor feedback.
2. There is consistent auditory-visual pairing of the symbols. When either of the modalities is relied on alone, it is not certain if the other modality is functioning in support or is supplying its association. This makes absolutely certain that the sound-symbol association is actually made.
3. The eye may be guided to follow the form of the word and take in details to insure the discrimination of distinctive features; to learn the perceptual skill of "looking," of scanning a figure. If the eye doesn't perform per-

ceptually, the hand does, taking in exactly the same information.

4. The meaningful pattern of the word is preserved and analysis is used within the total configuration. The elements are not separated from their context. The child is not required to "construct" or sequence or fuse or blend in the initial perceptual acts.

5. It allows the child to determine modality preference without superimposing an arbitrary selection. Tracing is withdrawn on any evidence that it is not needed.

6. It can be used to insure perception only, in the receptive aspect of the language process where the child simply traces and says the word, or it can be used to require perception and performance where the child must supply the response from memory. This includes reproduction where the child also writes as well as says the word.

7. It provides a triple mediation process in the input of visual or auditory information: (a) specific modality emphasis, (b) motion, (c) verbalization. The emphasis can be placed on the intake of visual information, on the intake of auditory information, or on motor performance itself, whichever presents the problem to the child.

8. It deals with orientation problems with implicit eye training. The eye is always guided by the hand in the left-to-right orientation in reading, the top-to-bottom in manuscript and the bottom-to-top in cursive writing. This can easily be made explicit by discussion. Constant physical experience of the primarily visual information is provided.

9. It enlarges the material to be perceived so that the child makes the discrimination more easily.

10. It uses a bold dark line in the presentation for a stronger image.

Fernald, too, must take her place with those educators who have understood the totality of the teaching-learning process and the relationship of activity and motion to learning.

Experimental Research and Kinesthetic Tactile Perception

The work of Montessori and Fernald is impressive. However,

it is largely based on empirical and intuitive knowledge of two great women and their own work was subjected to very little of what could be called scientific verification.

Fellows (1968) cites an explanation for the facilitation produced by tracing:

> If it is the case that a child fixates where he points, then tracing a figure with the finger will carry along with it a scanning of its contours by the eyes. After a little practice we would expect some stimulus generalization to occur. Operationally this means that the mere exposure of the figure will tend to produce some scanning of its contours even in the absence of overt tracing movements (p. 134).

He cites the work of Miller and Dollard (1941) which holds that the tracing enhances the distinctiveness of the stimuli, and that of Piaget and Inhelder (1956) which states that there is some equivalence between vision and touch. Piaget (1961), Reudel (1963) and Reudel and Teuber (1963) also support this position. The later authors suggest that there is a common aspect of perceptual activity that uses information from one channel or several so that invariant properties are extracted. This suggestion is also supported by J. J. Gibson (1966) and Eleanor J. Gibson (1969). Fellows (1968) suggested a theory of perception that was based on perceiving distinctive features; Gibson (1966) expands on this idea in his description of the senses as perceptual systems, and Gibson (1969) elaborates it even further to include detection of higher order structure.

Fellows also reports on the work of the Russians in this field. He quotes Pick's (1963) review for *Child Development*:

> The general theory predominant in Russian psychology is that percepiton is a joint function of the sensory input and feedback from the motor activity involved in insuring the reception of this input: the looking at, the listening to, the feeling of the objects in the external world.

He summarizes the work of Zinchencho and Lomov (1960) which concerns perception as the end of a process of stimulus exploration, and states that young children—three-year-olds—discriminated figures only upon following the form with a finger and that older children did not need this support. They state that when there is no tracing, eye movements are irregular and generally stay within the figure. They imply that the finger acts as a guide to eye movements, and with practice and maturity it is no longer needed. They also report that while the early tracing motions are clumsy, they are easily trained and that the young children tended to trace spontaneously the contours of the same figures. Whether the finger actually trains the eye is a debatable point and is losing support among theorists (Gibson, 1969, p. 229) but there is evidence of transfer of training and equivalence between touch and vision.

In the United States, Fernald carried out her original research in 1922. Later Coleman and Roberts (1958) found that children who have poor visual perception are helped by kinesthetic learning, but others may be hampered by it. This suggests the idea that this technique is best used for children who have problems which can be related to visual perception, and may not be adequate for children with other perceptual problems as well. While transference and equivalence between vision and touch is supported by tracing in the research literature, there is no discussion about its direct effect on some of the problems encountered in auditory discrimination, localization or the sequencing of sounds in words. Most of the research in intermodal function does not use language symbols as the stimuli; hence the results are of little use in dealing with this problem (Pick, 1970).

Cooper and Goeth (1967) and Blank and Bridger (1967) both report that modality functioning among certain disadvantaged poor readers may be unevenly developed and cross-modal shifting difficult. There may be difficulties in attaching verbal labels to stimuli within a given modality that may complicate cross-modal transfer in disabled readers. King (1964) found specific discrimination training beneficial in her work in visual discrimination training on learning to read words as did Muehl (1960) wth teaching the reading of a list of words to kindergarten children. Statts (1962), Popp (1967), Cronbach and Snow (1969), and Gibson (1969) all found that specific discrimination training was beneficial. There are apparently different effects on children who fall into the higher achieving group and this kind of teaching may actually get in their way (Cronbach and Snow).

Perhaps some of the most valuable research is that of Zeaman and House (1963) focusing on attention in discrimination learning. They report that the differences between bright and dull children are not in the slopes of their learning curves, but in the initial plateau; the difference in the length of time it takes the child to discriminate out the relevant stimulus cue—or to decide what to atend to. Berlyne (1960) argues that attention behavior may be facilitated by supplying the learner with information about stimulus properties, cues, and in training in looking for certain attributes in the situation.

In summary, kinesthetic teaching, or tracing, may be beneficial to the low achievers and hamper normal achievers. While touch supports vision, there is no direct justification for using tracing for the discriminations necessary in auditory perception. However, there may be some justification for using haptic or tactile perception or directed awareness of movement and touch to serve this function with hearing, as we shall see. Even with tracing, the auditory pairing which accompanies it as the child says the word may provide some discrimination training for the invariants of segmentation and sequence which are common to both vision and hearing. It is a very indirect way of teaching this skill, but may be sufficient for children with mild problems in this area.

While current research does not give unequivocal support to the idea that the hand teaches the eye, or that vision gains its meaning from touch, there is cross-modal equivalence of stimuli available to both vision and the skin. The eye can see what the hand can touch. Spatial and temporal order and therefore relationships are available to both. Visual perception has a wider array of stimuli available to it and therefore more differentiation is possible. Thus more invariants, more complex structure and relationships can be determined through vision than through touch. However, the use of the hand does follow a developmental sequence which is similar to vision in exploring and searching for distinguishing features. Looking behavior begins to develop before tactile and children reach visually before their limbs are controlled. Once touch develops and despite visual superiority, "new intermodal invariants can be extracted (Gibson, 1969, p. 368). It is entirely reasonably to use touch and movement to support vision when it seems to function inadequately in language symbol perception. We know it is effective. Exactly what is being learned is still uncertain, and possibly the most economical way to use it is not known. Still, teachers who use it systematically get improved visual perception and retention in the children they teach.

Three different suggestions for its use are offered: teaching the alphabet, teaching grapheme perception and teaching vocabulary or whole-word perception.

A. *Teaching the Alphabet*

This is suggested as a teacher-made material and would include a chart of the upper and lower case letters in random order, a set of tracing patterns, a manipulative alaphabet set (plastic, wood, or cardboard letters), a small slate and some lined writing paper (see complete illustration, p. 272).

	NAME						
DATE							
F							
D							
B							
ETC.							

Children who have persistent difficulty in learning the alphabet would practice recognition of the letters for *short* periods each day (not more than five minutes). The child would read the letters on the chart, receiving a plus (+) for a correct response and a zero (0) for an incorrect one. When an error occurred, the teacher would present the tracing pattern and have the child trace and say the letter. The child would also be presented with the manipulable letter and would be encouraged to feel the letter with moving fingers and hands while the teacher called attention verbally to relevant cues (a crossed *t*, a curve, slants, points, etc.).

The material would teach the alphabet either by name or by sound or both, depending on the teaching in the classroom or the severity of children's problems. (1) The material would pro-

vide a means for allowing for the repetitions that children frequently need to associate letter and name of letter and sound.
(2) It would provide perceptual skill teaching simultaneously to
differentiate form. (3) The teacher could present the material
in the classroom, but others could supervise practice. The
materials could be used by other children, the teacher's aides
or by parents. They could be used by a teacher in small-group
teaching within the clasroom or by special teachers. The main
idea would be to have material available that allowed for the
teaching in a systematic fashion. (4) Teaching differences in
letter forms, which may also be a critical factor in the reading
process, will be covered in Chapter 4.

B. *Teaching Spelling Patterns of Words*

The same technique could be used to teach morphemic or
the meaning bearing units within words. If a child seems to
have persistent difficulty with a particular morpheme, the tracing
could be used to differentiate its visual characteristics and to
systematically pair the visual and the auditory representations.
This is not suggested as a complete teaching approach, but for
spot teaching where the child seems to have great difficulty with
certain sound-symbol relationships. The number of letters and
position could be controlled as well as the form; that is, manuscript or cursive. The number of words can be controlled as well,
to allow for manipulation of the complexity factor. Using 8½ x 11
or 13 inch tagboard fastened by rings would allow it to be reused.

C. *Teaching Whole Words or Vocabulary Lists*

The same strategies would be applicable to teaching any word
the child might have difficulty learning. This can be adapted
several ways. The teacher can keep track of errors the child
makes in any reading, list them, and prepare tracing copies. The
success of this method will depend on how systematically the
teacher uses this approach. The child should study the words,
trace them, and be checked by the teacher or another to determine whether he retains the word after an elapse of time. Daily
checking is best. He traces any word he misses, and he must
get the word correct three times in a row before the word is
considered as mastered. Recent research has indicated that three

I

Restricted letter
sequence and position
Manuscript

II

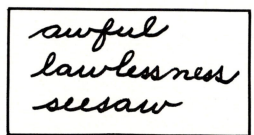

Longer letter sequence
and morpheme positional
shift
Cursive

Structure 4. In this technique, the integrity of the whole word is preserved. The preception or differentiation of detail and pattern is accomplished through tracing.

tracings on the initial presentation or study of the word increases the chance of retention (Berros, 1972). Whether he traces and writes from short-term memory or simply traces for differentiated perception depends on the degree of difficulty the child has. Writing from short-term memory is a more efficient learning strategy. The child must actively integrate the elements in order to reproduce the whole correctly. Writing takes more time, and should be allowed and encouraged.

This strategy can also be used with lists of primer words, when children are first learning to read or with "basic sight" vocabularies where additional discrimination training seems in order.

Tracing is equally suitable for older children; however, they frequently resist using this technique. It is suggested that if, after careful explanation of the function of tracing, the child

A primer list
Date

Page 1 of
Tracing Copy

Pg.	Word					
1	go					
1	saw					
1	have					
2	Mary					
2	cat					
2	om					
3	did					
3	will					
4	it					
4	see					

go
saw
have

Page 2 would contain tracing copies of the next three words on the list, etc. If a child makes an error, the page on the chart indicates where the word will be found on the tracing copy.

Structure 5. The Chart page can be prepared for each child; the Tracing Copy used for many children.

still resists, this be abandoned and only large print be used with verbal direction of visual attention. The child in this case would be required to write the word from short-term memory to insure perceptual accuracy and immediate integration of the elements in the word. *He would never be allowed to copy.*

Whole Word Pattern Perception

Tracing is used as a technique to insure percepiton of the salient cues in letters in order in words. Details, orientation, size relationships—all are discriminated with the use of this technique. The Simon and Simon (1973) model suggested that whole-word perception also was used in the recall aspect of spelling and different information was available in total form. While this discrimination is implicit in the tracing procedures, for some children it may be necessary to teach this explicitly. Spelling error analysis can determine for whom this will be beneficial. (See Chapater 3.)

There are two ways this perception can be taught. One involves boxing in the form to call attention to the most global concept available.

With the drawing of the ascenders and the descenders and unusual initial and final features, the child is helped to note features that can be guideposts that will help to establish the spatial relationships within the word. This may help to differentiate perception

This technique differentiates general shape:

GLOBAL FORM
(Boxing in the form)

grandfather

This technique differentiates detail of form, but is
limited:

SLIGHTLY DIFFERENTIATED FORM
(Drawing ascenders and descenders)

grandfather

This technique differentiates all details:

DIFFERENTIATED FORM
(Tracing the word)

grandfather

of the whole word that is used in the visual recall phase of
spelling, and provide for the whole relatively undifferentiated
pattern discrimination that is needed in the visual recognition
phase of reading. Teachers can select, or use all three techniques,
depending on the degree of differentiation needed.

Two Common Visual Problems

Low-achieving children frequently encounter two very common problems when they read. One involves "look-alike words,"
where there may be only one difference in word form and the
other relates to difficulties with the visual shifts which are
required.

Look-Alike Words

When children continue to miscall certain words or letters,
it may be quite helpful to pair the word which was the stimulus
with the response the child made and "force" the discrimination
of detail. Usually these errors are made on words which differ
on only one characteristic or detail. E. Gibson (1969) and Pick
(1970) make the point that in discrimination training, emphasis
needs to be placed not only on attributes but on differences.
While they discuss letter perception, the same discrimination
value would hold for word perception.

Because these errors are so common in beginning reading, a

list of the most common errors is presented here to be used as forced discrimination training exercises. These words are taken from the Fitzgerald and Fitzgerald Basic Integrating Core Vocabulary (1965) and space is provided at the end for individual errors the child may make. It would be of greater benefit, if time permitted, for the teacher to use error as the source of content, and simply make up similar exercises as the errors occurred.

Procedure: The teacher tells the child the two words to be discriminated. They are typed on a page. The words are pointed to by the child as he says the words after the teacher. (Examples follow) He then says the words as they are presented in the exercises as quickly as he can correctly make the discriminations. The teacher follows his progress, making immediate corrections as he proceeds. If errors are made, the child repeats the reading of the words until he can make the required discriminations correctly. Teachers may use preferred reinforcement techniques but should limit the time spent in this activity to two or three minutes a day.

PRIMARY LIST

1. we me me we me we we me
2. at it it at at at it at
3. in on in in on on in on
4. am an an am an am am an
5. it if if if it it if it
6. is as is as as as is as
7. has his has his has his has
8. far for far for for for far
9. fast first fast first first fast
10. hot not hot not not hot not
11. every very every very very
12. full fall full full full fall
13. her here her here her her here
14. how now now now how now how
15. give gave give give gave gave

16. how who who who how who how
17. get got get get got got get
18. come came come come came come
19. on no no no on on on no
20. own now now own own now now
21. us use use us use us use
22. new now now new now new now
23. white write white write white
24. some soon some soon soon some
25. will well will well will well
26. ran run ran run run ran run
27. then them then then them them
28. saw was was saw was was saw
29. these those these those those
30. there three there there three
31. where were where where were
32. went want went want want went
33.
34.
35.
36.

INTERMEDIATE LIST

1. we me we we me me me we we me we we me
2. at it it at at it at at it it at   at at
3. in in in in on on on in in on in on on
4. am an an am an am am am an am am an an
5. it if if if it it if it if if it it if
6. is as is as as as is as is is is as as
7. has his has his has his has his his has his
8. far for far for for for far for far far for
9. fast first fast first first fast first fast fast
10. hot not hot not not not hot hot not not hot
11. every very every very very every every very very
12. full fall full fall fall full fall fall full
13. her here her here here her here here her her

14. how   now   now   now   how   now   how   now   how   now
15. give   gave   give   gave   gave   give   gave   give   give
16. come   came   came   come   come   came   came   come   come
17. how   who   who   who   how   how   who   how   how   who
18. get   got   get   get   got   got   get   got   get   get   got
19. on   no   no   no   on   on   on   no   no   on   no   on   on
20. own   now   now   own   own   own   now   now   now   own
21. new   now   now   new   new   now   now   new   new   now
22. us   use   use   us   use   us   use   us   us   use   use   use
23. white   write   white   write   white   write   write   write
24. some   soon   some   some   soon   some   some   soon   soon
25. will   well   well   will   will   well   well   well   will
26. ran   run   ran   run   run   run   ran   ran   run   ran   ran
27. then   then   them   then   them   them   then   them   then
28. saw   was   was   saw   saw   was   saw   was   saw   saw   was
29. these   those   those   these   these   those   these   those
30. there   three   three   there   three   there   there   three
31. where   were   where   were   were   where   were   where
32. went   want   went   want   want   went   want   went   went
33.
34.
35.
36.
37.
38.
39.
40.
41.
42.
43.
44.
45.

The words are presented in two type sizes. While the larger type is intended for use by primary grade children, it can be used effectively by older children who evidence difficulties with visual discrimination. The large print provides a stimulus condition which makes details more easily discerned. The child moves from correct perception in large print to discriminating the same differences in smaller print.

The same technique is applicable to errors involving letters which are easily confusable:

b d b b b d d b d b b b d d d d b

p q p p p p q q q p q p q p p q p

These can also be presented in two sizes of print to facilitate the discrimination. Because of the repetitious nature of this exercise, the teacher should be watching for signs of fatigue or boredom and discontinue the activity temporarily, going to a regular intermittent teaching sequence and changing the reinforcers used to maintain active attention.

When regular intermittent schedules of teaching are used in any rote teaching, the time sequence of teaching itself is exploited as an aid in learning. The combination of the isolated nature of the task and the need for repetition increase the tendency of the child to become inattentive. Instead of practicing a skill every day, a teacher may schedule the practice every third day, or for three days in a row, and then include a two or three day lapse. The scheduling can be individually planned, but the essential point is that it is preplanned.

Frequently, if a child is on a planned reinforcement program, simply changing the reinforcer such as verbal praise, physical contact, tokens, check marks, or whatever has been selected, can increase attention and active participation on the child's part. In rote teaching involving isolated skills, teachers need to observe children carefully to determine when changes might be beneficial. Either disinterest or fatigue are reliable indicators that changes in schedule or reinforcement are in order or even abandonment of the technique entirely.

Visual Shift

In reading, a common source of difficulty occurs as the child "tracks" or moves from left to right across the page or shifts from the end of the line to the left of the page to begin a new line of print. Shift problems may also be noted as children glance at pictures to verify meaning and cannot find their place as their eyes return to the text. There are tracking programs available which attempt to deal with this problem; however, they have children look for letters in lines of letters. This is not exactly related to the problem the children have. When children exhibit shift difficulties or when eye movements involve frequent regressions, two possible explanations should be considered. In regressive eye movements, the child is probably uncertain of the letter, digraphs or words he is encountering. The problem may not be visual motor dysfunction but lack of "decoding" skills. The child is trying to pick up "cues" from context because he cannot determine the word from the word-attack skills he has at his command. He frequently "miscues" (Goodman, 1965) which can indicate a language problem. A linguistic study of cues and miscues in reading should be thoroughly explored by the teacher before beginning to train the eye with "tracking" programs.

With shift difficulties, the child has not judged the amount of distance involved in the shift. The amount is very consistent, but is two-fold. The eye must travel back across the text and down at the same time. The eye moves and drops. If the child has not discriminated the amount of space involved in the drop, he will end up in the wrong place.

One of the possible solutions to this problem is having the child practice estimating the distance involved in the drop and shift. He can be directed to use his fingers to help "physically" experience the distance, i.e. he uses his fingers to "measure" the distance. This technique should be used immediately following the error. If the child is using a "decoding material" the correction can occur immediately; if the child is reading a text for information or pleasure, "immediately" can be delayed until the conclusion of the session. Perceptual teaching should always be separated from reading which involves getting information and enjoyment.

With very low-achieving children, sporadic teaching is often ineffective. If the technique is used, it should be used consistently following some predetermined schedule. Providing the training immediately following the error is of course the ideal way because the child understands why he is doing something. But providing it regularly at a later time is the second-best route and just as effective. This is a better solution to the problem than the frequently used one which involves using the child's finger, a marker or a pacer, because it reqires the child to deal directly with the underlying problem, judging distance, instead of providing a support condition which by-passes the problem.

Again, a word of caution. Visual shift problems can accompany uncertainty about words or meaning. This should be explored for teaching attention, for these problems may be distracting the child's attention from the shift's perceptual demands.

Proprioceptive Teaching

While kinesthetic teaching, using tracing and verbalization, is an invaluable support for visual perception, it deals only tangentially with some of the common difficulties children have in auditory perception. The hand can help the eye and pick up some of the same perceptual information, but does not serve the same function for the ear. However, haptic (tactile) and kinesthetic factors are involved in articulatory-auditory responses and making the child aware of their function should serve as a perceptual support condition. Awareness of the sensations of the body itself is called *proprioceptive information.* The reliance on learning the physical formation of the sounds in order to help in discriminating them is a technique which is commonly used by speech pathologists and therapists, but only incidentally by teachers.

Two very common problems for which this technique is used are the articulation of various consonants and the discrimination of the short vowels. When these are found the usual teaching method is to repeat the associations until the child learns. Deliberate use of the proprioceptive cues is suggested as an additional support condition. Proprioceptive cues should be used in somewhat the same way as tracing, continuously or even as warm-up exercises, until the child makes the discriminations which allow for the articulation or association without hesitation.

From differentiation theory and linguistic theory we assume that phonemes possess distinctive features and are created through articulatory contrasts anchored in resonances, stops, frictions, and explosions. Vowels are classified by the shape of the mouth-space and consonants as plosives, fricatives, dentals, labials, etc. It is the perceptual information in these actions which we wish to highlight for the child. This information also comes from touch and movement, but the cooperating body areas differ. The skin, the vibratory mechanisms of the larynx and the ear as well as the muscles of the mouth and movements of the jaw joint are involved. Proprioceptive teaching simply directs the child's attention consistently to these body sensations and movements in order to develop active and explicit awareness of the distinctive features and contrasts, rather than assuming passive and implicit awareness. With tracing, the eye is being directed to distinctive features in visual stimuli in order to detect invariants and structure; with proprioceptive teaching, the ear is directed to the distinctive features in auditory stimuli and the skin, muscles and joints serve the function of supplying the redundant information common to touch and hearing.

Tongue position is the critical factor that differentiates the vowel sounds. The tongue is placed in a particular position in the mouth and a voicing sound is produced and vibrates in the larynx. The changes in tongue position are slight, and this makes the differentiation more difficult.

Lefevre (1964) presents a vowel trapezoid, McLean (1974) a rectangle, and the Lindamoods (1971) a circle. While there are slight differences in their classifications, all of them deal with the vowels as those which are high, middle or low and produced in the front, center or back of the mouth.

The Lindamoods have adapted this classification system for teaching, and include it in a program designed for teaching auditory discrimination skills. Teachers can understand the principles and adapt them for use with individual children. One of the most important aspects of the teaching suggested by the Lindamoods is that the teacher and the child share an overview of how all of the vowel sounds are made, so that they have a broader understanding of what they are learning. The chances of abstracting invariants and structure in the phonemic system should be greater if, as the Lindamoods suggest, children receive direct instruction in sound formation. This is because of the increased awareness of the physical sensations and the differentiation of the phonemes it supports.

The vowels are singled out for discussion because they are not only difficult to discriminate visually and auditorially, but five symbols stand for twelve sounds. This increases the ambiguity with which the child must cope. They also occur in the middle of words which, according to the laws of serial position, is the last thing learned in sequential material. The same techniques are of course suitable for teaching consonant discrimination.

TEACHING DECODING

In the initial stage of learning to read, the child is introduced to symbols for his verbal language. Many theorists have suggested that beginning reading is essentially a decoding process and emphasis should be placed on learning the sound-symbol relationships (Chall, 1967).

Most children learn to read no matter which method is used to introduce reading (Bond and Dykstra, 1967), and they learn the code incidentally if it is not directly taught.

For the low-achieving child who has not learned to read, code emphasis needs consideration. However, it could be a seriously limiting form of instruction unless it were included in an appraisal of the child's total language needs in general and unless it assumed its appropriate place in the reading process specifically.

The last chapter placed reading in a development hierarchy related to language and emphasized the importance of auditory skills. Especially important is the child's knowledge about the segmentation and sequence of sounds in spoken words. It should have great bearing on the choice of method of code instruction.

There are two approaches to teaching decoding; one is synthetic and the other is analytic. They are popularly known as "phonic" or "linguistic" methods. The major difference is that phonic methods teach the names and sounds of the alphabet and sound blendings and are usually limited to teaching these associations in single words. They assemble words, building them from known elements. "Linguistic" methods teach through spelling patterns which are organized according to a classificaiton system of spelling rules and increasing complexity of vowel and consonant patterns. They usually do not teach the names or sounds of the letters and they do not teach sound blending.

The child is enabled to generalize this knowledge from the patterned support. The "linguistic" approach is used to teach patterns in lists of words and in reader format. If this approach is used in a reader, meaning emphasis must be restricted because of the control of the spelling pattern. The intent is to provide enough regularity in the spelling patterns and to introduce diversity slowly so that the ambiguity is kept to a minimum and the child is able to generalize. "Linguistic" is used with quotation marks because linguists are interested in the structure of language and all of its meaning-bearing patterns and the application of linguistic theory in the development of these materials is extremely limited.

Some of the newer "linguistic" decoding materials use systematic reinforcement and charting of knowledge of results as a method of teaching the phonemic-graphemic relationships. Everyone goes through the same material which deals with single words in lists, but rate and reinforcement may vary as well as repetition and they are criterion referenced in terms of accuracy. One even includes timed sentence reading to provide for generalization in the act of reading (Monterey Language Program, 1972).

In teaching low-achieving children important curriculum considerations are theoretical approach, content, format, and hierarchy of learning tasks. However, they are not more important than individual differences in children. From our previous discussion about invariants in language, two were considered basic to function in both the pronemic and graphemic systems. These invariants were *segmentation* and *sequence*. Children need to be aware that there are individual sounds in words and that they follow each other in predictable sequences; the same is true for letters. These are "entry level" skills. The newer decoding materials assume that children know this about verbal language and that they will "discover" or generalize it about graphic language. The performance of some low-achievers demonstrates that the former is not always true and that the latter frequently does not occur. The most important thing for the teacher to be aware of in these approaches is what they do not teach so that compensation can occur.

"Linguistic" materials teach patterned whole words and do not allow for individual letter-sound teaching or for blending. Phonic methods teach segmentation and sequence to everyone, whether it is appropriate teaching or not.

When a child fails in the decoding aspect of reading, the teacher should first determine whether the child has distinguished or is aware of the individuality of words in the speech-stream or sentence; second, whether he has distinguished phonemes in words and their sequence in verbal language; third, that he has sufficiently distinguished the letters to attach a name or a sound; and last, that he can maintain the sequence visually or understands the left to right orientation of graphic language.

When the preceding problems are discovered, words can be distinguished by counting them in sentences, hand signals can be used to indicate beginning and ends of words and position of sounds (Chapter 1); sound spelling techniques can be used to teach segmentation and sequence at a verbal level, with or without letter names (Chapter 1); letters can be distinguished through verbalization of salient cues (Chapter 4), and sequence can be taught through tracing (Chapter 3). An individually determined program of decoding should be taught to low-achieving children, based on these considerations, and all other teaching of reading should make up for the limitations of this emphasis. The other reading activities should also be carefully planned; an overemphasis on the mechanics of reading for the low achiever is just as limiting as it is for any other group of children.

TEACHING VOCABULARY

There are two instructional areas in vocabulary development related to teaching reading. One involves learning "sight vocabularies" and the other relates to increasing the number and meaning of words that are available to the child to make meaning more precise and enhance comprehension.

Lefevre (1964) as do many linguists, argues for a meaning emphasis in all aspects of reading instruction. Even in word study, an analytic approach is emphasized. An effort is made to teach elements in context. But some words are relatively less "meaningful." These words are called *structure* words. They present great difficulties to many children.

These words, about 300 of them, can be classified into five groups. Essentially, they are words which help give meaning to other words.

1. Noun Markers—a, the, some, any, three, this, my, few . . .
2. Verb Markers—am, are, is, was have, has, had . . .
3. Phrase Markers—up, down, in, out, above, below . . .
4. Clause Markers—if, because, that, how, whom, why . . .
5. Question Markers—who, why, how, when, what, where . . .

There are also conjunctions such as and, but, for, nor, or, yet and so; proposers, such as please, if you please, if you don't mind, and so on. Starters are casual expressions such as Well, Oh, Say, Look, Now, Why, O.K., Listen (Lefevre, 1964).

Nearly half of the Dolch Basic Sight Vocabulary consists of structure words. From this list Lefevre (1964, pp. 134-137) selects the following as examples:

by	were	which	where	what	this
are	all	is	goes	from	me
a	at	into	around	to	has
all	any	if	his	because	the
it	an	many	but	after	not
in	had	may	both	about	of
I	have	as	four	can	we
did	him	am	every	so	could
fly	its	does	eight	five	seven
hurt	before	her	how	six	like
no	start	down	get	got	don't
please	on	or	you	your	yes
under	ten	they	my	much	must
myself	off	over	out	our	one
was	two	us	up	upon	with
some	shall	she	who	would	why
when	their	them	that	these	three
			those		

Lefevre argues against teaching the words in isolation because in order to gain meaning they must be learned as words which signal the syntactical structure of meaning-bearing language patterns. If they are taught alone with a primary stress, they may not later be read with the intonation patterns of speech and be lost in lending meaning to the words in context.

This presents us with a dilemma. In order to differentiate word forms and patterns we need to single words out and, in order to get their meanings and the meanings they help to convey, we need to learn words in context.

Probably the best solution to this problem is for the teacher to understand which words are structure words and to emphasize them in the sentences in which they occur in reading; teach them in the sentences in which they occur when errors are made, or at least in phrases; and lift the word for tracing study to differentiate its segments—their details, orientation and sequence—when errors are persistent. Closure should be brought to this activity by reading the word again in the original context in which the error occurred, but correctly.

With these words, both meaning and perception must interact to help memory and so both require teaching attention. If both kinds of teaching are done systematically and are based on child error, there will not be a tendency to study lists of words which are arbitrarily selected because most children who have reading problems miss them. This approach lends itself to individualized instruction, but requires some record-keeping devices on the part of the teacher as well as the ability to identify a word as a structure word. If word study is always based on error, or the fact that the child missed the word in a natural reading situation, the act of studying an individual word gains added meaning for the child. He knows why he is spending extra time on the word, and attention can be given to both perception and contextual meaning during the regularly scheduled "missed word" study period. The words that individual children miss, that they do not know by sight, will vary and teaching from error allows for complete individualization in this area. If the word and the page number are recorded as errors occur, they will already be in "lists" and can be reviewed, traced and easily read in sentences and phrases.

Developing Word Meaning

Probably, the single most important factor which will make a difference in teaching vocabulary is the allotment of *time* given to it. If time is scheduled to teach the meaning of words, children's vocabularies will reflect it. Most vocabulary development is based on an informal set of procedures which, sporadically employed, may be insufficient for the low-achieving child.

Weintraub (1968) states that wide reading is not as effective in learning new words as direct instruction. Direct instruction in vocabulary development has many facets and, in reading, decisions need to be made about whether word study is done before or after the reading period and what procedures can be most effective in increasing this form of word knowledge. Because word knowledge and academic success are so closely related, it is worth looking at some of the suggestions available in the literature in this field.

Pflaum (1973) suggests that learning new words and an extension of meaning of old words should be a major objective. Stating that the use of context is the major means for vocabulary extension, she suggests that teachers include in their activities in this curriculum area:

1. Direct experience with the concepts of words,
2. the use of comparison and contrast,
3. the use of familiar language associations,
4. context,
5. class discussion,
6. affix study, and
7. word derivation.

She also indicates that the approach used should be inductive. Concepts that are well known should be presented first, and children should develop attributes of the word with other words they already know. For example: woman—human, female, adult. Some of her suggestions include presenting a word and related words for analysis: lake-stream-river-pond-ocean. The words are given in categories and the child must name the category. Words can be given which share a relationship and the child names the relationship. Multiple meanings of words should be presented in several contexts.

Deighton (1959) feels that the use of context alone is a limited technique. It will not help with strange words and only one meaning is usually revealed. The entire meaning is not explained and context gives only clues. It is also slow. The ways in which context functions to reveal meaning is through direct definition, example, modifiers, restatement and inference. He states that word analysis gives only one meaning of a word, that in teaching it would be of value to use (1) base words, (2) words in combination, (3) synonyms and antonyms, (4) contrasting words and (5) derivatives.

Langer (1969) expresses a broader point of view. "Comprehension does not depend on vocabulary itself, but on the ideas the vocabulary represents" (p. 383). Reading is a thinking process, and vocabulary development should be placed in this context.

1. The role of actual experience should be emphasized. Role playing and dramatization are invaluable tools.
2. Categorization is of value. New experiences should be related to old ones.
3. Purposeful reading which involves answering questions based on concepts is helpful. Convergent and divergent thinking can be developed. Convergent thinking deals with facts and inferences or what the writer is implying. "Divergent thinking requires questions which extend and challenge the writer's logic, evidence and conclusions" (*ibid.*, p. 384).

Cohen (1969), in relating vocabulary development to the early childhood period, suggests simply piling up examples to illustrate meaning. It is valuable to provide the description of a function or procedure that the word represents with a great deal of detail. Mood itself can be used to define words, as well as meaningful context. Contrast and comparison are valuable and using similes is also helpful. Familiar experiences which are linked with the concepts presented will extend meaning.

Dean (1970) suggests deliberately picking long words or "sesquipedalians," funny words or nonsense words. Strickland (1962) reinforces vocabulary goals as both depth of meaning and precision of meaning. Depth of meaning involves many associations and precision involves exact definition.

Weintraub (1968) summarizes by saying that there are actually four different vocabularies that require attention: listening, speaking, reading and wirting and that they are highly related. The most effective techniques for building vocabulary relate to (1) context, (2) previous experience, and (3) studying root words.

Following Weintraub's suggestions, teachers might consider teaching vocabulary in relation to the communication process, setting times during the day or week when they attend to this specifically and also deciding which of the teaching suggestions will form their set of procedures for developing meaning. The main point being made here is that neither time nor procedure should be casually determined.

A Suggested Vocabulary Development Sequence

For teachers working with severely language-limited children, it may prove valuable to consider another aspect of vocabulary development. A surprising number of children who are in the low-achieving group do not possess a complete vocabulary relating to their own bodies. This might be a good place to start if the teacher is taking stock of the vocabulary that exists in the child's listening or speaking repertoire. Next, the teacher might examine the vocabulary as related to spatial, temporary and quantitative concepts. Many of these are structure words and present difficulties to children in reading. The Boehm Basic Concept Test (1967) provides a differentiated list from which to start. The vocabulary of the classroom may present difficulty to some children, and the objects in the room—their relationships, uses and functions—can serve as a source of words. The language of teacher direction is also a very specialized vocabulary which may not be clearly understood by the child, and bears some scrutiny by the teacher as a source of teaching material. The vocabulary of the playground or of the community might follow, and the choice could vary in unlimited fashion depending on the classroom activities. Curriculum areas provide the major content for vocabulary development in schools; arithmetic, reading, soical stuides, music and art can all be used for developing listening, speaking, reading and writing vocabularies of the children. Special student interests are particularly valuable sources of words because of the relationship of an individual's desire to learn the meaning lent by the context of the lesson.

If time is provided for study, and if context experiences and root words are consistently explored to increase the meaning of words which are selected from various curriculum areas, children's vocabularies should increase.

COMPREHENSION

The discussion about building vocabulary is a good introduction to the discussion of comprehension. A vocabulary with depth and breadth serves the same relationship to comprehension that differentiation of letter form serves for word perception. It is an "entry-level" skill. Essentially, reading comprehension involves thinking and the same skills involved in receiving information discussed in listening comprehension apply to reading comprehension. The cognitive processes used by the child do not differ; the mode of intake varies.

Compensating for Skill Emphasis

This discussion of comprehension will not deal with the breakdown of skills usually discussed when comprehension is covered in texts. Instead the experience story will be advanced as a technique for use with all low-achieving children where any langauge process functions inadequately. Its use is suggested on a daily basis to supplement, complement and integrate all forms of language instruction. Because so much emphasis in the teaching of the low achieving child is placed on cue training, skills and details, some integrative vehicle is needed which, used regularly, can make up for the inadequacies and disassociation inherent in this form of instruction. While it may be necessary and beneficial to provide skill teaching—and this is a commonly accepted teaching practice—it is not so common to find that teachers understand the need to compensate for its limitations.

Levine (1970) makes a very important point in relation to the usual teaching practices which develop comprehension skills. We cannot teach comprehension as we now conceptualize it as a separate skill. Comprehension comes with experience and familiarity with a body of knowledge, and there is probably little transfer between comprehension in different subject matter fields. When a basal series is used to teach reading, developing comprehension consists of asking questions about literal meaning. When workbooks are used to develop comprehension skills, they may deal with nonliteral comprehension to some extent, but they are paper and pencil tasks and not experientially based. Levine offers a solution to this problem: a vast increase in the quantity of reading provided and expected of the low-achieving child, *in school*.

Frequently, one of the factors in the background of the low-achieving child is inadequate adult-child verbal interatcions. There simply has not been enough talking. While increasing the amount of reading done by the low achiever is an invaluable adjunct to any program for developing comprehension, by itself it may not make up for this particular deficit. Pairing this increase in reading with consistent use of the experience story is suggested as a solution. The experience story, as suggested here, is a vehicle for integrating language function with experience as it is guided by the teacher. The discussions are as important as the writing of the story or essay and should be viewed in that light. It is not just another activity which occupies the child while the teacher attends to other duties. It is the means by which the teacher individualizes instruction in comprehension, guides the child's thinking, develops vocabulary, teachers language structure, and integrates knowledge. It is an ideal medium for compensating for skill teaching, and at the same time can expose verbal and graphic language areas which require specific attention.

The Place of the Reading Series

Teachers need materials which provide for continuity in teaching skills. The basic reader serves that function well. Children need to read what others have written and they need to read to others and share discussions about the concepts presented. Essentially, the basic reader shared in a group provides for the oral reading experiences children need. Many of the new readers are little more than "decoding" exercises, and if that is the case teachers will have to compensate for the incompleteness of the material for oral reading experiences. Many basic reading series try to cover all of the language arts to some extent, but for certain children they will be inadequate because they need more emphasis in a particular area. The experience story is not being suggested instead of a basic reader since a reader can serve as the hub of a skill development program. It is being suggested as a complement to a reader, and because of its essentially integrative function in the language arts the experience story can perform a needed service. Where readers serve the receptive function in the language arts, the experience story serves the expressive one.

Because so much emphasis is put on the experience story here, "revisiting" this form in relation to the needs of the low-achieving child is in order.

The Experience Story Revisited

Many low-achieving children are the products of poverty. Its effect on learning to read deserves special consideration. This issue is one of the most pressing challenges that American education faces. While it would be comforting to believe that the solution lay in the selection of one method of teaching over another, this is simply not the case. In order to solve the problem, educators will have to face the complexities of the dilemma and respond to them, openly and creatively. While education is a powerful force in shaping the behavior of children, it is not the only force and it always reflects the philosophy and wishes of more powerful forces in society. These forces are economic and political and it is here that change must come. Recognizing that reading method alone is inadequate as a solution to the problem, and that major basic alterations are needed, it is still possible to meet this challenge more effectively in teaching than we have done. The language-experience approach to teaching reading meets many basic needs and will here be developed as a partial solution, because in the development of a technology of teaching, we are losing sight of the position of reading in the total communication process as it relates to social interaction.

Tax (1968) points out that the Coleman report of the Civil Rights Commission of 1967 presented the view that compensatory education in black ghetto schools has failed. It stated that school achievement by black students was increased when they were in integrated classrooms; that the compensatory programs in ghetto schools could not make up for the importance of the influence of social milieu, class and peer factors on achievement. This presupposes that the transmission of white middle class culture is the only way to pass on an achievement orientation. If blacks were determining goals, policies and operation of ghetto schools, we might find an entirely different achievement situation. In most ghetto schools culture is being passed on though one link, the teacher, and "Students of acculturation know that it is impossible to impose the culture of one group on another by providing only a single, weak link. The crux of the matter with regard to education is the question of whose culture is to be transmitted (Tax, 1968, p. 5)."

This is an important aspect of reading failure. *Reading and cultural values cannot be separated.* Hess (1968) describes the effects that poverty in urban life has on the behavior of the black mother. He describes the lack of power, prestige and alternatives for action in the physical and social environment which limit the choices of residence, education and employment and lead to social and physical immobility. These bring with them low esteem and a sense of incompetence and passivity. They also lead to a simplification and lack of diversity in the experience world and a restriction of the variety of the forms of language avaialble for communication. This grows out of the limitations on the choices for action and movement in the environment. It ends in a rejection of intellectual in favor of practical thinking.

Ghetto and lower-class members become isolated and receive less information and so they less effectively form judgments on the factors which affect their lives.

In listing factors which affect the child's reading readiness scores and reflect the circumstances of the home, Hess suggests that the amount of time the mother spends reading to the child, the number of people in the house or the crowding, the mother's attitude toward the outside world, the amount of initiative she demonstrates and her belief that the world offers opportunities, her membership in community organizations and activities in community projects all are correlated with the child's reading success. Hess (1968, p. 98) also indicates that social class and behavior control methods are related and that there is an inverse relation between the two. Parental warmth is also a factor in the child's reading success. What Hess demonstrates is that "social structure of society is connected with the cognitive performance of the individual in the structure."

Middle and lower class members use language differently to cue children to appropriate behaviors. Bernstein (1964) has used the example of the middle class mother who quiets her child by saying, "I'd rather you made less noise, darling," and the lower class mother who commands the same behavior with "Shut-up!".

In discussing the relationship of language to the development of reading skills, Hess acknowledges its importance but suggests that it forms one of a "cluster of variables." He also calls attention to the teaching style of the mother and suggests that clear directions, models, and requests for performance as feedback are correlated with reading success.

In discussing the language limitations of the "socio-economically handicapped," Stern (1968) suggests that language limitations can be divided into three areas: (1) listening comprehension, the inability to follow directions and to understand the meaning of verbal presentation, (2) language production, the child's inability to communicate verbally, especially in describing and interpreting or asking questions about the environment to adults, and (3) verbal mediation, the inability to use language at the abstract level, categorizing, organizing thoughts and problem solving, drawing inferences from given information. She makes the point that the disadvantaged youngster starts school with a six-month handicap and its grows as he goes through school so that by the time he is in the eighth grade he is reading at third grade level. In specifically describing what constitutes the language differences which are apparent, Bernstein (1964) is cited as using the term "restricted" for the lower class and "elaborated" for the middle class language system. Restricted language refers to the use of incomplete or simple sentence structure, limited vocabulary, repetitious use of conjunctions and limited use of adjectives and adverbs. Stern goes on to question the success of perceptual training programs and states there is a difference of opinion about the results of early training in cognitive skills.

One of the best discussions of this problem is presented by Kohlberg (1968). He states that:

> Specific types of preschool academic and linguistic training, even if immediately successful, are unlikely to have long-run general beneficial effects and that programs directed toward raising general psychometric intelligence are unlikely to have marked success . . . more generally, cognitive-developmental theory does less to suggest or support radical new preschool cognitive-stimulation programs than it does to clarify the child-centered developmental approach to education expressed in its broadest form by John Dewey. The approach departs more from traditional child development concerns in providing a systematic analysis of the cognitive-structural and cognitive-interest of the play, aesthetic, constructive, and social activities which form the heart of the preschool, than in suggesting narrowly "cognitive" activities in the preschool (p. 1056).

Kohlberg makes the point that the stimulation in the environment of the low socio-ecomonic group in this country is relatively constant throughout life, and the stability of early intelligence tests as a predictor of later behavior is due to the constancy of the deprivation throughout childhood. In commenting on the ideas of Bereiter and Engleman (1966) as they attempt to translate Bernstein's (1970) ideas about "restricted" and "elaborated" codes of the lower and the middle classes, he suggests that "this is best done through integration so that it is picked up through modeled behavior, rather than through direct teaching." Modeling will occur if integrations wins out as a point of view in this country. If segregation occurs however, in terms of the major cities in the United States becoming ghettos, language changes may be slower, but achievement may be greater because blacks will have some degree of control, at least at the local level, and more to say about curriculum content. The cultural dichotomy will be somewhat lessened.

To teach reading as a decoding process or separate it from the cultural life of the child, or from the communication process itself, is a short-sighted solution.

> Much of the context of our schools is unwittingly drawn from aspects of the symbolic world of the middle class, and so when the child steps into school he is stepping into a symbolic system which does not provide him with a linkage outside (Bernstein, p. 347).

If, in addition, as Bernstein points out, the "deficit in the child" position is taken by the school, it places the entire burden of inadequacy on the children and the family, and it leaves the teacher and the school free of such charges. This position is not supported by current cognitive learning theories in education, or by any sociological appraisal of the relationship between society and education.

Staten Webster (1968), in his review of the research on reading programs, isolates specific learning problems associated with poverty. First, there is the lack of attentiveness, and knowledge of the environment is limited. The limitations and the homogeneity of experience increase the amount of retardation as the children advance in school. There are also auditory discrimination and visual discrimination problems. (As we have noted, these may be related to undifferentiated perception due to inadequate attention behavior.) Vocabularies are smaller and there are unique articulation problems. The isolation of the poor contributes to the limitations in language which include deficits (or at least differences) in syntactical use and its concern with concrete rather than abstract ideas. Cognitive style also feels the pinch of poverty and the poor are more motoric in style preference. Visual motor output is preferred over auditory vocal. There are also problems in self-esteem. In summary, he states:

The foregoing problems have been identified as being those which inhibit the educational development of disadvantaged learners. Regardless of the fact that some of these factors perhaps have a greater impact upon reading achievement than do others, they should be given attention by those planning reading programs designed to aid the disadvantaged learner (Webster, p. 6).

The problems of poverty and the value of cultural heritage are never separated. They are equated. The child is regarded as deficient, not the school nor its method.

There are many educators who take exception to these positions and who feel that the differences in language are quite secondary to the fact that the school maintains and reinforces the social, cultural and economic position of those in the lower class. Labeling differences in language as inadequacies in lower class children may create attitudes in teachers which serve to maintain a superior-inferior relationship which has a pervasive and depressing effect on learning. The differences in language, symbolism, cognitive style and methods of control may be quite secondary to the broader social status relationships of the learner and the teacher. It would be naive to assume that the teacher or a method alone could deal with such overwhelming social problems in the relationship of education to those in the lower socio-economic levels in this country. However, methods can make *some* differences and awareness can foster *some* shift in relationships.

From discussion about the problems of teaching children who have come into schools without the prerequisite skills necessary for learning to read and lacking perceptual, cognitive, language and social skills, it is obvious that a narrow view of the teaching of these children will not produce readers. The best methods would be those that would provide for opportunities for the increments that have been noted "in training programs," and the broad general supportive continuing stimulation necessary to maintain and develop skills as the child goes through school, and those which value cultural differences. Any program aimed at developing reading skill will also have to develop sensory motor or perceptual awareness, language, cognitive and social skill and will best accomplish this in an environment that values communication as a social asset, and does not consider reading as merely a disassociated rote learning process or a score on a reading test.

When reading is regarded not as an isolate but as part of language skills and experience, it becomes more apparent why the prerequisite skills are important. The child must learn to listen, to speak, to read, and to write about something. These skills are interrelated and reading and writing are dependent on listening and speaking skills. Speaking and listening are learned incidentally in the family, while reading and writing involve structured teaching in the school. The question that needs to be asked and answered by research is whether structured teaching outside a natural context of those skills that are usually learned incidently will provide a base solid enough to support the later learning and, even more important, a continuing desire to learn. As has been indicated before, the questions do not only involve skill but motivation and cultural attitudes and values, and the most important ability of middle class schools to be flexible enough to use divergent methods and to allow for some social mobility of the learner.

Two aspects of the programs that have been carried out seem obvious. In general, with systematic teaching there is improved performance in the specific taught. The transfer of this training to reading is less well supported (Stauffer, 1967). Very little research is available which attempts to deal with the problems broadly. Most of the research involves either training programs or reading methods, and the emphasis is not on analysis of individual need or on valuing and enhancing cultural, social or economic differences and relating reading and wirting content to them.

Those methods which attempt to build from experience are called Language Experience approaches. Usually they are used only long enough to make the shift to another approach, basal reader, linguistic reader or programmed instruction. This occurs because it is difficult to individualize a language experience approach for a group of children. It is slow and time consuming and because there is not a tradition which gives more than lip service to the importance of personal cultural experience and its relation to differences in communication skill. Most reading programs are judged by scores on reading tests, not by a description of the child's reading behavior. Unfortunately, our goals are more words correctly read, not more books enjoyed.

Teaching reading is a matter of extending the use of language. It involves attention to the many aspects of the communication process and cannot be considered as a separate subject or an isolated skill. Success in learning to read is inevitably dependent on the development of listening and speaking skills which precede its teaching and all are equally dependent on the social and emotional experiences which the child has had in his early years. These cannot be separated in the child except for purposes of discussion.

A complicated process when it is taught to children who learn easily, its complications more than multiply when we mix the inherent difficulties in teaching reading itself with the intricate difficulties of children who do not learn quickly or easily in our schools. Successful teaching of reading to the group we designate as "handicapped" or "deprived" children is totally dependent on our abiilty to value them in terms of their individual differences and to relate those differences to the total communication process. This includes its expressive and receptive phrases and their feelings about learning skills; this teaching takes effort, concentration and time.

Adult-Child Verbal Interactions

One of the major problems in teaching low-achieving children is finding vehicles which provide reciprocity in language function between children and teachers. In most teaching-learning situations the teacher is the sender of messages and the child is the receiver. This is a passive language role. As many of the children have had insufficient earlier adult-child language experience, their school experience does not compensate for this difference. The experience story offers an opportunity to reverse this process and to stimulate the flow of language as well as requiring exchanges which place the teacher in the receiving role.

Low-achieving children usually have a variety of problems

related to the use of language, many of them peripheral to the academic problem and more closely related to cultural, social and emotional factors such as attention, the ability to accept instruction in a group, the possession of motivation to pursue unrealistic goals or achieve in rigid schools, to maintain interest in the face of great irrelevance in learning and repeated failure. Our teaching must include some provision for facing these problems. We cannot come armed only with inappropriate methods and materials and we cannot look only at the child as inadequate. We must consider the appropriateness of the demands of the school.

Academic Skill or Motivational Uses

The experience story provides a vehicle with enough flexibility to allow attention to be directed at either the needed academic or the motivational skills. It can serve as a bridge between home and school where there are differences. It supplies a medium for instruction in all areas of communication, listening, speaking, writing, reading and spelling which are meaningfully related to personal experience. It furnishes a natural means of teaching the reorganizational language skills involved in listening and reading and giving back information verbally or in writing; This may be extremely difficult for some children with language, social or cultural differences. It provides practice in these skills and demonstrates and maintains these relationships which, with teacher explanation and direction, can be made quite clear to the child. The relationships of the communication system need to be considered part of the necessary instruction of children in teaching the language arts. Too frequently it is considered teacher information and the child is left to imply the generalizations. The group of children exhibiting difficulties in mastering language skills cannot be counted on to generalize about them. Most children have no idea about how verbal and graphic language are related. The problem does not lie in their lack of ability to understand; the relationship is not taught.

Motivation

Perhaps the greatest strength of the experience story for classroom as well as individual teaching is that it provides for problems of motivation. Personal interests and experience can be tapped and children can explore in great depth an area which is fascinating to them. It is this aspect which makes it such a valuable tool, for in the pursuit of an interest the child fouses his attention through natural motivation and can become totally involved in learning. It is this framework of personal interest which sustains him as an active learner as the teacher analyzes problems and takes time out to provide the necessary practice in deficient skills.

Its Use Does Not Preclude the Use of Other Materials

The use of the experience story need not preclude the utilization of any other material, programmed readers, linguistic readers, culturally based readers, perceptual training material, cognitive skill games or any of the new materials that teach specifics so well. It is not a substitute for these methods and materials. It is concerned, instead, with the development and extension of the structure and content of the child's own language system, which is usually abandoned too soon for many, many children. We use it to introduce reading and then push it aside as we focus on reading from books. The use of the experience story in one of its forms should be maintained consciously as a language teaching strategy all the way through the elementary school, especially for the low-achieving child. It is a bridge within the communication process and between school and society.

Meets Four Goals

Austin (1963, p. 36) states four goals which are achieved with the use of the experience story:

1. The creation of interest in, and a favorable attitude toward, reading by children who discover that they can read what they have written and later what others have written.
2. The integration of the communication process.
3. The development of an understanding on the part of chil-

dren that reading is an important form of communication.
4. The fostering of creative expression.

Strengths

Perhaps the fact that the whole approach is based on the thinking of the children themselves is one of its main strengths. R. V. Allen (1963), a leading proponent of this method of teaching, has stated:

> These experiences which have been selected for the basic framework of the program are ones which, when implemented at the classroom level, require the selection of learning experiences which generate productive thinking, allow freedom of expression, stimulate individuality, value ingenuity, satisfy curiosity, and promote personal satisfaction to the extent that learning to read becomes a lifelong experience which requires more maturing and more complex skills and knowledge (p. 88).

Allen lists twenty experiences which are exploited in this approach:

1. Sharing experiences,
2. discussing experiences,
3. listening to stories,
4. dictating,
5. telling stories,
6. developing speaking, writing and reading relationships,
7. making and reading books,
8. developing awareness of common vocabulary,
9. expanding vocabulary,
10. writing independently,
11. reading whole books,
12. improving style and form,
13. using a variety of resources,
14. reading a variety of symbols,
15. studying words,
16. improving comprehension,
17. outlining,
18. summarizing,
19. integrating and assimilating ideas, and
20. reading critically.

This program is not conceptualized, Allen goes on to point out, as a "reading period."

As it develops, it gives depth of meaning to art and and construction activities; it is the vehicle for conveying meaning of social studies emphasis; it encourages exploration and discovery in science and mathematics; it builds spirit and understanding into the singing of songs and playing of games. It places the "creative thinking process" at the heart of the instructional program (p. 89).

These goals achieved by Allen for classroom teaching are identical for individual teaching. The unique opportunity in the approach to teaching in individualized teaching is that it is specifically adapted to each child. It makes certain that he understands and can perform. For the child between two cultures, the black, the chicano or the culture which is common to poverty, the experience story can provide another link between home and school. This step is not even considered in most reading programs and the child must abandon the wealth of experience which has been his heritage when he steps into the school and faces "Dick and Jane."

Limitations of Programmed and "Linguistic" Methods

Programmed instruction and "linguistic" decoding approaches, while they have much to commend them, do not provide enough verbal performance in terms of interaction with adults and other children, or in terms of self-exploration. They do not deal with thinking skills or with the problems of relating reading to the meaning-bearing elements of verbal language. These must be reconstructed in the receptive act of reading to yield meaning. When limited aproaches are used, it is critical that the teacher compensate for their inadequacies in the total language practice she provides.

Jones (1965, p. 130) points out that "The use of natural child speech should lead to more rapid learning than does the use of unnatural stilted sentences, such as are used in early readers, for these do not make sense to the child." She argues for natural language and against the notion of repetition because of perceptual disintegration that occurs with loss of meaning with the repetition that readers use. Familiarity is necessary but not excessive repetition.

Most of the authorities agree about the desirability of using the language experience approach to begin and introduce reading, but then they diverge. Paul Witty (1963) states:

> Certainly we agree with linguistic scholars who assert that children's natural oral expression should be used in their initial reading instruction. But how far should this practice be carried? To what extent and by what means should materials for reading instruction be enriched and extended further at various levels? What types of materials are essential in a balanced reading program that gives full recognition to the importance of interest, motive and need as well as to the role of varied forms of oral expression? (p. 107)

Witty indicates an awareness of the need to place reading in its proper framework, broader than an isolated process. The point of divergence among authorities comes, not over the understanding of the interrelationships in the communication progress but of the how to teach and when to teach questions.

While linguists are quite aware of the totality of the communication process, when they design materials to teach reading they come up with constricted points of view, as exemplified in most of what are called linguistic readers and programmed instruction. *It still remains the lot of the teacher to design and implement a balanced reading program for each child.*

There are two major points of view in the translation of linguistic principles to reading programs. One point of view stresses "letter-to-sound" relationships. These are simply reformulations of the older phonics approach. The other stresses meaning-hearing patterns, not word meaning as used in basal readers, but intonation, word order and syntax. Tabachnick (1963) points out that language deals with sound and social interaction. He notes that there is a structure of expression and a structure of content. Linguists so far have only attended to the structure of expression, the sound structure of the language, and have not been able to deal with content structure or the interaction of the two. This is where language and experience merge. This meeting is critical for meaning, and it points to the need for exploiting the content structure unique to individual children—the personal meaningful language of each child.

When linguists write readers, they are more interested in

the structure of expression, and they ignore content to a great extent. They almost entirely ignore individual differences of the learner, except for the provision of speed in programmed learning.

Chall (1967) reviews the research and summarizes the field for IRA stating: "the real promise of linguistics and perhaps its greatest contributions to reading instruction will ultimately come in its application to the understanding of the comprehension process." That lies in the future.

The issues in teaching reading are by no means settled and teachers are going to need to know and be familiar with a great many methods and materials, learn to be *observant* of children's behavior in response to the route they have chosen to pursue in teaching, and become extremely *adaptive* in responding to the behavior they see, so that changes can be made to facilitate learning. To a large extent, the skill of the teacher is the major determinant of the program and process for the child. We know that we can identify children early who may encounter difficulties in school, and we also know that there is much we can do to lessen these difficulties. This includes early education and enriched educational programs that provide prereading skills; enrichment should continue throughout school as long as needed by the children. The early education should provide for diversity of experience, increased opportunity to hear and use language, specific training programs in perceptual skills, and learning to work in groups. The early education should focus attention through interest and play, and include planned adult-mediated learning or tutoring, and closer relationships between school and home. A specific reading method is not the answer alone for the children who do not learn. But the reading program should, whether it is individual or group:

1. Use the child's speech to help him understand and value his own experience and to elaborate on both;
2. Record the child's speech to help him understand the relationship of experience, speech and writing, and point out this relationship to the child;
3. Use the writing of the child's speech to help him understand the relationship of sound to symbol;

4. Read the written speech to get meaning and to help him understand the relationship of symbol to sound;
5. Use the mistakes the child makes to teach him exactly what he does not know;
6. Continue with this approach until the child's listening, speaking, writing and reading skills are adequate;
7. Include these activities, regardless of any other method or material being used.

A language experience approach can be used for teaching, listening, speaking, reading or writing as well as for spelling or thinking. It is an ideal vehicle for developing self-awareness and for validating children's likes or dislikes, feelings, opinions, and wishes. It also can be used to develop a child's verbal language with an emphasis placed on sentence structure.

Syntax

Lefevre (1964) points out that in analyzing language from a structural point of view, three levels can be isolated: phonemes, morphemes and syntax. *Phonemes* are the basic sound units and the smallest class of significant speech sounds. There are nine simple vowels, three semivowels and twenty-one consonants in American English. There are also four levels of pitch, four degrees of stress on syllables and four junctures or ways of termination of speech. *Morphemes* are the basic meaning-bearing units of language. They include word bases or roots, prefixes, suffixes, and word-form changes and inflections. These are of major concern in teaching decoding.

Syntax, however, includes patterns of morphemes into larger units such as noun or verb groups or clusters, prepositional groups, clauses and sentences. There are four signaling systems in American English: intonation, syntactical function order in sentence patterns, and structure words as well as word-form changes. *Intonation* involves pitch, stress and juncture. Juncture is only partially represented by capitals, periods, semicolons and question marks. *Syntactical function* order includes four important sentence patterns which can be modified or expanded through substitution, inversion and transformation. *Structure words* are those which have few referents outside the language system itself and are relatively lacking in meaning or content. Word-form changes include plurals, possessives, verb parts and adjective comparison. Reading is not simply a matter "decoding," although decoding certainly may be a facilitating and necessary condition for reading.

Strickland (1962) agrees with Lefevre when she states:

> It is possible that children need help to recognize and understand the entire phonemic scheme of English, not only the basic phonemes that are built into morphemes but also the suprasegmental phonemes of pitch, stress, and juncture as they use them in oral speech. Such knowledge might help children better turn the stimulus of printed symbols into oral langauge patterns for both comprehension and interpretation (p. 106).

Lefevre (1964) supports a large view of teaching reading in its relation to verbal language.

> Writing and print are thus mnemonic devices whose main function is to effect recall of entire language patterns, sentence level utterances in particular. True knowledge of reading and writing processes begins with such study of the interrelationships of language patterns and their graphic counterparts (p. 4).

Obviously, teaching these relationships cannot be accomplished with ditto sheets or work books or programmed material entirely. Somewhere, in all children's education and especially in the low-achieving child's education, someone must take the time to make the relationships meaningfully explicit.

One of the most important opportunities provided in the use of the expeirence story is the chance for general language development, not just vocabulary development. It provides the logical occasion for very individualized attention to sentence structure itself. Low-achieving children frequently use very simple form and the teacher has direct access to the prevailing form in the child's speech. Possible goals might be to vary sentence type, to introduce transformations and inversions and to teach the use of questions, commands and requests as variants of statements. Including prepositional phrases and clauses which are combined in basic sentences to extend meaning could be another goal. Helping children use adjectives and adverbs to refine meaning is easily done in this form. Discussing subject verb agreement is appropriate as is choice of pronouns. Using more complex speech forms or more appropriate ones and then reinforcing them through reading, provides familiarity with this sentence structure which will later be necessary when the children read books written by others which use these forms. The decision about what to include in instruction can be determined through direct observation in the teaching. Developing an awareness about language form and alternative ways of stating ideas is an invaluable aid to comprehension.

Comprehension

Hockett (1968) has presented a hierarchy of skills for both reading and listening comprehension:

1. *Inferring connotative word meanings.* Passages are presented which contain unfamiliar words;
2. *Identifying mood, humor, etc.* Passages for listening are of the exposition, narration, prose type;
3. *Providing examples by details.* Having listened to a reasonably short passage, the student is able to provide the detailed examples it contains, when given the main idea;
4. *Reinstating sequence of ideas.* Having listened to a passage containing a sequence of ideas, the student is able to reproduce the sequences.
5. *Identifying the main idea.* Having listened to a reasonably short passage (from two to five sentences), the student is able to state in his own words the general principle or principles being communicated.
6. *Predicting sequences of thought.* A sequence of ideas is presented, without a completion or a conclusion. The student is then asked, in effect, "What sort of idea does it seem likely the speaker will present next?"
7. *Inferring the speaker's purpose.* The passages are mainly of the persuasive sort. After listening to a passage, the student is asked this kind of question: "If I followed the speaker's intention, I would . . ."
8. *Applying the standards to judge persuasion.* Passages listened to are of the persuasive sort. The student is asked to identify the class of device used by the speaker in persuasion: side-tracking, card-stacking, bandwagon, plainfolks, testimonial, transfer, big

general ideas, name-calling. Logical argument is also included as an alternative.

9. *Inferring main ideas from specifics.* The student listens to a passage which is terminated before the main idea is presented; what are given are specific ideas (examples) leading to the inference of the main idea. Following such a passage, the question is: "How could these specific ideas (events) be summarized as a main idea?"

10. *Judging logical validity.* The passages here are largely of the expository sort, including persuasions, and are chosen to exhibit correct and incorrect deductive logic.

11. *Identifying sequence inconsistencies or ambiguities.* Passages are constructed to contain inconsistencies in the sequence of ideas, for example, by placing a sentence out of order. This kind of inconsistency or ambiguity is carefully distinguished from logical inconsistency (validity).

Listening comprehension has been presented in several organizational frames of reference (Chapter I). The discussion of comprehension always comes back to the same general issues, and Schreiner (1969) lists those elements which determine successful comprehension as:

1. Level of vocabulary,
2. syntactical functioning,
3. set of mind,
4. mechanical reading skills, and
5. teaching at appropriate level and sequence for growth.

He also lists two basic types of comprehension:

1. Literal
   a. Fact and detail
   b. Main idea of passage or selection
2. Nonliteral
   a. Making decisions and judgments about reading
   b. Cause and effect relationships
   c. Inferences
   d. Evaluations and criticisms
   e. Determining author's intents

Supporting the argument presented in this chapter about comprehension, Levine (1970) makes a critical observation. *Comprehension is not a separate intellectual ability.* She also says that the skill of word recognition can be applied universally to all print using our alphabet and that comprehension does not necessarily enter into the experience of word recognition. It is also different for different subjects and comprehension skills cannot be easily transferred from subject to subject. Her conclusion is that word recognition be given more emphasis and the amount of reading done at school be greatly increased. The differences in point of view between the argument that Levine sets forth and that is supported in this chapter is that word recognition is an "entry level" skill for comprehension and that while comprehension skills may differ from subject to subject, the process of comprehension and those processes involving thinking do not. The skills in comprehension involve such issues as getting the main idea, sequence, detail and simple inference. Those involved with nonliteral comprehension are issues involving deductive or inductive approaches, convergent or divergent thinking and a hierarchy of steps to arrive at a conclusion.

Developing Thinking Skills

As teachers work with children helping them record their thoughts, they have an invaluable opportunity to develop critical thinking skills. Shotka (1960) lists eight steps in critical thinking:

1. See and state a problem,
2. recognize what can be taken for granted,
3. assume what is true for the sake of testing,
4. give reasons for testing,
5. get evidence (reading, or by teacher, observation, survey and experimentation),
6. evaluate evidence by finding bias, validity, reliability,
7. put findings together and organize them, and then
8. draw conclusions.

Teachers can use these eight steps as their guide in helping children to develop comprehension and active critical thinking.

Taba (1965) has suggested that in the group of children who are regarded as having low ability (as measured by intelligence tests) there are many who are slow absorbers, and that when the amount of information to be assimilated is reduced and opportunities for pacing and transitions are provided, the students can function abstractly. Teachers can question children in ways which guide them in the thinking process which involves their actiivty, not teacher activity, for them. Taba suggests that teachers question children both on the substance of what is being discussed and with an eye to cognitive process. Questions may be asked which relate to the management of learning such as approval, disapproval, disagreement, management and reiteration. Questions may also be asked which focus or refocus, deviate or extend thought on a particular level or shift to a higher level. The teacher is not a controller of thought, but elicits, times, paces, and lifts thought. She feels the child must be active, that the development of thought follows a sequence from simple to more complex and abstract, that there is a sequential order in which the thinking must precede, and that there must be a constant reorganization of the intake of information with the existing conceptual scheme in the child's mind.

There is no better vehicle for this theory than the experience story. If teachers begin to think of this activity not simply to record a trip a child might have taken, something he particularly liked, or a dream or fantasy (which are common subjects for this activity), but as a vehicle for individualized teaching of the whole cognitive process of language and thought, the experience story will begin to assume its proper role in the teaching of low-achieving children.

The Experience Story in Four Different Forms

There are a variety of forms the experience story can take, depending on the problems the child may have, or on the teaching plan.

1. *The child can dictate a story to the teacher, or a group of children can compose a story together.* The story is recorded on the blackboard, a chart, taken by typewriter or tape recorder, or inscribed in longhand. *The children are asked to illustrate the story.* The children are not expected to read the story as "reading material," but only to read it incidentlly, with the teacher's help, in order to understand that this reproduction, which is graphic, stands exactly for what was said. Two skills are being developed

in this form and the teacher must be very clear in the teaching objectives. One of the goals involves the use of expressive language with the teacher as stimulator or model, depending on the needs of the children. If the child possessed some expressive skill, the teacher would act as stimulator, encouraging the child to speak, helping him with questions to structure and convey his ideas to others. If the child had little expressive skill, the teacher would act as a model, providing the language behavior expected from the child and rewarding him for performance, for copying or imitating. The goal would be to establish a behavior which was lacking or very meager in a child so that it could be encouraged, fostered and elaborated. As the lessons began, the teacher would provide the exact form expected from the child. S(he) might be working on speaking in sentences rather than phrases or single words. Later, s(he) would demonstrate to the child a variety of ways that ideas may be expressed: changing word order, using adverbs and adjectives, inserting clauses or phrases which make meaning more exact. Word meanings would be developed and particularized, elaborated and embellished, so that the word would have more significance for the child. A good beginning is: "There is another way you can say that." As the child progressed, the teacher would shift to help elicit or start the expression, serving only as guide. These activities are primarily designed to develop oral-aural language skills and are specifically separated from visual and visual motor tasks or auditory skills in their integrative interaction with graphic symbols. They demonstrate to the child the relationship between his language and forms of writing, and value his experiences and his oral participation. They do not ask for his performance in either writing or reading. The teacher helps the child use those skills which were designated earlier as basic to listening and speaking, but here the child is integrating processes in meaningful and interesting activities, not practicing specific skills.

Another objective of these activites would involve the conceptual content of the drawings accompanying the stories or discussions. The teacher would help the child plan the drawing, eliciting or calling to his attention the variety of possibilities for inclusion. The aim would be a widening of the child's awareness of drawings as an expressive avenue of communication, aiding the child to select suitable graphic themes and details which would convey the meaning of his language. Just as s(he) had served as model in stimulating the production of oral language, here s(he) might demonstrate by drawing what s(he) expected (if reticence is based on fear of failure or inadequate skill.) Through comparison, s(he) would lead the child to notice similarities and differences which would help focus his attention on pertinent details or ideas. This would also help to enrich the imagery available to the child for the future use of language. In all of the teaching for the child who is handicapped there is an absence of the Victorian notion of the basic goodness and virtue in struggling with tasks that are difficult. The teaching creates the success of the child by breaking up the tasks, so that he can come to know that learning is enjoyable.

2. *The child can dictate the story to the teacher and s(he) records it—only as a holding action—dictating it back to the child if the problem involves thinking and writing simultaneously.* We take the ability to perform these skills for granted, assuming that all children who can perform them separately can perform them simultaneously. This often is not the case. The child might be encouraged to begin with short sentences if he demonstrated that he could not remember his thoughts. The goal would be remembering a short sentence and writing it from memory. The teaching would provide for "rehearsal" of the sentences to fix them in the child's memory, and the teacher would serve as prompter. The teacher provides actual models of elaborated sentences and discusses the kinds of words and phrases which lengthen them—adjectives, adverbs, dependent clauses, and so forth. As the child gained confidence and skill, the sentences would be lengthened. This problem is one which is not restricted to elementary age children; it is prevalent in older children as well.

3. This variation on the experience story is particularly suited to older children but is also valuable and useful for the younger ones. It is always up to the teacher to assess the problems and

make the decisions about which approach, or combination of approaches, will be most fruitful. Here, *the teacher reads to children material which is too difficult for them to read themselves, but which they can deal with conceptually and which meets their interest needs.* They "process" the material and rephrase what has been read to them, using their own language to formulate the ideas. The teacher takes the reprocessed material in dictation by hand, on the typewriter or by tape recorder to be transcribed later. The child uses the recorded version as his "reader." Because he knows the content and the vocabulary before he rereads, he is able to read quite difficult material using contextual clues and preknowledge to aid him, and he demonstrates to himself and to others that he can read, something which he does not believe himself capable of doing. This is an especially effective technique with hostile, negative children, or with older children who reject the material available at their own reading level, for it enables them to explore a wide variety of materials and ideas and it holds their interest. This is an effective technique for older nonreaders in a particular subject area—science, social studies, history, and so forth.

4. *The children write, illustrate and read their stories with or without the aid of the teacher.* The goal is supplementary language experience. This can be especially valuable where programmed or linguistic materials are being used and the "process" of reading is emphasized. General skills are emphasized rather than a specific one of the other three forms of the experience story.

A Group Technique for Using the Experience Story

Wozner (1971) describes an interesting adaptation of the Fernald Method used in Israel as a remedial reading technique for groups of between six and eight children. "The Weekly Text," as the method is called, was designed for use with children who in this country would be described as "culturally disadvantaged" or "educationally handicapped."

This method has three basic principles: (1) teaching a story as a unit, (2) student choice of subject matter and words and (3) use of an analytic approach—from whole to part. The story stands for the whole and the letters, standing for sounds, represent the smallest part. This is conceived as a hierarchy whose components are arranged from: idea—sentences—words—syllables—sounds. There are five stages which are covered each week.

Stage 1 involves the initial discussion. The children are grouped by age level and on the first day of the week they sit in a circle and talk, sharing experiences, feelings and fantasies. Each child is encouraged to take part and at the end of ten minutes or so the teacher asks the children which of the stories they would like to write. At the outset of this method this is a difficult choice but, as the children learn the expectations and procedures and the group becomes more cohesive, this becomes routine. The teacher then writes the story on the blackboard. The teacher reads the story to the children first and then they read it individually or in chorus. This stage presents opportunities for expressive language, for possible corrections which are carefully explained by the teacher and very rarely does the teacher veto the children's choice. In the beginning it is preferable to encourage the children to write short stories.

Stage II involves breaking the story into its components. On the following day the teacher brings two posters into the classroom on which the story from the preceding day has been written. The children discuss for ten minutes or so—this is always the first activity of every meeting. Then the teacher practices reading the story with the children. This is made lively and interesting through variations and games. The second poster is cut into sentences and the children practice reading these. After a period of sentence reading, each sentence is cut into words and the words are read as flash cards. Again games are made up to enliven this activity.

On the third day of the week the stories are presented to the children in ditto form. Then individually they repeat the preceding steps, cutting the story into sentences and finally into words.

Stage III involves a Rehearsal Procedure. In this stage the children are asked to reconstruct the story from the words which they have cut. They paste the words on another paper and practice in this actiivty word order, sentence rhythm and structure.

Stage IV. On the fourth day all the students again read the story. They now move from the words to individual symbols. The story is again presented on a poster, and the teacher colors consonants or vowels which are to be studied. There is a period of teacher-directed study from the poster. Attention is first called to the element as a part of a known word and then as a unit by itself. The teacher keeps track of the letters which have been studied in order to insure that all are covered. Games again are played to insure that all children participate in the whole-to-part analysis.

Stage V involves a generalization of the use of the story components. On the last day of the week the children are asked to use the words they have studied in a new context. They are encouraged to write new but smaller stories using the words of the larger one. They take their work home and share it with their parents. At regular intervals the stories written in preceding weeks are reread.

Wozner lists five strengths which are inherent in the use of this method. First, every child reads and experiences the rewarding feeling of success. Second, reading a self-generated story motivates and encourages children to want to read—especially emotionally disturbed children who frequently are quite egocentric. Third, a gradual distancing process occurs which enables the child to create distance between himself and the world outside. This happens as the process starts with the child's idea and ends with letter study. Fourth, personal language is enhanced at the same time as the reading skill is developed and they are paced together. They represent two aspects of the communication process and are taught simultaneously. Last, perceptual and conceptual rigidities are broken as the child is helped to generalize by writing and reading new stories made of the words which are familiar through the week's study.

There are also advantages to the group work for the child who is in need of remedial teaching. The child receives support from the group as he realizes he is not the only person with difficulties in learning to read. He also learns from the practice activities of the other children. There is an opportunity to use competition positively to motivate interest.

This is an interesting adaptation of the Fernald approach. Teachers could use this method as an adjunct to their teaching where programmed or linguistic approaches were the mainstay of the reading program, in order to provide for oral language development and to tie speaking and reading of verbal and graphic language together meaningfully.

The Weakness of the Language-experience Approach

While the language-experience approach offers great richness and variety in terms of valuing cultural and social diversity, dealing with motivation, general language skill building in listening and speaking, and in visual perceptual training in the motoric areas involved in handwriting, it has one major weakness which has prevented many teachers from using it for greater lengths of time when this would be beneficial for the children. It does not provide a systematic approach to problems involving learning sound-symbol relationships unless it is used in the Fernald Method (1943) with tracing. Even when used with this approach the "system" or "method" is indirect and the sound-symbol relationship is established through repeated auditory-visual pairing with kinesthetic tactile reinforcement as the binding agent. No attempt is made to structure the introduction of sounds or to provide more repetition than occurs naturally in the speech of the child. Admittedly this way of presenting the assoications allows some children to "discover" the relationships, and it can teach perceptual awareness about words not possible with strictly auditory-visual synthetic methods. It is an indispenable technique for working with severe visual perception and memory problems.

Dr. Fernald had a clearly formulated conception of the gestalt of the individual language system of the child. She understood the value of building on this in the inital stages of reading or remedial reading. She understood interest and choice and its effect on involvement in learning. She was clear and adamant about using an analytical method of teaching which preserved meaning as the prime unit and purpose in reading. Her use of the kinesthetic tactile modalities as reinforcement provided for increased attention and focus on the task, additional input of relevant information to the central nervous system, and instruction in the awareness of distinctive cues in word perception. She was also a tremendously dynamic personality and stands, even in this distance in time, as a guardian of her method. For no one has used kinesthetic-tactile learning—separated from her method—to teach sound-symbol relationships systematically or in any material. Even Montessori, dedicated as she was to movement and learning, did not exploit its potential in word perception.

While the "Weekly Test" suggested by Wozner is a very effective group adaptation of the Fernald approach as far as the expressive receptive relationships are concerned, and activity in word study is exploited by cutting up the sentence, and the teacher structures the study of sound symbol relationships, the kinesthetic aspects of learning is not involved as Fernald intended it to be used. This, of course, is because of the difficulties inherent in group tracing or words. The limitation of the method means the teacher must consider whether the skill teaching implicit in the method is sufficient or requires direct and separate instruction. The adaptation, however, is an excellent one and is easy to use.

The "No-comprehension" Reader

It is not uncommon to find children who read or "decode" very accurately but have no comprehension of the meaning of the text. These children usually have had teaching which has emphasized word attack skills. They have learned what they have been taught and have also been limited by its limitations.

Broadening the Meaning Base

The solution to this problem is to place full emphasis on meaning and comprehension. This means building vocabulary primarily through experiences which are deliberately linked to other similar or related experiences. Daily writing, with teacher-child discussion about content and about how best to express the child's thought, is invaluable. This can lead to discussion about word forms and sentence structure. In the rereading, the child can learn about intonation and its relation to meaning. Implicitly and explicitly, he must learn that reading involves recreating speech. Personal interests, science and social studies projects, retelling a familiar story, or even rewriting a textbook used can serve this activity well.

Limit the Amount

The child should also have direct guided experience in understanding what has been read from a book. A good technique for accomplishing this is to limit the amount that the child reads before he pauses to extract meaning. In the initial phase of this teaching, one sentence would be sufficient.

Using Imitation and Modeling

The teacher first demonstrates abstracting meaning by reading the sentence orally and rephrasing it. Other words are used or word order is changed or the number of sentences is increased to make meaning more explicit. The child is then invited to read the same sentence and to rely on the teacher's verbal model or to modify it: "You can say just what I said or change it and say it in your own way using other words." The instruction remains at the one-sentence level until the child is proficient and fluent in rephrasing and restating meaning. Sentences are added one at a time until the child can handle a whole paragraph. The teacher gradually withdraws the model as the child demonstrates skill, moving in only when support is required. This technique aims at the whole process of abstraction, not at the specific skills of comprehension as they are usually taught. The objective is not to retrieve information through questions, but to have the child spontaneously extract meaning at a more global level so that it later can be retrieved by questions. Again, it is an "entry level" skill that is usually expected to function spontaneously.

One of the difficulties in teaching low-achieving children is that language frequently does not convey conceptual meaning. The child does not know what cognitive operations are required and verbal explanations alone do not convey to him what he is to "do."

Modeling allows the child to view process and to incorporate it in his behavior repertoire without risking failure. Once he establishes the pattern of cognitive action, he can make minor changes and, as he generalizes through repeated experiences, then functions independently.

Silent Reading

Once the child develops competence in oral reading, the instruction is paralleled for silent reading but without the imitation and modeling. The limit to the amount, plus immediate verbalized abstraction, is practiced first. When the child can read silently and restate the meaning orally, he is encouraged to simply stop at the end of a sentence and restate it to himself in thinking or silent language. The child is being guided through the process he will eventually continue on his own. The number of sentences is increased until a paragraph can be understood, then a page, a chapter, or a story. The restatement is increasingly delayed to develop skill. As soon as the child comprehends, teaching attention shifts to fluency and speed; time and accuracy and amount all become variables which are manipulated to increase competency.

FLUENCY

For many children who have difficulty learning to read, fluency presents a particular problem. Such children read slowly, unevenly and without "expression." Phrasing is inaccurate and punctuation is ignored. This may be related to language, perception or motivation factors in the child and to a teaching methodolgy to which many low-achieving children are subjected. Basic reading is viewed as "word study." The decoding emphasis in basic reading largely ignores the larger structures of verbal language and their relation to successful oral reading and comprehension.

Teachers frequently admonish children to read with "expression" without explaining what that means. They may even demonstrate sporadically, giving examples, or they may call children's attention to punctuation and tell them that a comma indicates a pause and a period indicates a full stop. Very few language arts texts provide more than perfunctory guidance in this area.

Lefevre (1964) states that children who are in the beginning stage of reading already use the basic signals and structures of language well, and that as reading and writing instruction begins, these should be brought to a level of consciousness. "He should be given practice in speaking and oral reading of familiar patterns, with emphasis upon the native intonations" (p. 43). In beginning reading a great deal of time is spent in perceiving the relationships of sounds and symbols within words. Very little time is spent on learning the signals which distinguish sentences. Those children who have had a heavy emphasis on decoding use these skills only in decoding and have limited experience in reading for meaning.

Stating that "we should teach him the relationship of entire sentence patterns—in his own speech—to their graphic counterparts, that is to say to langauge structures as represented in the systems of writing and print" (p. 44), Lefevre feels that the teaching of reading should proceed from verbal language to graphic and that whole sentence patterns should be learned first and then the details or phonemes emphasized. This is, of course, one of the major reasons for the emphasis in this chapter on the experience story. Expression in reading is to a large extent dependent on *intonation*. It provides the rhythm, cadence and facility which amplifies and underlines meaning. Using the experience story to make the child aware of the intonation in personal language form and its graphic representation is not fully exploited in the teaching of low-achieving children. Teachers give this area some attention in beginning reading, but for the low-achieving child the teaching should be explicit and continuous throughout his educational experience.

Teachers themselves need to understand the function of intonation in sentence sense in order to help children use it to retrieve meaning from print. A brief summary of some of the high points of Lefevre's discussion may serve as an introduction to this subject.

Basically, intonation involves two different signals—*syntactical* (grammar or structure) and *interpretive* (meaning). They are difficult to distinguish; while syntactical signals are obligatory, tone of voice or interpretive signals are optionals and superimposed on the basic syntactical structure. Tone of voice or interpretive signals are subjective and express bias, attitude and feeling; therefore they often vary from speaker to speaker and by dialect. The elements of intonation are stress, pitch and juncture. They serve as signals with facilitate, enhance or modify meaning.

"Primarily, English utterances are understood as sentences because they end with one of the signaling patterns, not because of word order" (p. 52). Falling pitch and voice-fade indicate completion. Medium or heavy stress occurs only on the last or concluding word of an utterance. Usually, only one word in a sentence receives heavy or maximum stress. A fading and then a rising indicates that the utterance is not complete and will continue. Any series of utterances uses this intonational pattern. The fade-fall is indicated in print by a period, the fade-rise usually by a comma. The fade-fall concludes declarative statements, commands and many questions. It is often preceded by falling pitch. It is also the intonation used for any word uttered alone. It is not without reason then that it is the intonation used by the child who reads word-by-word, not actually focusing on either structure or meaning in sentences.

When a statement is converted to a question the fade-rise ending is utilized. It is used with a request for repetition and an expression of surprise, incredulity, relief, regret or disbelief. The intention of the reader determines whether he will use fade-fall or fade-rise with questions. Only the question mark is available in print, but context furnishes clues. Questions most frequently require the fade-fall intonation and often they are preceded by falling pitch. There are two ways in which speech can end; it can end abruptly or trail off. Also, pitch may rise or fall slightly or be sustained.

Stress can be used to distinguish many grammatical structures. *Stress* means loudness and there are four degrees: heavy, medium, light and weak. In his advice to teachers about using stress, Lefevre states:

> The main thing is to be able to locate the medium and heavy stresses often associated with a rising pitch, and in general to realize

that while four distinctive degrees of stress exist in the intonation system, you do not have to be conscious of them all at all times in order to use them properly. If your oral reading is fluent and easy, it will serve as a good example for the children to follow (p. 73).

This leads directly into some suggestions for teaching the nonfluent child. First, some verbalized instruction about the use of intonation should be provided. The experience story offers a vehicle for relating verbal to graphic language, and some of the discussion should take place during the sessions when the child records his own verbal expression.

Using a Tape Recorder

The child should have *regular* opportunities to read and be recorded so that he and the teacher can discuss the different uses of intonation in conveying the meaning of the text. Stress, pitch and juncture can be dealt with in ways that will allow the child to hear himself change and monitor his own intonation. If this is to be an effective teaching strategy, the regularity of use and predetermined teacher-child evaluation procedures become critical factors. The child should be aware of the problems the procedures are intended to solve. The teacher's use of the recorder for motivation and direct instruction—with its use in all correction —is frequently slighted.

Using Modeling and Imitation

Another technique which is invaluable in helping children use intonation effectively is providing a model and asking the child to copy it. There are two ways in which this can be done. One is for the teacher to perform while the child listens, and then the child repeats, using the intonation patterns the teacher has provided. Another technique is the more formalized method called the Neurological Impress Method (1962) which provides for simultaneous performance by child and teacher. The teacher sits slightly behind the child and reads slightly ahead of the child while both share the same book. The child is encouraged to "lean on" the example of the teacher. In this technique no discussion occurs; the practice in performance fixes the behavior.

Again, if it is intended to improve intonation, the regularity of its use will be a determining factor.

Reducing Impulsivity

Frequently nonfluency is related to a lack of attentiveness and an inadequate "set for accuracy." This problem can be dealt with by setting absolute accuracy as a teaching objective. In this case, instruction moves away from the meaning of the text. When this is done, it should not occur in the reading period. (Reading for meaning and enjoyment and all skill teaching should be separated in time, so that the enjoyment of the content or the search for information is not diluted.) The time spent on a task like this should be limited, but regular. The teacher asks the child to read one sentence without a mistake and with proper intonation. In order to predetermine success, some instruction, rehearsal and practice can be provided before the child performs the reading task. The child is told that the teacher will signal if he has read correctly and may proceed to the next sentence. A dropped paper clip is usually a good signaling device because it need not divert the eyes from the page. If the child makes a mistake, the teacher withholds the signal and the child searches for his mistake and rereads until he reads correctly.

Speed

Nonfluent readers often read very slowly. Teaching to this problem directly is frequently helpful. When manipulating speed, the teacher needs to be certain that the child is reading below his instructional level so that he is familiar with the vocabulary and sentence structure. Timed one-minute drills are valuable and often enjoyable for the child. The teacher or child record both speed and accuracy over a period of time to provide the child with information about improvement. Increased speed alone can often enhance comprehension because the child may have learned to read so slowly that he destroyed or distorted the natural rhythm and intonation which supports comprehension. The pressure of timed drills may provide the "set" or intent which allows the child to improve.

A wealth of reading material which is easy and interesting is one of the best ways to deal with the speed factor in reading performance. Nothing improves reading performance so much as spontaneous reading on the part of the child. When planning is done around the speed factor, spontaneous reading is an important support condition and should not be neglected.

MOTIVATION

Teachers can use two kinds of motivation to help children learn. One is *intrinsic,* the other *extrinsic.* Intrinsic motivation has two aspects. In the child it can mean the possession of general achievement motivation or interest in a particular subject or field. In content it means material which is interesting to the child. In low-achieving children, achievement motivation often functions at a low level. Sometimes they don't bring it to school with them as part of their early social learning; sometimes failure has simply buried it. Curiosity, which is a basic behavior in human beings, has been suppresed or not supported by adults in the child's life and many of the children may not be able to state an interest or even pick one out of the array presented.

When children fail in reading, one of the basic subjects taught in school, they fail in their own expectations for achievement as well as that of the school's. The child who fails in reading cannot be expected to maintain his motivation to learn, and it is up to the teacher to try to arrange the learning situation so that the child succeeds. Traditionally, we have seen the low-achieving child as basically inadequate and not much emphasis was put on teaching him. More recently (Hunt, 1961), "intelligent" behavior as meaured in achievement tests is viewed as largely learned. During this same period, low-achieving children have been barraged with extrinsic motivation as reinforcement theory (Linsley, 1968) has been translated into strategies for use in the schools. Behavior modification techniques work very well on specific skill teaching and many children have learned to "decode" using these approaches. Unfortunately, all have not learned to love reading and many read as little as possible. The rationale is that the child needs the skills in order to read and there is never any time or planning allotted to reading itself. One of the main goals in an individualized program is to rekindle some of the natural achievement motivation that is built into all children. Bruner (1966) states it well: "The will to learn is an intrinsic motive, one that finds both its source and its reward in its own exercise." The only way that a child can renew this sense of accomplishment and receive the reward of doing, is by doing. With so much time spent on skill teaching for the low achiever, little time is left over for the pleasure in reading.

Teachers simply need to consider developing pleasure and enjoyment in spontaneous reading as an equal goal to skill teaching for the low-achieving child. This means helping children pick and develop interests about which they might like to read and then providing a wealth of reading material at an appropriate level. The appropriate level for pleasure reading is considerably below the instructional level so that the child can read by himself. It may also mean "tempting" the child with subject matter that may be exciting. Animals are a source of interest to young children; learning about their habits and ways of living can offer unlimited opportunities to coordinate reading and writing and discussion. Ditmars (1914) offers a wealth of information about reptiles which is fascinating to children and his book about strange animals is awesome. The characteristics of bats, horses, owls, to name a few, all offer stimulating content which can capture the attention and involvement of the child. While developing interest in spontaneous reading will be limited by the selection and availability of books at an appropriate level, the interests that are available for the experience story approach are unlimited. Science experiments, cars, diving, surfing, sports, clothing, personal care—all can be of interest to a particular child. If the child cannot state an interest it is up to the teacher to find content areas which might develop into individualized interests and capture his curiosity.

Incentive Reading

Following this line of discussion relating to motivation, incentive reading can often get a low-achieving child started. The leisure reading is required by the teacher but planned with the child; he decides ahead of time how much he will read each day and what the content will be. The teacher provides a wealth of material at an appropriate level from which the child may choose. Sometimes the child may be sent to the library to browse and pick out books. If this is done, the librarian should be apprised of the child's reading level so he does not pick out books which are too difficult. The ease of reading is one of the most facilitating conditions for the success of this approach. The kinds of incentives for this leisure reading will vary, depending on what is motivating to a particular child. A good deal of discussion about content and the child's evaluation of what has been read should be part of this strategy. With very young children, teacher attention is one of the most valuable reinforcers. Here taking time to discuss the reading or being read to can be the incentive. With older children attention, privilege, time, a mark, a token, a toy, or food are possibilities. The list is endless and depends on the child. The main points in an incentive reading program are that time for spontaneous reading without instruction is provided, is expected, occurs regularly and is reinforced, with knowledge of the reinforcer known ahead of time.

SUMMARY

When children fail or perform poorly in reading, there are six areas which require deliberate consideration in planning instruction. The first is *developing perceptual skills*—visual, auditory or visual-motor. Kinesthetic teaching is suggested as a support for visual perception, proprioceptive teaching, for auditory and judging distances for visual motor perception. The second area is decoding and decisions are made regarding the suitability of a synthetic or analytic approach. Some children will not generalize the sounds of the letters of the alphabet or the sequencing or blending of sounds. The teacher will need to decide which approach is suitable for a particular child. The third area is *building vocabulary*. Developing word meanings requires careful planning as well as providing strategies for learning those particular words which present difficulties because they are less "meaningful," the "sight vocabulary." The fourth area involves *teaching comprehension*. It is an area which usually gets short shrift in the instruction of low-achieving children because of the emphasis on teaching decoding. Comprehension involves thinking and time should be allowed for developing thinking skills as well as just getting the literal meanings. The experience story is offered as a vehicle for teaching which integrates all of the communication skills. It should be included in the daily instruction of the low-achieving group of children all the way through school. *Fluency* is the fifth area about which specific teaching decisions must be made. The teaching in this area should develop an awareness on the part of the child about the role of intonation in expressive and fluent reading. Speed is another factor which may require direct teaching attention. The sixth and last area which requires teacher attention and decisions is *motivation*.

Motivation is not placed last because it is regarded as least important, but because of the emphasis on skill development explored in this book. The child may need motivation in school as well as to read. Again the experience story provides a vehicle which can help meet this need. Interests and projects can be developed which require reading, discussion, writing and re-reading. Provisions should also be made for spontaneous reading on the child's part, without instruction.

If the teacher considers all of these areas when planning instruction instead of basing her plan on the more limited and less elaborated decoding-comprehension dichotomy, the children will have better chances of learning. Some of them may even become achieving children and escape from the "low achiever" classification.

BIBLIOGRAPHY

1. Allen, R. V.: The language-experience approach in reading instruction. In Clelend, D. L. (Ed.): *New Dimensions in Reading, A Report of the Nineteenth Annual Conference and Course on Reading.* Pittsburgh, July 8-19, 1963.
2. Astin, Mary C.: Teaching reading to the kindergarten child. In

Cleland, D. L. (Ed.): *New Dimensions in Reading, A Report of the Nineteenth Annual Conference and Course on Reading.* Pittsburgh, July 8-19, 1963.

3. Baker, R.; Gray, B.. and McClain, L.: *Monterey Reading Program.* Monterey, Behavior Science Institute, 1972.

4. Bender, L.: *Visual-motor Gestalt Test and Its Clinical Use.* Research Monograph No. 3. New York, American Orthopsychiatric Assoc., 1938.

5. Bereiter, C., and Engleman, S.: *Teaching Disadvantaged Children in the Preschool.* Englewood Cliffs, P-H, 1966.

6. Berlyne, D. E.: *Conflict, Arousal and Curiosity.* New York, McGraw, 1960.

7. Bernstein, B.: Elaborated and restricted codes, their social origins and some consequences. In Gumperz, J., and Hymes, D. (Eds.): *American Anthropologist Special Publication,* No. 6, Part 2, *66:* 55-69, 1964.

8. Berros, M.: Personal communication. Fernald Clinic, University of California, Los Angeles, 1972.

9. Blank, Marion and Bridger, W. H.: Deficiencies in verbal labeling in retarded readers. *Am J Orthopsych, 36:*840-847, 1967.

10. Boehm, A.: *Test of Basic Concepts.* New York, Psychol Corp., 1967.

11. Bond, Gil and Dykstra, R.: The cooperative reading research program in first grade reading. *Reading Resch Quart, 2,* Summer 1967.

12. Bruner, J. S.: *Toward a Theory of Instruction.* Cambridge, Harvard U Pr, 1966.

13. Bryan, T. H.: Learning disabilities: a new stereotype. *J Learn Disabil, 7, #5,* May 1974.

14. Chall, J.: *Learning to Read: the Great Debate.* New York, McGraw, 1967.

15. Chall, J.: Research in linguistic and reading instruction: implications for further research and practice. *Int Read Assn Conf Proc, 13,* pt. 1:560-571, 1969.

16. Cohen, D. H.: Word meaning and the literary experience in early childhood. *Elem Engl, 46:*914-925, 1969.

17. Coleman, J. C., and Roberts, R. W.: Investigation of the role of kinesthetic factors in reading failure. *J Ed Resh, 51:*445-451, 1958.

18. Cooper, J. C., and Goeth, J. H.: Interactions of modality with age and with meaningfulness in verbal learning. *J Ed Psychol, 58:*41-44, 1967.

19. Cronbach, L. J., and Snow, R. E.: *Individual Differences in Learning Ability as a Function of Instructional Variables.* Stanford, School of Ed.; Washington, DHEW, Bureau of Elem & Sec Ed., Eric Reports Ed 029-001, March 1969.

20. Dean, L.: Increase vocabulary with word elements, mono through deca. *Elem Engl, 47*:49-55, 1970.

21. Deighton, L. C.: *Vocabulary Development in the Classroom.* New York, Bureau of Publications, Teachers College, Columbia Univ., 1959.

22. Dewey, John: *The Child and the Curriculum.* Chicago, U of Chicago Pr, 1960.

23. Ditmars, R. L.: *Strange Animals I Have Known.* New York, Brewer, Warren and Putnam, 1931.

24. Ditmars, R. L.:*The Reptile Book.* New York, Doubleday, 1914.

25. Dolch, E. W.: *The Dolch Basic Sight Word Tests.* Champaign, Garrard, 1942.

26. Fernald, Grace M.: *Remedial Techniques in Basic School Subjects.* New York, McGraw, 1943.

27. Fitzgerald, J. A., and Fitzgerald, Patricia G.: *Teaching Reading and the Language Arts.* Milwaukee, Bruce, 1965.

28. Fellows, B. J.: *The Discrimination Process and Development.* Oxford, Pergamon, 1968.

29. Frostig, M., and Horne, D.: *The Frostig Program for the Development of Visual Perception.* Chicago, Follett, 1964.

30. Frostig, M., et al.: *The Marianne Frostig Developmental Test of Visual Perception.* Palo Alto, Consulting Psychologists, 1964.

31. Geake, R. R., and Smith, D. E.: *Michigan Tracking Program.* Ann Arbor, Ann Arbor Publishers, 1962.

32. Gibson, Eleanor J.: *Principles of Perceptual Learning and Development.* New York, Appleton, 1969.

33. Gibson, J. J.: *The Senses Considered as Perceptual Systems.* Boston, HM, 1966.

34. Goodman, K. S.: A linguistic study of cues and measures. *Elem Engl, 42*:639-643, 1965.

35. Heckleman, R. G.: *A Neurological Impress Method of Reading Instruction.* Merced, Merced County Schools, 1962.

36. Hess, R. D.: Maternal behavior and the development of reading readiness in urban Negro children. In Douglass, M. P. (Ed.): *Claremont Reading Conference, 32nd Yearbook.* Claremont, Claremont Press, 1968.

37. Hockett, M. G.: A hierarchy of skills in listening comprehension and reading comprehension. Ph.D. dissertation, Berkeley, 1968.

38. Hunt, J. McV.: *Intelligence and Experience.* New York, Ronald, 1961.

39. Jones, Margaret H.: Some relationships between reading and listening. In Douglass, M. P. (Ed.): *Claremont Reading Conference, 29th Yearbook.* Claremont, Claremont Grad. Curric. Library, 1965.

40. Kephart, N. C.: *The Slow Learner in the Classroom.* Columbus, Merrill, 1960.

41. Kirk, S. A.; McCarthy, J. P., and Kirk, W. D.: *The Illinois Test of Psycholinguistic Abilities.* Urbana, U of Ill Pr, 1968.
42. King, Ethel G.: Effects of different kinds of visual discrimination training on learning to read words. *J Ed Psychol, 55*:325-333, 1964.
43. Kohlberg, L.: Early education: a cognitive developmental view. *Child Ed,* Dec. 1968.
44. Langer, J. H.: Vocabulary and concepts. *Elem Sch J, 69*:381-385, 1969.
45. Lefevre, C. A.: *Linguistics and the Teaching of Reading.* New York, McGraw, 1964.
46. Levine, I.: The fallacy of reading comprehension skills. *Elem Eng, 47*:672-677, 1970.
47. Lindamood, C. H., and Lindamood, P. C.: The Lindamood auditory conceptualization test. *Teaching Resources.* New York, New York Times, 1971.
48. Linsley, O. R.: *Training Parents and Teachers to Precisely Manage Children's Behavior.* Lawrence, University Bureau of Child Research, 1968.
49. McLean, J.: Language development and communication disorders. In Haring, N. (Ed.): *Behavior of Exceptional Children, An Introduction to Special Education.* Columbus, Merrill, 1974.
50. Montessori, M. M.: *The Discovery of the Child.* (Trans. by Mary A. Johnstone.) Madras, India, Kalakshetra Pubs, 1962. (Rev. and enlarged ed. of *The Montessori Method.*)
51. Montessori, M. M.: *The Absorbent Mind.* 3rd. ed. (Trans. by Claude A. Claremont.) Adyar, Madras, India, Kalakshetra Pub., 1961.
52. Montessori, M. M.: *The Secret of Childhood.* (Trans. by Barbara B. Carter.) Adyar, Madras, India, Kalakshetra Pub., 1962.
52a. Montessori, M.: *The Montessori Method.* New York, Schocken, 1964.
53. Muehl, Siegmar: The effects of visual discrimination pretraining on learning to read a vocabulary list in kindergarten children. *J Ed Psychol, 51*:217-221, 1960.
54. Pflaum, S. W.: Expansion of meaning vocabulary: strategies for classroom instruction. *Elem Engl, 50*:89-93, 1973.
55. Piaget, M.: *The Origins of Intelligence in Children.* New York, Int U Pr, 1952.
56. Pick, A. D.: Some basic perceptual processes in reading. *Young Children, 25*:1624-1681, 1970.
57. Pick, H. L.: Some Soviet research on learning and perception in children. In Wright, J. C. and Kagan, J. (Eds.): *Basic Cognitive Processes in Children.* Monograph 28, No. 2, *Soc Resh Child Develop,* 185-190, 1963.

58. Popp, Helen M.: The measurement and training of visual discrimination skills prior to reading instruction. *J Exp Ed, 35*:15-26, 1967.

59. Reudel, R. G.: Cross Modal Transfer Effects in Children and Adults. Paper, APAP meeting, Philadelphia, August 1963.

60. Reudel, R. G., and Teuber, H. L.: Decrement of visual and haptic Muller-Lyer illusion on repeated trials: a study of cross-modal transfer. *Quart J Exp Psychol, 15*:125-131, 1963.

61. Salomon, G.: Heuristic models for the generation of aptitude treatment interaction hypothesis. *Rev Ed Resh, 42*, No. 3:326-342, 1971.

62. Schreiner, R. L.: A logical analysis of reading comprehension skills in social studies. Paper, IRA, Kansas City, April 30-May 5, 1969.

63. Shotka, J.: Critical thinking in the first grade. *Child Ed, 36*, No. 9, 1960. Reprinted in King, M. L.; Ellinger, B. D. and Wolf, W. (Eds.): *Critical Reading*. New York, Lippincott, 1967.

64. Simon, D. P. and Simon, H. A.: Alternative uses of phonemic information in spelling. *Rev Ed Resh, 43*, No. 1, 1973.

65. Smith, K. U. and Smith, W. M.: *Perception and Motion*. Philadelphia, Saunders, 1962.

66. Statts, C.: The effects of discrimination pretraining on perceptual behavior. *J Ed Psychol, 53*:32-37, 1962.

67. Stern, Carolyn: Systematic instruction of economically disadvantaged children in pre-reading skills. In Douglass, M. P. (Ed.): *Claremont Reading Conference 32nd Yearbook*. Claremont, 1968.

68. Stauffer, R. G.: The first grade reading studies: findings of individual investigations. Reprinted from *The Reading Teacher*. Newark, Inter Read Assoc, 1967.

68a. Stern, Carolyn: Systematic instruction of economically disadvantaged children in pre-reading skills. In Douglass, M. P. (Ed.): Claremont Reading Conference, 32nd Yearbook, Claremont Reading Conference, Claremont University Center, Claremont, California, 1968.

69. Strickland, Ruth G.: The language of elementary school children: its relationship to the language of reading textbooks and the quality of reading of selected children. *Bulletin of the School of Education,* Vol. 38, No. 4. Bloomington, Ind, U Pr, 1962.

70. Strickland, R. C.: Vocabulary development and language learning. *Ed Horizon, 50*:150-155, 1972.

71. Taba, H.: The teaching of thinking. *Elem Engl*, XIII, 1965. In King, M. L.; Ellinger, B. D., and Wolf, W. (Eds.): *Critical Reading*. New York, Lippincott, 1967.

72. Tabachnick, B. R.: Reading and the language arts. In Robinson, H. A. (Ed.): *Proceedings of the Annual Conference on Reading*. Supplemental education monographs. Chicago, U of Chi Pr, 1963.

73. Tax, Sol: Self and society. In Douglass, M. P. (Ed.): *Claremont Reading Conference 32nd Yearbook*. Claremont, University Center, 1968.

74. Webster, Staten: Research in teaching reading in disadvantaged learners: a critical review and evaluation of research. Paper, Convention of the International Reading Association, Boston, 1968.

75. Weintraub, S.: Developing meaningful vocabulary in reading. *Read Teacher, 22*:171f, 1968.

76. Wepman, J. M.: *The Wepman Test of Auditory Discrimination*. Chicago, Language Research Associates, 1973.

77. Witty, Paul: Remarks on B. Robert Tabachnick's paper. In Robinson, H. A. (Ed.): *Reading and the Language Arts*. Supplementary Educational Monographs. Chicago, U of Chi Pr, December 1963.

78. Wozner, Yaela: Technical report. Paper presented in the Learning Clinic Seminar, Counseling Department, San Francisco State University, 1971.

79. Zeaman, D., and House, B. J.: The role of attention in retardate discrimination learning. In Ellis, N. R. (Ed.): *Handbook of Mental Deficiency*. New York, McGraw, 1963.

80. Zinchenko, V. P. and Lomov, B. F.: The function of hand and eye movements in the process of perception. In Pick, H. L.: Some Soviet research on learning and perception in children. *Basic Cognitive Processes in Children,* Monograph *Soc Res Child Dev, 28*(No. 2):185-190, 1963.

CHAPTER 3

TEACHING SPELLING

SPELLING CONTENT IS particularly well suited for the development of visual, auditory and motor skills. It is usually taught as a separate subject, deals with single or groups of words which can be selected to meet individual needs, receives a regular time allotment in most daily classroom schedules, and the semantic, meaning and comprehension demands are much more limited than that required in reading. By far the best way to teach it, even for low-achieving children, is to make it an integral part of the language arts program, but most often formal spelling is based on the use of a spelling book. It would be more advantageous for the low achiever if a distinction were made in teaching practice so that skill training and "meaningful" use were not confused. One should not be substituted for the other as is frequently the case; both should be planned for in the daily schedule if individual children show by either the number or type of mistakes they make that either perceptual skill or meaning emphasis in teaching would be beneficial. Frequently both are needed.

Most teachers use a "teach-study-test" procedure and use repetition as a remedial strategy. More teaching strategies would become available if the teacher had a clearer understanding of the spelling process itself. The most important considerations in using spelling as a perceptual training medium are related to the teacher's ability to interpret individual patterns of spelling errors and to tie these to the processes which spelling may entail. Individual differences in the visual, auditory and motor processing strategies preferred or used efficiently, or not in use, are clearly visible in the errors made by spellers. These are usually ignored

132

as a source of diagnostic information in remedial and compensatory teaching.

Simon and Simon (1973, p. 117) describe four different processes which spellers may use: memory or direct recall, spelling by sound-symbol association, a successive matching process involving trial and error in retrieving parts of words and whole words and last, using rules. Elaborating on each of these processes, they characterize:

1. Direct recall—as spelling of words which are associated in long-term memory with pronounciation and meaning.
2. Direct phonemic spelling—as based on stored sound-symbol associations supplemented to some degree by rules which determine these.
3. Generate and test process—as stored sound-symbol associations which are combined with the recognition of trial spellings. This is used in the sounding out and for the whole word.
4. Each of the above modified by morphemic information. This process may make use of rules, e.g. "When adding "ed" or "ing," double a final consonant preceded by a short vowel." The recognition of morphemic components gives access to spelling information.

In their comments on each of these processes, the Simons state that direct recall requires rote learning and, unless the words are overlearned, they are likely to be forgotten rapidly. Direct phonemic spelling produces very low accuracy even when conditional rules are learned (which is another major problem for the low-achieving child). The generate-and-test process will not produce accurate spelling by itself because it uses incomplete visual recognition information, but it does allow the speller to use that information which is held in long-term memory and is also comprised of his knowledge of all of the words in his reading vocabulary. (If the word has been seen, there will be some recognition information stored.) In describing this process, decoding words sound-by-sound and recoding them letter-by-letter is accounted for as well as recognizing words at the level of the whole word. In summary, while no one method can produce accurate spelling, teaching attention to various combinations tailored to individual needs might make great differences in accuracy.

A distinction between recognition and recall in relation to spelling is clearly stated in the Simons' discussion: "In order to recall a stimulus, we need complete information about the stimulus, else we could not reproduce it. In order to recognize the stimulus, we need only sufficient information about it to enable us to distinguish it from other stimuli that are possible in that context (p. 117)."

In support of this point, most teachers have had the experience of finding that when the child knows that the word he has written is incorrect, even if he erases and tries to make changes, he does not recall it more accurately. The child recognizes inaccuracy, but cannot recall enough detail to correct it spontaneously.

The most interesting view of the spelling process in the Simons' discussion is centered in the idea that spellers may actually make use of a trial and error in performance. The intriguing ideas of spellers recognizing and recalling correct form as they sequence the sounds and letters as they spell and compare the whole word with a stored image, suggest possibilities for teaching emphasis. In the researchers' analysis of the errors made by computer simulation and by typical students, the errors are described as phonetic, morphemic and semantic—a very meaningful categorization for instructional purposes.

It is also possible to look at these three types of errors in individual differences in spelling performance. Phonemic errors could be regarded as indicating auditory or visual perceptual difficulties. These are considered as a single group of errors because of the essentially cross-modal nature of the sound-symbol associations. Morphemic errors include this group but also yield information about an individual's knowledge of rules governing the ways in which parts of words can combine. Semantic errors indicate insufficient experience with the concepts the words represent, disregard for context or with what is called "word meaning."

Often, based on some diagnostic information, children will be classified as "auditory" or "visual" learners. This usually is an overgeneralization based on insufficient information. Because of the cross-modal demands in spelling, the process cannot be described as visual, auditory or motor—but the errors can give very good clues as to what is occurring in these three modal areas. The same information can also be viewed from a linguistic frame of reference and spelling errors analyzed in relation to the structure of language. When they are viewed in terms of perceptual modes, characteristics of the learner are in focus. When the errors are analyzed in relation to language structure, the characteristics of content are in focus.

The Simons' "generate and test" model of spelling has some interesting implications for teaching and is worth looking at in detail. It describes an enroute matching process used in spelling and a comparison made at the whole-word level as well. (See Figure 2, Chapter 1.)

This is a simple and informative model of the spelling process which focuses on cognitive and linguistic issues, and pictures, but ignores descriptively the matching act which the Simons postulate. If children were directed to choose correct forms from lists of possible but incorrect spellings, it might simulate to some degree the matching process used in the recall aspect of the spelling process and force those discriminations which are needed. Spelling proficiency is tested in this manner on several standardized tests but no systematic teaching material utilizes this tactic. (See Appendix for sample exercise based on words from "demon" lists.)

Spontaneous spelling always involves motor activity as words are written, but the perceptual-cognitive processes which are clearly defined in the model may precede motor function in practice. In other words, if the images are clear the writing will be accurate. This is the position supported by E. Gibson (1969); it is implicit but rather circular in the teaching strategies of Fernald (1943), Gillingham and Stillman (1960), Montessori (1964), and Slingerland (1971). All of these teachers support a multisensory approach to taking in information; this means they use tracing, verbalization and manipulation in learning letters and words. The cognitive process is receptive in tracing and one which involves developing recognition skills in these activities. Drawing and writing are expressive acts and involve the guidance of a tool—a pencil, pen, crayon or brush. Recall, the more difficult cognitive process, is demanded. This may explain to some extent the suppressive effect that writing seems to have on performance in some children. It is not the writing that causes the difficulty, it is the act of recalling. This explanation cannot be relied upon entirely, because many children have poor handwriting whether they copy (where no image is required) or perform spontaneously (where an image is required). As clear initial perceptions are important directors of motor activity as well as vital to the ability to recall a good image, it should make the teacher aware that very careful teaching is in order when words are first presented. Word study becomes a very important aspect of spelling ability. The common practice of writing the word five times and using it in a sentence may not develop a sufficiently differentiated image.

Word Study

In most spelling programs, word study is not distinctly divided into activities directed toward developing imagery and those involved in knowledge of the structure and meaning of words. These are intermingled in the study activities. Testing takes care of remembering. If a child misses a word, usually the only recourse is repetition of whatever strategies were used in the first place. As spelling process is rarely discussed in the teaching of spelling, neither do spelling programs foster matching teaching activities to perceptual cognitive attributes or needs of individual children. They deal entirely with issues related to the structure of content.

The predicament in spelling instruction is that problems exist in the inconsistencies in the sound-letter correspondences, in the ways in which words are pronounced, and in the unique ways in which individual children process perceptual information. These become confabulated in spelling instruction and usually repetition is the only teaching alternative regularly exploited. For the poor speller, this frequently serves as negative re-inforcement.

A great deal of recent research has been directed at studying the sound-symbol correspondences (Venesky, 1967; Hanna, 1966). Relatively less research is available on the information processing strategies that children use when they spell and on suitable instructional practices related to these issues. Even the studies on visual and auditory factors in spelling do not provide a clear description of function in the perceptual act of spelling or of common performance patterns. They link auditory and visual perception and memory but in an undifferentiated manner, skirting the issues involved in individual modality preference as well as the spelling process.

Word knowledge, spelling and reading proficiency are consistently linked in research studies and there appear to be high correlations between vocabulary development and spelling ability (Townsend, 1947; Russell, 1946). Plessas and Ladley (1963) suggest that

> these results indicate the need for (1) regular systematic spelling instruction, not incidental spelling instruction; (2) avoidance of teaching spelling through reading [they feel this practice can have adverse effects on word recognition and comprehension during the reading process]; (3) reading failure is not the cause of poor spelling, but a child who is unable to recognize a particular word will surely encounter serious difficulty in trying to spell it (p. 145).

As vocabulary and word meaning scores have such high correlations with spelling ability, children should be taught both word meaning and orthography in spelling instruction. Attention should also be paid to individual style in modality strength or to the information processing strategies the child prefers.

Familiarity with words and the frequency with which children are exposed to words may explain the consistent correlations between vocabulary tests and spelling tests. The more children see the word, the greater the possibility of the storage of a differentiated and clear image. One other point might be added: It would be of value to the children if the teacher were able to analyze spelling errors in an organized frame of reference and could provide adapted instruction to meet the needs which were determined. The development of linguistically-based spelling programs will provide better-organized content, but as the learner always appraoches the task with his own perceptual style, the organization of content (as it is currently being interpreted) is not the only relevant issue in spelling instruction. Error analysis has much to offer in this area and will be discussed later in this chapter.

Word Knowledge

It is possible to consider word knowledge with more specificity than as word meaning and word study. Other areas are:

1. Word selection—Which words?
2. Word meaning—Verbal definitions and concept development.
3. Word structure—Phonological and morphological considerations.
4. Word perception—Error analysis, pattern awareness, discerning salient visual cues, appreciating the difference between what is heard and seen, serial position effect, the effect of syllable stress, training in auditory sequencing and visual memory, the effect of word and list length; complexity as a problem; differentiating recognition and recall activities.
5. Word production (see chapter on Handwriting).
6. Learning management—The number of words, the number of letters, distribution of practice and recall patterns, feedback and proofreading, knowledge of and analysis of errors, the use of reinforcement, the use of records.

Before dealing with these specifics, it might be valuable to enumerate the issues in teaching spelling in the research literature and briefly summarize some of the findings.

Some General Issues in Teaching Spelling

According to Horn (1969) the major concerns in the research on teaching spelling include an examination of the causes of the difficulty, which words should be studied, how many and at what rate should they be introduced, as well as when specific words should be studied. Other issues involve contributing factors to spelling ability such as teacher interest in teaching spelling, pupil motivation, study habits, family socio-economic level and special visual and auditory and motor abilities and disabilities. Attention is also given to the issues of direct instruction vs. incidental learning, list vs. contextual study, self-selection, grouping by linguistic principles, recall and overlearning, visual-auditory syllabic presentations, dictionary use, kinesthetic techniques and programmed instruction, oral spelling and the place of games.

Some Results of the Research

Stating some of the findings from Horn's (1969) review may also be helpful in considering the issues.

1. List presentation of words is more efficient than their introduction in context. (p. 1288)
2. The principles used to group words must involve few exceptions. (p. 1288)
3. Calling attention to "hard spots" is not as efficient as studying errors on an individualized test basis. (p. 1289)
4. Each word should be learned beyond the point of one successful recall (p. 1289)
5. Distributed learning is more effective than mass learning for word study. (p. 1289)
6. Presenting words in syllable form does not enhance learning. [This probably is a useful technique for *some* children.] (p. 1289)
7. Dictionary use is basic to any spelling program. (p. 1289)
8. Kinesthetic techniques have proved successful with poor spellers. (p. 1289)
9. Games make a positive contribution to pupil motivation. (p. 1289)
10. There are positive correspondences between phonic knowledge and reading and spelling. (p. 1290)
11. Teaching meanings of spelling words is unnecessary since their meanings are already known if the writer is encoding his thoughts to be read. [But not if he is studying lists.] (p. 1290)
12. Speed and legibility have average correlations of about .20 with spelling. (p. 1290)

13. Speech aberrations and differences such as articulatory difficulties and inadequate command of American English are related to spelling disabilities. (p. 1291)
14. Unaccented syllables distort vowel sounds. (p. 1291)
15. There are obvious advantages to developing proofreading as a skill. Studies show that students do not do it systematically. [Research is inconclusive as to its effectiveness as a teaching strategy.] (p. 1291)
16. The value of learning rules depends on whether it has wide application and few exceptions and if it makes differences in the ability to learn. According to Horn (1954, p. 1291), "Other researchers feel uncertain about which rules should be taught and which discovered by the student, which ones are likely to be misapplied, which ones are intuitively used though not able to be stated by the student." (p. 1291)
17. Words of great difficulty must be treated as individual learning tasks. (p. 1292)
18. Spelling ability is highly related to visual perception, visual discrimination and visual memory, and sound perception and discrimination. (p. 1287)
19. Reading words in context temporarily improves a reader's spelling of those words but direct study is needed for long-term retention. (p. 1290)
20. "All but 63 of the 222 most persistently misspelled words are among the 1,000 words of highest frequency in reading, thus indicating that reading alone will not insure spelling mastery" (Fitzgfierald, 1951, cited in Horn, 1969, p. 1290)
21. Test-Study procedures are superior to Study-Test procedures. (p. 1292)
22. The corrected test technique is the most efficient single procedure for learning to spell, when children understand the purpose of the pretest, immediately correct errors and realize that the correction of the pretest errors reduces later test errors. (p. 1292)
23. When teaching rules, one should be taught at a time. They should be taught inductively with word examples which exemplify the rule. Both positive and negative instances should be presented. After teaching, the rules

should be used and reviewed, rather than only verbalized. (p. 1292)

Many of these conclusions will be discussed as the six areas to be covered in this chapter are explored.

Cahen et al. (1971) in their summary of the research note several studies which are of particular interest:

1. Gibson (1969) looked at errors and found that they fall into four categories: *additions, omissions, substitutions* and *inversions*. This research found high correlations between the first three and suggested that they probably involve similar psychological processes and that inversions seem to differ from the other error processes. This will be discussed in greater detail in Error Analysis.

Bloomer (1964) looked at word length, sound discriminability and shape discriminability, meaning and frequency (the greater exposure to the word, supposedly the easier the spelling task) and found them important in accurate spelling. While Cahen cites a Bloomer study (1959) which found the study of configuration to be superfluous in spelling mastery, Crosland and Johnson in an earlier study (1928) had found that words with ascenders and descenders (an important configuration detail) were easier to spell. This will be discussed in greater detail in the discussion on teaching configuration and awareness of salient visual cues.

One spelling program was mentioned in the Yee (1971) article which is of considerable interest. He cites a program developed by Schonell (1942) in which words are grouped by the auditory or visual similarities they contain and emphasis is placed on the articulatory and graphic responses with attention to the "utilitarian worth" of the words being learned. One study (Personke, 1963) indicates significant gains for children who were instructed using this approach. This supports the idea of using the visual and auditory differences and similarities in words for grouping, not simply spelling patterns. While this approach does not observe the child's function and adapt the approach, it does deal with two critical problems in spelling—hearing sounds in order and visual memory.

The current practice is that of groping words according to "linguistic principles." "Its purpose was to establish rules for translating spelling to sound [that is, to read] and it distinguished between rules based primarily upon phonemic and morphemic considerations and rules based primarily upon orthographic considerations" (Horn, 1969, p. 1288). Whenever there is a discussion of phonemic considerations in spelling, there never is any importance attached to the fact that the speller may not be able to differentiate the sounds in order in words at the verbal level. This is always taken as a "given" in all spellers. All of the emphasis in translating so-called linguistic principles is placed on regularity of the correspondences and whether the child will be able to generalize the ability to use a spelling pattern if he has enough experience with it. Words are organized in presentation so that the fact that there is some pattern is clear. The orthographic considerations take precedence over the phonemic ones in most teaching materials. Because spellers start with sounds in spontaneous spelling, at least in the learning stages, this needs more attention than it usually receives. However, the first subject to consider in discussing a spelling program is which words should be taught in order to deal with some of the issues.

WORD SELECTION

For the child who is having spelling difficulties, the basis on which words are selected may vary from those selection procedures used with general populations. Not only do children have problems with the spelling "demons" which may largely represent a group of words which are structure words, orthographically irregular and requiring visual memory and strong associations, but children may also have auditory sequencing problems which means they do not verbally respond appropriately to sounds in order in words. Words may be selected to meet a particular need or strength in the child.

List Study and Spontaneous Spelling—
A Distinction in Process

In spelling study, when lists of words are used, the task is very close to the decoding aspect of the reading act and quite different from what occurs in spontaneous spelling when the individual is generating the stimuli and responses himself. He is not reading something which has to be remembered. He is remembering something which has been read or heard, often infrequently and in the distant past. In list study, which is common spelling teaching procedure, the child "reads" the list. He is only required to remember it for a limited length of time, usually one week. The hope is that he will remember it forever, but usually inadequate teaching teaching procedures are provided for long-term retention and lists of inadequately learned words result. The "poor" speller is overwhelmed by inadequacy, his own and that of the teaching procedure. For many children the patterned word lists may provide a support condition during the study period and they are valuable, along with the linguistic ones, for that reason. However, when spontaneous spelling is the goal, teaching strategies should match the task. Errors need to be analyzed for they may be one means of solving the problem. Groups of words may be related by topic, by auditory or visual pattern, or by spelling or "linguistic" pattern. They can be dictated to children in a different form from which they were learned to determine the child's ability to remember and use the word. Overlearning, or continuous tested performance, is another helpful strategy. Lists of individual errors can be kept in spontaneous writing activities as well as in list learning, to cover both kinds of needs.

List learning can be valuable because of the control the teacher exercises over the choice of words, the spelling patterns, or the letter or list length. The selection of words can be made on several bases:

1. *Meeting Self-concept Needs*

The teacher may wish to support a child in learning words that other children in the class are learning. This may be valuable for developing self-confidence in the child. The amount of practice, the perceptual modes used for support, the incentives and reinforcements can be varied to accomplish this. Children can receive peer and adult approbation for successful performance. Success can be visible to the child and others.

2. *Using Demon Lists*

This can be a valuable strategy for developing skill with words that present special memory problems. Among such problems are silent letters and "homographs" or words spelled alike but pronounced differently and varying in meaning, e.g. "lead" as a verb versus "lead" as a noun. Homologs are words spelled and pronounced alike but different in meaning, e.g. "list" meaning to itemize and "list" meaning to learn or tilt (Cahen, Craun and Johnson, 1971, p. 287). Homonyms are also common to demon lists. These are words that are spelled differently and with different meaning but are pronounced the same, such as *to, too, two* and *their* and *there*. There are also words that are highly similar in elements and different in meaning and pronounciation such as *three* and *there*. Capitalized possessives also appear and again these require visual memory. Plessas (1963) presents a list of the most common homonyms encountered in grades 3 through 6 spelling lessons. He found that certain errors increased between certain grades; that children tended to write familiar words in place of unfamiliar ones and that there were dominant homonyms. He listed as such: *know, one, red, hear, week, wood, roll, hole, your flower, there* and *road*. His suggestions for teaching rely on increasing associations with meaning. This could be included with "forced discrimination training" where (1) an emphasis was placed on the differences in meaning, (2) consistent practice was provided in using and differentiating these words throughout grades 3 through 6, (3) kinesthetic experience was increased in the initial learning of these words in order to enhance the discrimination process and to increase the possibility of reliance on motor memory as a supportive means of differentiating the words, (4) incentives were provided consistently throughout the training to increase learning motivation, and (5) the learning situation was teacher- or peer-supervised in order to provide immediate reinforcement of correct responses. [Teaching suggestions are the editor's interpretation of "increasing associations with meaning."]

Plessas' list and other "demon" lists are presented in the Appendix.

3. *Using Phonetic Lists*

For many children it may be valuable to restrict the visual memory problems and work on learning to hear and write sounds in order in words. Difficulties in auditory sequencing (hearing sounds in order) are very common in low-achieving children and when systematic instruction is indicated, using lists of totally phonetic words with no irregularities can facilitate learning. This does not mean using spelling patterns or linguistically grouped words but those where the correspondences are limited to "one to one." The teacher may need to develop these lists on an individual basis, especially if certain sounds are presenting difficulties for individual children.

4. *Lists Made of Individual Errors*

Lists of words which are made of errors which occur in the spontaneous writing of children may be helpful as study material and in an ideal teaching situation would be first choice. This can always be a supplemental strategy, no matter what other lists of words are used, especially if error analysis is used and special teaching provided for the diagnosed needy areas.

5. *Word Lists in Curriculum Areas*

Frequently, teachers will find it necessary to develop specialized vocabularies to deal with math, science, social studies or some other area of the curriculum. Meanings may need to be developed as well as familiarity with the spelling pattern of the words. These vocabularies can be included in spelling lessons so that children can use the words in their spontaneous writing in these subjects. For the low-achieving child, the activity base in these areas can provide the direct experience which is necessary for concept development.

6. *Word Lists Based on Children's Interests*

If children are involved in special projects which are based on their interests or hobbies, special vocabularies can be developed around these topics. As spontaneous writing frequently occurs in these activities, the words can be filed or listed to serve as study lists.

7. *Standardized Word Lists*

Often it may be of value to teach from the basic word lists such as the Dolch (1942), the Fitzgerald (1951) or the Thorndike (1944). This could be included when extra attention to words which are also reading words seems indicated. When an experience story approach is being used with a child, a teacher may want to make certain that some structure and breadth is provided in the range of words with which the child develops familiarity.

It is very common to find that the child for whom the experience story is used has very good verbal skills and an excellent vocabulary. This child may also have "perceptual problems" and have difficulty remembering words. It is not uncommon to find in this approach that the child remembers what are considered hard words and has difficulty with what are considered easy ones. Studying "basic word lists" could have a place in such a situation. The best solution would be to make up the list from errors, but studying the standard lists might be more convenient for the teacher.

8. *Lists of Words of Controlled Length*

As word length is frequently a problem for the poor speller, control of this variable may be an advantageous teaching strategy. A teacher may wish to deal only with three- and four-letter words in initial teaching. These lists of controlled word length can at the same time control auditory sequence and correspondence or visual memory problems, depending upon the teaching approach to be used. Complexity in word length can be increased very gradually, letter by letter, until the child can handle this dimension of spelling performance.

9. *Linguistically Patterned Words*

Here the words are grouped according to spelling patterns and to stressed syllables, as well as changes which can occur in root words when affixes are added. This will benefit the child because each word does not present unique learning tasks. Even though the child may not generalize the rules which are presented in the lesson, the grouping presents a support condition in that the child's knowledge of what is expected of him in performance is given stability. He can rely on the pattern by stating it if necessary and if he does not remember it by saying "all of these words have 'ou' or 'ai'."

10. *Coping or "Survival" Lists*

These lists may be helpful for older children where vocabulary related to checkbooks, tax forms, job applications, drivers' licenses and practical living or vocational interests form the spelling list source.

11. *English-as-a-Second Language Lists*

When a child speaks very little English, the lists may be related to this issue, establishing first the vocabulary of the person, the classroom, the home, the community, needs or interests, or any content supporting verbal fluency.

12. *Disoriented Children Lists*

For those children who are not aware of the vocabulary of the body or who seem unaware of themselves in space and time —who have not been individuated by language related to their interests, desires, preferences—all lists might be personalized ones relating to the body, to interests, experiences, likes or dislikes, time, space or words which are chosen by the child. In this "therapeutic teaching" personal validation for the child takes precedence over curriculum content.

In summary, for the low-achieving child there are many ways in which a spelling list may be assembled for study. Taking into account the child's individual needs in the academic environment in which he is attempting to function rather than the exclusive use of an approved spelling book may make more sense and provide for more integration in spelling instruction. Because meaning is an important aspect of accurate spelling performance, it can be more broadly interpreted to include "meaningful" word selection.

Selection of the words which are provided for study can be a very important means of restricting or elaborating the demands made on children in spelling study. In remedial or developmental teaching, exact perceptual and cognitive skills can be given attention through careful selection of the words. It deserves very thoughtful attention from teachers of children with serious spelling problems.

WORD MEANING

Even though spelling provides well-suited curriculum content for developing word knowledge, it has certain limitations. Words which are provided in lists are isolated and not related to other curriculum areas or based on spontaneous need. While this is of value for the development of perceptual skill, it has definite limitations in the development of word meanings because of emphasis on verbal definition rather than direct experience or the need to "know." Carroll (1964, p. 178) has stated that word knowledge is "one of the principal tasks of teachers at all levels of education." Accepting this as a basic premise, some attention will be devoted to the teaching of word meaning in spelling because it must be assumed (1) that a child would not spell a word spontaneously which had no meaning for him, (2) that word meaning must exist before perceptual training is attempted, and (3) there is a definite relationship between word knowledge of which meaning is a factor and spelling success. A brief summary of some of the important aspects of teaching word meaning is in order.

In defining the terms word, meaning and concept, Carroll (1964) observes that *words* can be thought of as physical entities, spoken or written. *Meanings* are complex relationships of sets of words. They are rules of usage that have developed through socialization and communication. "A meaning can be thought of as a standard of communicative behavior that is shared by those who speak a language" (p. 187). *Concepts* are classes of experience formed in individuals independently as well as closely dependent upon language. A concept may be represented in language by a word which in imagery is visualized in a setting, has color, texture, "feeling," and has a variety of images associated with it in the mind of the speaker.

Usually, in spelling lessons, the meaning of words is taught through verbal explanations given by the teacher or read in the spelling book by the child. Frequently, dictionary work is assigned and the child looks up a formal definition. Sometimes the word is used in a sentence or in "context" to demonstrate meaning through use rather than in formal definition. Sometimes the teacher expands upon the meaning of words the child knows and often teaches a new concept, one that is unfamiliar to the child. Most of the word-meaning activities in formal spelling are based on some form of verbal definition and not much concrete experience is provided.

Concepts

Carroll states that:

. . . concepts are essentially nonlinguistic (or perhaps better, alinguistic) because they are classes of experience which the individual comes to recognize as such, whether or not he is prompted or directed by symbolic language phenomena. Because the experiences of individuals tend to be in many respects similar, their concepts are also similar, and through various processes of learning and socialization, these concepts come to be associated with words. The meaning of words are the socially-standardized concepts with which they are associated. One of the problems in teaching concepts is that of teaching the associations between words and concepts and this is analogous to a paired associate learning task (pp. 201-202).

As Carroll defines concepts, "they are abstract and often cognitively structured classes of 'mental' experience learned by organisms in the course of their life histories" (p. 180).

Successive Experience and Negative and Positive Instances

The individual must have a series of experiences that are in one or more respects similar; the constelaltion of "respects" in which they are similar constitutes the "concept" that underlies them. Carroll goes on to make the point that when the concept learning is developed from verbal explanation, the learner must be put through a vicarious set of experiences of positive and negative instances. He gives the example of explaining the concept of a lion to a child. He suggests that one discuss positive and negative instances, including a range of variations that could exist in real lions and the respects in which other animals differ from lions (p. 181). Many of the children with whom the suggestions being made will be used, will have poor knowledge of words, their meanings, as well as meagre experiences. The first implication for teaching is, of course, direct experience, concrete experience with the things, living organisms, people and animals, events or relations the words represent. These must be successive so that a stage of generality can be reached and the individual can recognize similarities and differences even though variations may be slight. Enriched word meaning rests on concepts which are developed in such successive experiences, verbally associated with words. The more chances the child has to experience and verbalize the concepts embodied in words, the more meaningful his vocabulary will be. If direct experience is not provided, then the quality of the verbal definition becomes even more important for the child with any kind of language problem. Teachers need to watch children to determine whether teaching negative instances verbally is helpful. For some children it might be very confusing. But teachers do need to remember to return to verbal definitions again and again to determine if the concept of the word is established.

Levels of Representation

Not only must experiences be successive and possibly contain negative and positive instances, but verbal langauge is itself representational and instruction in word meaning can be more effective if the definitions provided relate to the levels of representation when possible. The first level is the *Object Level* which involves real experiences with objects, places and events. By acting on the objects and experiencing events, the child is building a basis for some referents for later representational activities. The *Index Level* involves some part of the real object or its mark or imprint must be present to serve as a clue for identifying and mentally reconstructing the whole real object. At the Index Level, the child can construct the whole object when (a) only part of it is seen, (b) when it is perceived through senses other than sight, (c) when a part is missing, and (d) when an imprint or something causally related to the object is seen" (Weikert, 1968, p. 10). The *Symbol Level* involves something that stands for something else and resembles it in some way. The symbol is not the same as or part of the object it represents. It is chosen as a representation because it is in some way like the object it represents. Symbols include models, pictures, diagrams, maps and actions which imitate or pretend that an object is other than what it is (a stick for a horse). The degree of abstraction varies and it is helpful to children who have language problems to use simple abstractions and those as close to reality as possible. The last level is the *Sign Level*. Here, conventional and arbitrary representations occur. Words and their graphic representations are good examples of signs.

Carroll makes the point that, in teaching concepts in schools, there is a strong memory component involved in matching words and concepts added to the problems of concept learning itself. Successive presentations of definitions become critical. Children with spelling difficulties have special kinds of language-memory problems and these differ widely from individual to individual. When the problem involves verbal language as well as some specific perceptual nonfunction, the way in which meanings are developed becomes quite important. Carroll goes on to state: "The difficulties that learners have in attaining a concept are likely to be due to their inadequate mastery of prerequisite concepts and to errors made by the teacher in presenting in proper sequence the information intrinsic to the definition of the concept (p. 202)." The sequence to which he refers largely involves the steps in successive presentations which elucidate the positive and negative instances. In the development of a concept, the teacher might sequence the materials involved in relation to the levels of representation in order to develop meaning and deal with appropriate perceptual support strategies as well.

One has only to recall the standard spelling lessons which move on relentlessly with cursory word meaning activities and inadequate attention to the memory functions which defeat many children, to realize that *less* needs to be *better* developed by the teacher and more thoroughly learned by the child. It is not a simple teaching task, but neither is it hopeless.

Seven Suggestions for Teaching Word Meaning

Summarizing the suggestions for teaching word meaning, the verbal definitions can be: (1) given by the teacher, formally defined by dictionaries, given in use by the child, (2) definitions should be given which not only explain what something is but devote as much time differentiating it from what it is not (individual determination), (3) make successive presentations of definitions, (4) categorize words which are related in meaning, (5) associate concepts and link meanings in order to elaborate concepts, (6) use pictures, graphs, models, diagrams and other aids to deal less abstractly with the concepts and, finally, (7) wherever possible provide actual experiences with the concepts being taught in the words, the objects, events, people or relationships. This means that the integration of spelling with social studies, science, art and other "activity" subjects in the curriculum can provide the experience base which is the foundation of concept development. Verbal definition alone is simply inadequate as a strategy for developing word meaning. This is particularly true for the low-achieving child and supports the argument for teaching spelling in two ways—from spelling books and integrated with other subjects.

WORD STRUCTURE

One important skill in spelling involves sequencing sounds in words in internal language. This means saying the word as it is written or *thinking* the saying of the word. This process is learned as children learn the "encoding" aspect of spelling and, with proficiency, it telescopes as performance becomes more automatic. The way the child pronounces the word becomes very important. As written language is a representation of spoken language, some characteristics of the sound system are important. Two aspects of language deal with meanings *within* words; one is *phonology,* the other *morphology.*

Phonology

Bock (1969) presents an excellent discussion of these two aspects of language; his points are presented here in summary: As a child learns to speak, he becomes aware of significant differences among the sounds of the language he uses. The sounds that consistently make differences are called *phonemes* and they are not in themselves meaningful. Like units of a code, they only communicate meanings when arranged in certain conventional patterns. They are signalling units and they are produced by differences in voicing and tongue positions. In English, we learn to note these differences. There may be other differences used in other languages such as tone, loudness and speed of production which we have learned to ignore.

Most phonemes are produced in sequence. This is true of consonants and vowels. There is another type which occurs simultaneously with the sequenced ones, and that is *stress*. It can signal a change in meaning when everything else is held constant (content'—con'tent). *Tone* is also used (in questions) but not to indicate differences between pairs of words.

The number of phonemes used in English is about thirty-five. These are defined in a systematic way with the attributes of voicing and tongue position as the main characteristics used to signal differences in single syllabled words and stress added for words of more than one syllable. Also involved are plans and instructions or rules which limit the ways in which categories can be combined. Sounds in speech follow each other in certain patterns just as letters do in spelling. The consonant sound cluster *ldt* is not used to begin a word, but *br* is.

While many theorists differ on this point, Hodges and Rudorf (1965) feel that an alphabetic system is determined at the phonological level. They studied the positions of phonemes in syllables and in monosyllabic words. They found a remarkable amount of consistency in sound-letter correspondences. When they looked at the added dimension of stress, they found even greater consistency. They feel that, "the evidence indicates that the bulk of the words in a typical elementary school program can be spelled on a phonological basis and a smaller but still significant number of words can be spelled by correctly combining phonological and morphological factors such as compounding and affixation (p. 531)."

Other theorists view the problem a little differently; some feel that most spelling errors are made on words which are spelled in a phonetically ambiguous or irregular way (Simon and Simon, 1973, p. 128). Ambiguity may be a problem for all spellers, but many of the low-achieving children also have the problem discussed before, i.e. accurately establishing the sound sequence in words. While leaving out letters or substituting letters may be related to the ambiguity of which one to choose when the speller is aware that there is a sound sequence which must be represented, others leave out letters or substitute them because they do not sequence the sounds or are unaware of the segmented nature of verbal expression.

If children have not mastered the set of rules which govern the production of speech, this inadequacy may show up as a problem in spelling unless the children have extraordinary visual memories to compensate for this lack. Problems may occur when articulation problems, hearing difficulties, use of foreign languages, slurred speech, and ethnic, cultural and regional differences are present. The phonological aspects of speech—tongue positions and voicing, sequencing and stress—are very important in spelling and any distortion in the production can be reflected in errors in writing. Stress on syllables distorts sounds so that vowels are frequently not discernible. In spelling, if an element cannot be heard, it *must be* remembered. Even if a child hears a word globally, he may not be able to discern its parts well enough to be able to spell it. "Hearing" a sound presumes either a one-to-one correspondence or memory of a combination.

Morphology

Words not only have phonemes and single letters which represent them, but larger divisions called *morphemes*. Morphemes are composed of phonemes in sequence which are conventionally ordered and constitute larger parts of words which are combined to differentiate meaning. Morphemes include roots and affixes. Roots carry the basic meaning of the word and affixes change or modify it in a variety of ways. Affixes are of two kinds, those that precede the root, i.e. *ex*port, *de*port and those that follow it, i.e. port*er*, port*s*, deport*ee*. Most of the affixes in English follow the root. There are also compound words where two or more roots are combined to form a single word (portable). Words also carry information about number and tense, i.e. deport*ees*, deport*ed*. Words which stand alone are called "free" morphemes and sound clusters such as affixes which have limited meaning and do not stand alone. They are called "bound" morphemes. They add consistent meaning to many words (McLean, 1974, p. 462).

The morphological aspects of word structure are usually covered rather sporadically in spelling texts. With the advent of "linguistic teaching" more emphasis is given to this aspect.

Chomsky's (1970) suggestions for teaching spelling move

away from teaching by spelling pattern and word family to a broader consideration about how some words became the way they are, i.e. why they are irregular. In discussing the relation of spelling patterns to the sound structure of the language, Chomsky suggests a "deep sound structure" of the language that is not arbitrary. She cites Herbert Kohl's description of his own teaching in *36 Children* and suggests that teachers follow his lead and interest children in entomology—putting an emphasis on word meanings and word relationships including discussions of word origins and historical changes. She suggests teaching children to look for and be challenged by irregularities rather than simply memorizing spellings of words in isolation or even in groups. Memory for words is not only considered perceptually but cognitively as well. The child will be more likely to remember a unique spelling demanding "visual" memory if he understands something about its historical development.

Dialects and Spelling

Brengelman (1970) makes several points in discussing dialects and their influence on spelling performance. In his opinion, while English spelling is not phonetic, he feels there are connections between English sound and spelling systems that are worth exploration. The sounds are not represented indiscriminantly and the number of spelling alternatives for any given sound are severely restricted. With most consonants, only one spelling is likely and with the vowels seldom more than two or three.

He amplifies the points made by Bock about voicing, articulation and stress and includes sound features such as nasality and consonality, stating that with the introduction of a new distinctive feature in a word, a new character is required. Each character represents a combination of sound features and can show shifts. Unstressed syllables are spelled according to more complicated principles. The spelling of polysyllables is not based on actual pronunciation, but on morphological structure. He states that in some dialects, the spelling will have to be related to semantic rather than phonological features because the vowels may be insufficiently distinguished to differentiate them; for example, *cot*

—*caught, body—bawdy, sot—sought,* and so forth. We find agreement among all theorists on this point. He also states that permitted sound feature sequences differ in some dialetcs and gives the example of *wh* and *w* as reflecting phonological difference for some Americans and not others, and being arbitrary in British English.

It is perhaps also worth mentioning that anyone who lightly advocates changing a child's phonological system should realize what he is proposing: a tremendously difficult task . . ." (p. 136). He suggests: ". . . a teacher must be able to determine when a spelling difference can be related to a phonological difference and when it must be related to some higher level of language structure" (p. 137). His suggestions include developing relationships to semantic differences, and he lists the most common phonological elements which generate spelling errors (p. 135).

Brengelman's point of view supports a "meaning" based program of instruction, even when memory, which is regarded as a perceptual-cognitive skill, is an instructional goal. Simple repetition, the main present teaching strategy for dealing with error, is inadequate to deal with "perceptual problems." The six phonological elements which he feels are involved when dialects are present are:

1. Consonantal /r/ after vowels.
2. The pronunciation and spelling difference between the common consonantal clusters—*ld, nd, st, sts,* etc.
3. Distinguishing vowels which precede /r/.
4. Helping the child deal with low-central and low-back vowels: *cot—caught; body—bawdy; sot—sought; hock—hawk; don—dawn; nod—gnawed.*
   [Making the child aware of the difference in his particular articulation of the word so that he understands the difficulty in distinction and can develop an "intention to compensate" as a learning strategy. Ed.]
5. Understanding the effect of alveolar consonants on certain vowels—*do—dew* (*yuw* and *uw*)—in relationship to their own pronunciation.
   [Alveolar refers to the contact point of the tongue in mak-

ing the sound—the gum area above the upper teeth. With such problems, increasing the meaning base of the concepts in the two words and possibly teaching another pronunciation as a mediating or mnemonic device might be helpful. Ed.]

6. Calling attention to the /hw/ and /w/ sound and helping the child pick a learning strategy.

   [Exaggerated pronunciation, meaning amplified or increased intent to remember as compensatory strategies. Ed. suggestion]

A teacher could adapt several strategies in helping the child who spoke with a dialect:

1. Help the child *become aware* of his own pronunciation and how it differs from standard English and the areas in which he will need to compensate to improve his spelling.

2. *Attempt to change* some glaring differences in pronunciation by making the child aware of other ways of pronouncing words.

3. *Develop strategies for compensation.* Primarily, these would be kinesthetic teaching for memory problems, increased dependence on morphological (sound-symbol relationships), syntactical (grammar), and semantic cues (meaning) to enhance meaning and familiarity and increase the frequency with which the child was exposed to and required to spell the word.

Dialect is a very important part of an individual's identity and self-concept, and teachers should consider this carefully before attempting changes. Schools have subtle ways in which they make children feel inadequate, and finding a child's language insufficient may be one of hidden ways in which this occurs.

Rules

Shaw (1965) states that there are more than fifty formulated rules which govern the way letters are grouped into words. Agreeing with other authorities that rules are of limited value in spelling, he nevertheless lists six which he feels may be helpful if (1) they are applied, (2) if they are supplemented by visual and motor memory tricks or dictionaries (as every rule contains exceptions), (3) if the corollaries or the reverse of every spelling rule is learned as well. The low-achieving child may have as much difficulty in learning the rule as he does in applying it because many of the children have pervasive memory problems as well as difficulty in generalization. But as this may not be true of all low-achieving children, rules should be used as one support condition on an individualized basis. At least the teacher should memorize the most important rules in order to structure words by spelling patterns to provide additional practice when errors occur consistently in words where rules can be applied. Sometimes the teacher does not know the rules and for that reason they are emphasized. The six rules which Shaw (1965) has found to be most useful and which apply to the largest number of commonly misspelled words are:

1. *ei* or *ie* words: *i* before *e* except after *c* or when sounded like *a* as in neighbor and weigh (believe, receive).
2. Final *y*: If *y* at the end of a word is preceded by a consonant, change it to *i* when adding a suffix. If preceded by a vowel, retain *y* (try, tried, trying).
3. Final *e*: Drop silent *e* if adding a suffix beginning with a vowel, keep it if suffix begins with a consonant (believe-believing; hope, hoping, hopeless).
4. Inserted *k*: *k* is usually added to words ending in *c* before a suffix beginning with *e, i* or *y* (picnic, picnicked).
5. Doubling Final Consonants: In one syllabled words, or those accented on the last syllable, double the consonant if the suffix begins with a vowel and if the base word ended in a single consonant preceded by a vowel (except *x*) [begin-beginning, plan-planning].
6. The "one plus one" rule: Be sure both letters are included when:
   a prefix ends in the same letter with which the base word begins (dissatisfied),
   the base word ends in the same letter with which a suffix begins (accidenta*ll*y),
   two words are combined and the first ends with the same letter with which the second begins (boo*kk*eeping).

There are so many exceptions to the brief statements of the rules just given that they are almost useless for our purposes in this discussion. However, they will serve to emphasize classes of errors which teachers can use as the basis for exercises. It is for this reason that they are presented here. Other rules which are important and can be used to some extent to help the low achiever involve plurals, capitals, hyphens, apostrophes, and compound words. Shaw's summary of the rules for each of these areas serves as an excellent resource, but it does underscore the importance of learning to use the dictionary for both rules and spelling. Low-achieving children should receive extra emphasis in training in dictionary use.

WORD PERCEPTION

Psychological Behavior and Spelling Errors

In spelling instruction, not only is knowledge about the rules for combining sounds and letters necessary, but certain psychological attributes of behavior are important in determining teaching emphasis when errors occur. The analysis of errors in spelling can provide direct information which is individualized, about skill in hearing sounds in order, discriminating them and remembering those elements in the roots and affixes which require visual memory. As spelling tests deal largely with issues involved in phonological, morphological and semantic aspects of word knowledge, little attention is paid to hearing or producing sound, information processing or modality preference in most spelling programs. Most spelling instruction assumes the sufficient development of oral language as well as the manipulative skills required in writing. No spelling test provides for an analysis of spelling errors in relationship to the information processing strategy the child may be using or failing to use. Yet an analysis of the errors is an easy way to determine which aspects of word knowledge require teaching attention. Error analysis can direct attention to some of the phonological elements which may never receive the attention needed in order for successful spelling to occur. It can also pick out those particular morphological elements requiring visual memory which are difficult for individual children, and in the process can develop word concepts.

Error Analysis

Gibson (1969) has classified spelling errors in four categories: *omissions, additions, substitutions* and *inversions*. Stating that high correlations were found between the first three types, the conclusion is reached that these errors involve similar psychological processes. The lower correlations between inversions and the other three was taken to suggest that the inversion differs from the other error processes. While errors can be further categorized as an aid to individualization, examining these four areas in terms of possible process meanings may be of interest.

If a child omits a letter it may indicate that one of several things occurred. It may represent an auditory sequencing error (this can easily be checked to determine the sound-letter correspondence); it may represent a visual memory error; it is part of a dipthong or a digraph and is not remembered, or it may represent a cognitive-motor lapse. In a child's attention to the perceptual-cognitive and the motor aspects of the act, lapses and omissions occur as attention is directed to production activities. Either perception or attention may be at fault. When a child *adds a letter,* where the letter is added is important; in the error "witle" (*will*) the addition of the *e* may represent a motor error involving memory for sequence and automatic response. It is very common and expected to write *le* in final position. The child probably relied on motor memory. In the same word, the *t* substituted for the *l* indicates a visual discrimination error—*t* and *l* are similar in shape. It is possible that substitutions could be auditory—*chip-ship or lit-lid*. Errors of substitutions, omissions and additions could be visual-motor or auditory, but inversions are entirely visual and involve a single change in the letter, the orientation. This may partially explain the difference Gibson found in this class of error and this discussion provides some preliminary examples about how errors need to be considered.

Interestingly enough, in the Hodges and Rudorf study, eight phonemes have been identified as causing most of the errors: /a/ as in care; /e/ as in here; /oo/ as in food; /oo/ as in foot;

/u/ as in urn; /u/ as in circus; syllabic /'n/ as in button; and /z/ as in zebra. All require visual memory except /z/ which is used relatively infrequently.

Visual memory, at least in part, is a function of differentiated perception. Using errors to track perceptual inaccuracies could be very helpful in individualizing instruction. Patterns of visual and auditory strengths and weaknesses emerge when errors are analyzed.

In order to analyze errors in greater detail, a classification system or matrix of perceptual functions is presented as structure. The three modalities involved in spelling are the *visual, auditory* and *kinesthetic*. There are also some highly relevant skills which operate within each of the modes. The most important perceptual skills are those involved in discrimination. Actually, there are only two areas with which instruction is concerned: *discrimination* and *memory*. As has been stated, memory depends to some degree on the success of the initial discriminations. The characteristics or attributes of the letters and sounds in spelling which are most important are details, orientation-localization, and sequence. When these are arranged in a matrix, they allow for organized error analysis. Attention, an attribute of the learner, is also important and deserves close observation and evaluation by the teacher.

Before this matrix is filled in with common errors which exemplify each category and skill, it might be valuable to discuss briefly each of the skills.

Discrimination

As it is used in analyzing spelling errors, discrimination simply means the ability to notice details. The discriminations which need to be made in spelling are both visual and auditory. The auditory discriminations include differences between like sounds, such as *d* and *t, ch* and *sh*. The visual discriminations are between letters such as *c* and *o* or *b* and *d*. It is very easy to look at spelling errors and determine if the discriminations have been made and if they have not, whether they involve a detail such as the length of a stroke as is the difference between *n* and *h*, or the orientation of a figure as in *b* and *p*. Both of these errors

SKILLS	VISUAL	AUDITORY	VISUAL-MOTOR
Discrimination Detail Similarities & Differences Substitutions			
Memory Short term Long term 　　Letter span 　　List length			
Orientation 　Spatial (Letters) 　　Reversals 　　Inversions *Localization* 　Temporal (Sounds) 　　Initial 　　Medial 　　Final			
Sequencing Transpositions Omissions Substitutions Insertions			

Figure 3.

involve discriminations, but of different characteristics of letters. In the motor aspect of spelling, some errors involve perceptual discriminations and some involve inadequate motor control. Perceptual discriminations are evidenced in incorrect line relationships, spatial distance between letters and words, and the disproportionate size of letters. Evidence of poor motor control is seen in line qualities, such as wavers and the lightness or darkness of the line. These indicate pressure or grip problems which can cause fatigue and lack of control. Maintaining continuity may become a problem with either of these conditions. Letters may not be well formed because the hand is too flaccid or the grip too excessive to provide the proper degree of guidance of the writing tool—not because the discriminations have not been made.

Memory

Memory is a critical skill in all learning. In spelling, it is necessary for remembering word meanings and for making the associations between the sounds and letters—or combinations of letters—that stand for the sounds. There are some special aspects of memory which could be given more attention than is now customary. One concerns the particular difference between short- and long-term memory patterns in an individual. (The child can learn the spelling list each week, but in spontaneous spelling which requires long-term retention, errors occur.) The other pertains to the number of letters which a child can remember in a word and the number of words in a list which can be remembered before error occurs. Observing these two behavior patterns can give exact information about where to start in developing more efficient memory fucntion in children. These following "chunking" laws, which state that information which is processed tends to be taken in chunks of nine units if the memory is exceptionally good, seven units if average, and five if below average (Miller, 1956). The average list of words in a speller is twenty, and most of the errors occur in the second half of the list. Most low-achieving children can remember three-letter words (well below the five considered below average) or three words and is a good place to start when a severe spelling problem exists. Some children have difficulty with short-term auditory memory and ask for frequent repetitions of words or sentences. This can be an attentional, discrimination or comprehension problem and would benefit from teacher observation for more specific teaching objectives.

Some evidence of an auditory memory problem is also available in the fact that the word the child writes has little relationship to the sound pattern in the word, although there is some evidence of relationship to the visual configuration of the word. It is usually after the representation of the beginning sound that difficulties occur.

The information contained in the shape of the word will often yield some information about visual memory. Children frequently remember shape and confuse detail. Certain confusions must be clearly differentiated visually in order to be remembered because there is no direct sound representation or because there may be several ways of representing the same sound. *C-K, s-c, g-j, sion-tion, cian-cion,* are examples of this. *R* obscures the sound of the vowels which precede or follow it and capitals, possessives and hyphens all represent something about the word which has no direct sound-equivalent. One of the most frequent examples of this kind of difficulty is spelling which is completely phonetic with none of the "silent letters" represented. This pattern can be considered a strength as well as a weakness.

Several kinds of errors can be related to the perceptual-motor aspects of spelling. Children often forget how to form a particular letter or they will mix capitals and lower case letter indiscriminantly. Frequently there will be evidence of motor memory where frequently used sequences of letters are included inappropriately.

Orientation and Localization

These two skills are differentiated in order to observe spatial and temporal qualities in relation to sounds and letters. Letters have specific vertical and horizontal orientation which can be described as a "spatial relationship." Sounds occupy specific positions in words. Children often distort or change these in perception that involves recall. It can be helpful in observing error to differentiate inversions which involve vertical turns and reversals which involve horizontal shifts. The letter does not move out of its position in relation to the other letters in the word, but is rotated on its axis.

As sound involves temporal rather than spatial relationships, localization of sound in word position becomes an important skill in descriptions of errors related to the ability to hear sounds in words. The speller frequently needs to determine where sounds are in words, to label position of sounds or letters, or to name sounds and letters when given position.

Errors in spelling also follow the serial position curve. Less errors are made at the beginning or end of a word and most of the errors occur in the middle. The laws of serial position indicate that in anything which is learned in sequence, the first things are learned first, the last things learned second, and those in the middle are learned in alternating order, i.e. 135798642. The last things learned in words are the vowels which usually occur in the middle position. Wherever they are, they are difficult to discriminate since there are such small differences between them both visually and auditorially. According to this position law, they are the last to be learned in any word. As far as teaching is concerned, this simply means that the vowels need more instructional attention given to them.

Orientation problems are also visible in writing. Examples of difficulties with this are seen in letters which require a change in direction of the stroke, or a return sweep over a stroke which has already been made. Inaccuracies are often found in the lower case *t, i, d,* in cursive writing, for example. Closure may also be a problem in these letters. Reversals and inversions are examples here, as well as mirror writing, slant problems, improper or inconsistent margins or writing strokes in manuscript which start from the base line up, or writing which begins at the bottom of the page and proceeds upward. Mirror writing is a good example of the orientation problem; extreme paper rotations are also indicators of some difficulty in this area.

Sequencing

It was pointed out earlier that one of the invariants or commonalities between sounds and their symbols is sequence. Both letters and sounds occur in order. In spelling, however, auditory sequencing occurs first because the process begins with a spoken word or one which is thought. It is quickly followed by visual sequencing as the word is written, and the two may occur simultaneously. In this area the common errors are omissions, substitutions, insertions and transpositions. These always can occur because of lack of attention. Frequently, they indicate a discrimination difficulty such as a substitution of a *d* for a *t* or vice-versa; this is an auditory error. It also could be interpreted as a visual error in that it is a tall letter in correct position. General form, not detail, is represented. A *t* might be written for an *l*. This is also a visual substitution where general form rather than detail has been discriminated. An omission can indicate a lack of the ability to think sounds in order, as when *rember* is written. This also could be interpreted as reliance on visual memory which was inadequate. Omissions can also indicate a visual memory error as in the case when letters are doubled, when accent or stress obscure sound-letter relationships or when mispronunciation occurs. Insertions frequently occur because of mispronunciation or because visual memory fails. [There's a tall letter someplace in the word, but which one and where has not been clearly differentiated.] Insertions also occur because of the interference in memory of sequences which have previously been learned. The example of *will* written *witle* is such an error. Often *tle* is written at the ends of words; as writing begins attention may lapse, motor memory is functioning, and such an error is the result.

Transpositions are spatial and temporal sequencing errors and they occur both in speech and writing. Called "spoonerisms" in speech (after a professor who had this problem) they involve changing the position of the sounds in a word or words in a sentence. *Psghetti* is an oft-heard mispronunciation of *spaghetti* in the young child's speech. Such errors as "I date the ate" for "I ate the date" or "That man is weldom selcome" for "That man is seldom welcome" are quite common. These errors are not so frequently recorded in writing. Those that do occur usually involve the shift of letters in words, such as *again* written as *agian*, *receive* as *recieve, third* as *thrid*.

Maintaining continuity in the sequence in words as well as sentences is a common difficulty in writing. There usually are breaks in the writing or write-overs that make this problem easily visible in cursive. Older children who prefer manuscript writing frequently have this difficulty; they stay with the previously learned form because of the discreteness of the letters which does not require the same degree of control in continuous writing and allows time between each letter.

WORD PRODUCTION

The Visual-Motor Channel

Since writing requires the integration of eye and hand, perception and movement are intermixed. Much information is available about this skill in spelling performance. In written lists of words, knowledge of letter forms can be observed as well as consistency in the use of manuscript or cursive form, capitals and small letters, apostrophes or hyphens. All of these errors indicate inadequate initial perceptions (from a perceptual point of view and inadequate meaning from a linguistic point of view). There is also information about line awareness, spatial relations between letters and words and the orientations of letters in manuscript and, in cursive, transpositions of letters. Line quality also can provide information about grip and pressure. Use of this information can individualize teaching and meet exact needs.

In language activity involving writing, it is often difficult to distinguish between visual and motor difficulties. The thesis supported in this book is that if the perceptions are sufficiently discriminated there will be a better chance of remembering and of producing an accurate representation. Whenever an error occurs, the stimuli should be regarded in the light of the perceptual as well as cognitive demands they make and the errors interpreted in this frame of reference. The chart which follows provides a modality referenced framework for the most common errors which do occur.

A Sample Analysis

The following sample for an error analysis will clarify use of the matrix in categorizing visual and auditory performances. In spelling these are of greater importance than motor skill and will

PERCEPTUAL DIAGNOSIS THROUGH SPELLING AND WRITING ERROR ANALYSIS

SKILLS		AUDITORY	VISUAL	VISUAL - MOTOR
D I S C R I M I N A T I N G	Details	Sound similarities ch - sh; d - t; p - b; f - v; etc. Short vowel sounds Stress Mispronunciation	Letter similarities t - f; c - e; h - n; m - n; g - y; vowels, etc. Word similarities come - came; am - an	PERCEPTUAL AND/OR PERFORMANCE PROBLEM MANIPULATIVE CONTROL – line character- istics, grip, pressure, speed, fatigue point, fluency LINE RELATIONSHIPS – Starting-stopping problems, line awareness SPATIAL RELATIONSHIPS – Judging dis- tance between letters and words SIZE RELATIONSHIPS – inconsistency in relative size of large and small letters VISUAL SHIFT PROBLEMS – from board or near copy or return sweep at end of line

M E M O R Y	Spatial
	  Form
	  Span
	  Letter
	  Word
	Temporal
	  Immediate
	  Delayed
	  Test
	  Spontaneous
		Short term - needs
		  repetition
		Reliance on visual
		  skill only
			Configuration
			Letter span
			Confusions - c - k; s - c
			  g - j; sion - tion; cian - cion;
			R difficulties
			Capitals - possessives;
			Reliance on auditory skill only
			Word span
				Letter formation
				Consistency in use of form – manuscript or
				  cursive
				Motor Memory – automatic responses – le at
				  ends of words

O R I E N T A T I O N	Spatial
	  Direction
	  Temporal
	  Localization
	    of position
		Error clusters in
		  Initial
		  Medial
		  Final positions
			Reversals b - d; saw - was;
			  etc.
			Inversions y - h; p - d;
			  u - n; w - m; etc.
			god - dog
				Letters requiring return sweep – t – d; a – c;
				  g – h – n; etc.
				Reversals
				Inversions
				Mirror Writing
				Bottom to top of line stroke: of page use
				Slant problems (alignment and symmetry)
				Margins
				Paper Rotations

S E Q U E N C I N G	Serial
	  Position
	  Order
		Insertions
		Omissions
		Substitution
		Reliance on visual
		  skill only
			Transpositions
			  ai - ia; oa - ao;
			  ie - ei; etc.
			  god - dog
				Continuity

Figure 4.

be dealt with first. This spelling example was obtained from a nine-year-old child in the fourth grade who read at primer level. He was asked to attempt the words even if he was not sure of how they were spelled. The words are from Level I of the Wide Range Achievement Test. [Handwriting sample too light for reproduction.]

Word	Written	Analysis
1. go	go	correct
2. cat	cat	correct
3. in	in	correct
4. boy	buy	*Visual memory error*: vowel diphthong — not phonetic. Visual memory for configuration main-tained. Visual discrimination error.
5. and	and	correct

Word	*Written*	*Analysis*
6. will	witle	*Auditory sequencing error*: did not check by saying the sounds. Relied on visual memory. Visual memory for configuration maintained. (*tl* a discrimination error.) *le* indicates function of motor memory.
7. make	makey	*Visual memory error*: (necessary for silent *e*). May have remembered and confused *e-y* word ending ru*le* (*e* is silent but *y* is pronounced *e*). Possible visual-auditory confabulation. Motor memory may be working—*ey*.
8. him	hma	*Visual memory error*: transposition of incorrectly discriminated vowel. May indicate use of auditory sequencing (*h -m -ah*). Visual configuration maintained. Exaggerated pronunciation.
9. say	say	correct
10. cut	kat	*Visual memory error*: c - к confusion. Visual discrimination error *u - a*. Auditory sequencing questionable (may have sounded because of presence of к - т in correct sequence and either not discriminated the vowel sound or not remembered its visual equivalent.
11. cook	loc	*Visual memory error*: c - к confusion. Transposition of *C*. Reversal of word. Visual discrimination error *l - k*. Configuration maintained in reversal. Probably no auditory sequencing.
12. light	lit	*Visual memory error*: Omission of *gh* — confiuration not maintained. Phonetic spelling. Auditory sequencing probably operating.
13. must	mast	*Could be a visual or auditory discrimination error*: Visual configuration maintained.
14. dress	rjes	*Visual memory error*: *rj* for *dr*—a transposition of an imperfectly discriminated *d* (lacks closure and line orientation). Letter configuration maintained. Omission of final *s*—same phonetic relationship present but probably relying on visual memory primarily. *rj* might be a mispronunciation of *dr*.
15. reach	reha	*Auditory sequencing and visual memory error*: might have caught *ch* if there had been a phonetic check. Transposition and omission of *a* might have sequenced phonetically, exaggerated and prolonged the pronunciation and omitted *ach* in the writing act. Fatigue may be setting in.

Word	Written	Analysis
16. order	ore	*Auditory sequencing error:* omission relying on visual memory. Visual configuration deteriorated —fatigue.
17. watch	wah	*Auditory sequencing error:* omission relying on visual memory. Configuration deteriorated — fatigue.
18. enter	ntoer	*Visual memory error:* auditory sequencing operating, visual memory necessary for *en.* May have remembered and transposed the *e.* Discrimination error involving the *o.* Approximate configuration maintained.
19. grown	gona	*Auditory sequencing and visual memory errors:* *Gr* is an auditory error. An omission and *on* written *o* is a visual memory error. Probably relying on visual memory—fatigue.

Summary of Analysis

This child possesses some auditory and visual skills but none are firmly established. He can sequence sounds in words. He demonstrates visual memory for the configuration of words. There is some evidence of the use of motor memory. There are problems in visual discrimination and sequencing. Visual memory involving letter span is three letters long before errors occur. He does not systematically check sound against what he writes. He tends to rely on either phonetic skills or visual memory. He does not move back and forth between the modalities. He is not certain of vowel sounds, either auditorily or visually.

Brief Summary of Teaching Suggestions for Case I

1. Establish definite and secure auditory sequencing skills by sounding out phonetic words.

2. Increase letter span in words orally—first start with three-letter phonetic words, then four, five, six (see *Sound Spelling*). When successful here, include writing (at first, only phonetic words).

3. When succesful with writing phonetic words, begin emphasis on visual memory, discrimination and sequencing problems —use tracing.

4. Select words from Demon Lists.

5. Start with three at each study period (see *Group Teaching Suggestions*). Increase meaningful activities in spelling study— use errors in spontaneous writing.

6. Go through procedure for *15 Suggestions in Teaching Spelling to Develop Perceptual Skill* (see Appendix).

Analysis of Errors—Case II

The samples which follow are the efforts of a nine-year-old boy in the fourth grade with mild visual memory problems and severe visual motor ones. He was described as being exceptionally able, scoring high in intelligence tests, an excellent athlete, well liked by other children but performing poorly in any academic activities which required expressive language, written and verbal. As our interest is in the perceptual motor aspects of spelling performance, the psycho-dynamics of the school performance is not under scrutiny. In this case, however, in the instructional planning for this child, it would be well to look at the adult and peer relationships in the classroom and carefully manage the learning situation. Even spelling reflects children's feelings about learning and concepts of themselves as performers as we shall observe in some of the samples that follow.

In Figures 5 and 6, the words presented are a combination of homonyms and patterned words. Except for *built-build*, which require auditory discrimination of the final sound, all of the other words require visual memory. They include silent letters and double letters and patterns where the sound correspondence is approximate (*does*).

In these samples motor problems in handwriting include knowledge of letter form and knowledge of how various letters are to be joined. There are many erasures and write-overs indicating both difficulty and uncertainty about form. Erasures are always indications of uncertainty, not necessarily lack of knowledge, and frequently the child needs guidance and positive verbal reinforcement in the performance area to develop self-confidence in his judgment. The size and the uneven line quality indicate difficulties with motor control. This may mean inadequate muscle strength in the fingers and hand. Even through this child is described as an excellent athlete (baseball) in which the arm and

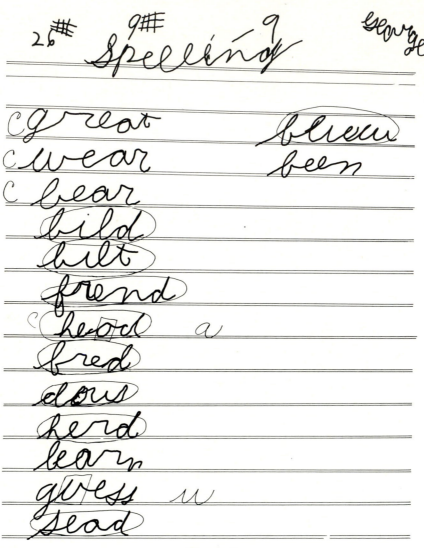

Figure 5.

hand are used, writing requires tool guidance and specific visual-motor integrations related to language which is, so to speak, an entirely different ball game. The frequent difficulties with the joining of letters may reflect both lack of firm knowledge about form and sustaining power or endurance. Perceptually, spacing between letters presents less of a problem than do line relation-

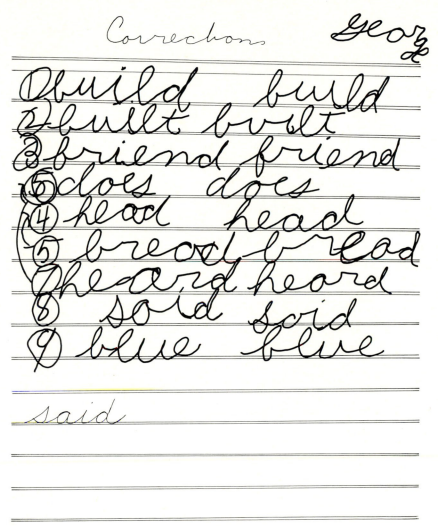

Figure 6.

ships, letter form, closure of o's, d's, etc., and size relationships.

Figure 6 represents the teaching strategy that was employed to deal with error. Repetition is the teacher's tactic and, in this case where only two repetitions were required, the child is able to spell the words correctly but the motor problems are more evident, possibly reflecting his negative feelings about the assignment.

Figure 7.

Figure 7 represents quite clearly the frustration with the task of writing, and while *maybe* is written relatively clearly, the disintegration of control intensifies in the ensuing performance as margins, line relationships, size, spacing and form all deteriorate.

In Figure 8, a poem about daffodils, while the verse spacing is maintained, initially *daffodils* is inconsistently spelled but ends

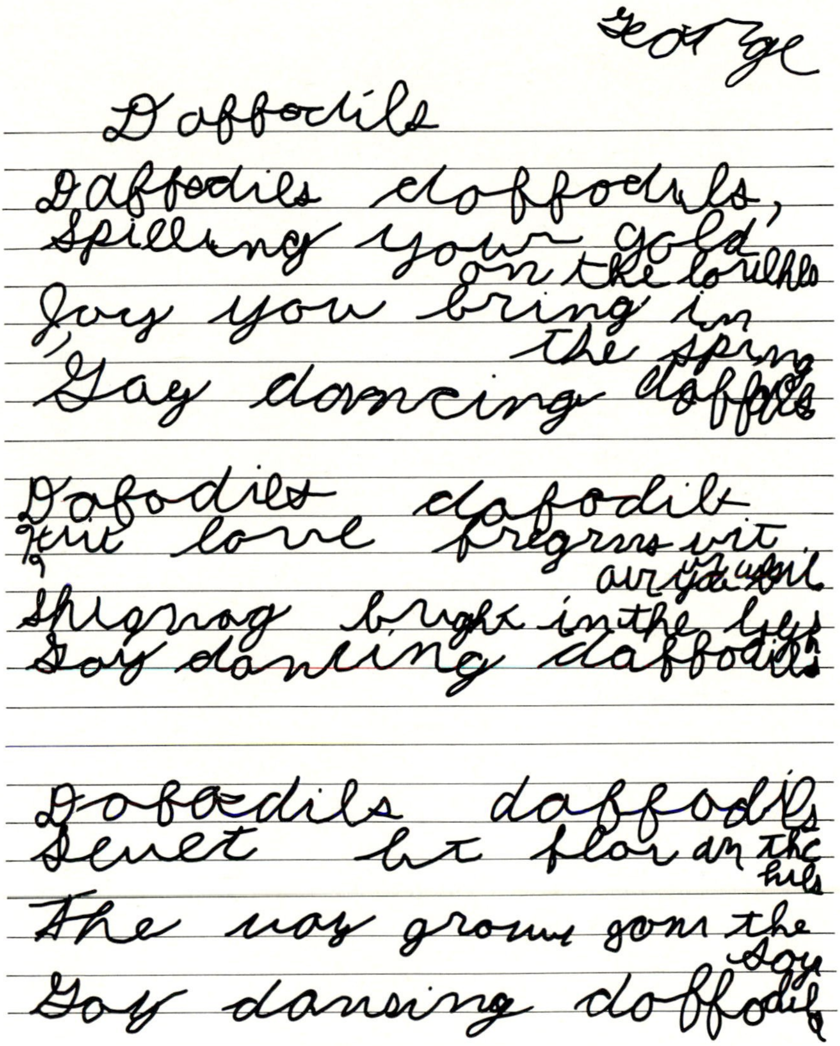

Figure 8.

correctly spelled. *Fragrance* is spelled *fregrns,* indicating good auditory sequencing and poor visual memory. In the last paragraph, most of which is unintelligible, *dancing* has deteriorated to *dansing.* This much writing is too difficult for this child and the problem is not being dealt with by the teacher. The child

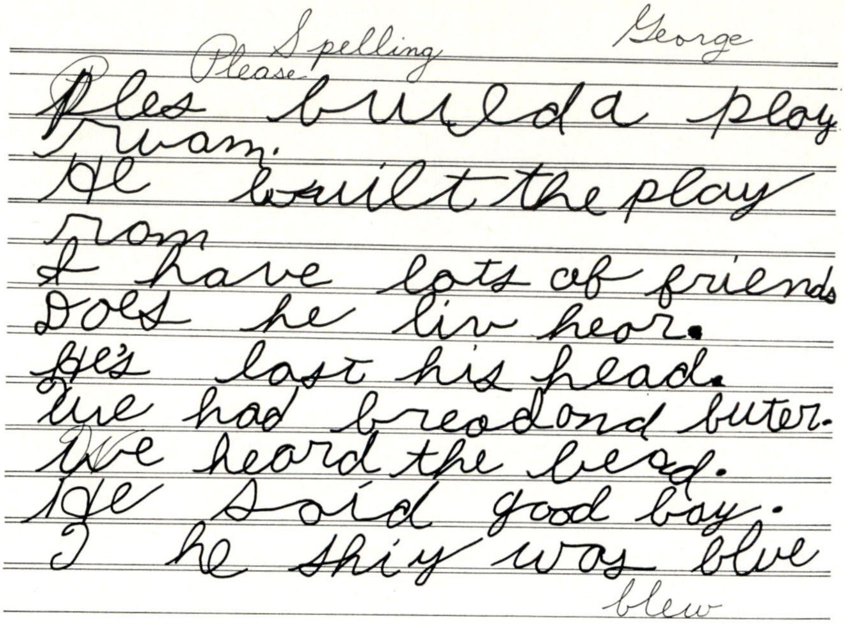

Figure 9.

is not so inadequate, but the teaching demands are not related to his needs.

In Figure 9, *please, playroom, live, hear, butter, goodbye,* are all examples of visual memory errors. The assignment required use of the words in sentences. *Bird* spelled *berd* in the seventh sentence, might be an auditory discrimination error, but probably is a visual memory one, consistent with this child's perceptual performance. The last sentence indicates his correct use and spelling of *blue,* but incorrect memory of which *blew-blue* he was supposed to have used. The teacher has written the correct one below.

In Figure 10, the teacher has written *Recopy* in ink at the head of this page. Asking this child to recopy this without reducing the amount and providing guidance in setting specific perceptual characteristics of the writing as objectives, simply constitutes reinforcement of the problem and inadequacy which exists and is in fact handicapping teaching. In this example, even the name is misspelled. It could well be the expression of frustration and anger rather than simply a perceptual failure.

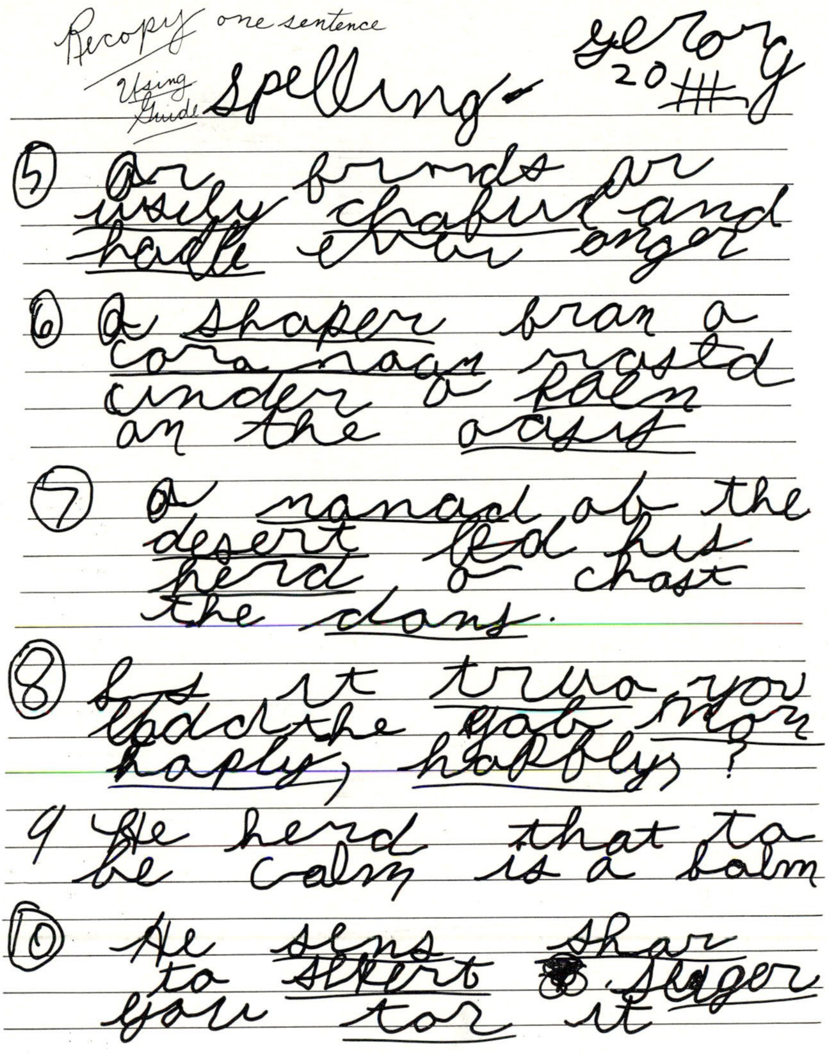

Recopy one sentence
Using Guide Spelling - *George*
20

⑤ *[Our friends are usually cheerful and*
handle their anger]

⑥ *[A shepherd burns a*
caravan roasted
cinder o rain
on the coast]

⑦ *[a nomad of the*
desert led his
herd to chase
the clans.]

⑧ *[Had it true, you*
had the job more
haply, happily?]

⑨ *[He heard that to*
be calm is a balm]

⑩ *[He sens*
to alert shar
you tor Stager
it]

Figure 10.

Suggestions for Teaching

The very first requirement for helping this child is to reduce the amount of writing required. As this child is having physical difficulty with writing, it is hard for him to meet the teacher's demands. Teaching suggestions include:

1. Reviewing all letter forms individually and analyzing every erasure for the difficulty in form or joining it represents. Practice

should be supervised so that attention can be verbally directed.

2. Providing exercises in strengthening the fingers and the muscles of the hand and arm.

3. Providing direct instruction in maintaining quality and enduance.

4. Reducing the number of words required and using a test-teach-test approach.

5. Using tracing to deal with the visual memory problems. (See teaching suggestions in the Handwriting chapter for additional and more complete suggestions).

With systematic instruction, this child should show immediate improvement. The problems are very clear.

Figure 11 is the spelling test of a third-grade boy. In observing this test for instructional goals, the first errors which are apparent involve incorrect use of capital letters. This represents a visual memory lapse and also a lack of understanding about meaning and use of capital letters. While the sample does not represent a severe spelling problem, it is evident that visual memory exists for five-letter sequences, auditory sequencing is also functioning (*ntr* for *enter*) and that teaching goals should be directed at increasing letter span and the ability to deal with more complex visual memory demands. An error like *dress* written *deass* may mean that reliance was placed on visual memory rather than on auditory sequencing in this word. Some training should be provided in systematically saying the word and responding to the sequenced sounds.

In Figure 12, the student does well with the first list of words and both *adjucate* and *matereal* indicate that auditory sequencing is functioning and the lapses are in visual memory. Handwriting performance deteriorates as failure occurs and frustration mounts. This child did fairly well on the first half of the list, where words were probably more familiar. This indicates that the words on the last half of the list may never have been seen by the child and the spelling is simply a sounding out. There is no stored information to fall back on. For this youngster, visual memory may not be such a great problem, but limited experience with reading and word study may be part of the difficulty.

WIDE RANGE ACHIEVEMENT TEST

Reading, Spelling, Arithmetic from Pre-School to College
By J. F. Jastak, S. W. Bijou, S. R. Jastak

COPYRIGHT, 1965 by
Guidance Associates
1526 Gilpin Avenue
Wilmington, Delaware

Printed in U.S.A.
1937, 1946, 1963
Revised Edition
1965

Name__*Damon*_____ Birthdate__*9-12-59*__ M. F. Chron. Age_____*8-10*_____

School_____ Grade_*3*__ Reading Score_*42*_Grade_*2.3*_Stand-Sc*86*%ile__*18*_

Referred by_____ Spelling Score_*29*_Grade_*2.3*_Stand-Sc*86*%ile__*18*_

Date_____Examiner_____ Arithmetic Score*26*Grade*2.8* Stand-Sc*92*%ile _*30*_

Percentiles and Standard Scores corresponding to grade ratings and age may be found in the Manual.

Level I–Spelling–Grade Norms.

Score	Grade	Score	Grade	Score	Grade	Score	Grade	Score	Grade	Score	Grade
1	N.5	12	Kg.4	23	1.5	34	3.0	45	5.7	56	10.3
2	N.8	13	Kg.5	24	1.6	35	3.2	46	6.0	57	10.9
3	Pk.1	14	Kg.6	25	1.7	36	3.5	47	6.3	58	11.5
4	Pk.2	15	Kg.7	26	1.8	37	3.7	48	6.5	59	12.2
5	Pk.3	16	Kg.8	27	2.0	38	3.9	49	6.8	60	13.0
6	Pk.5	17	Kg.9	28	2.2	39	4.2	50	7.2	61	13.8
7	Pk.7	18	Gr.1.0	29	2.3	40	4.5	51	7.7	62	14.5
8	Pk.9	19	1.1	30	2.5	41	4.7	52	8.2	63	15.2
9	Kg.1	20	1.2	31	2.6	42	5.0	53	8.7	64	15.9
10	Kg.2	21	1.3	32	2.7	43	5.3	54	9.2	65	16.7
11	Kg.3	22	1.4	33	2.9	44	5.5	55	9.7		

Level I

Test	Cumul Score
Copying	
1 point	1
per	to
mark	18
Name	
1 letter	19
2 letters	20
Spelling	
1 point	21
per	to
word	65

Level II–Spelling–Grade Norms.

Score	Grade	Score	Grade	Score	Grade	Score	Grade	Score	Grade
0	Kg.2	11	4.0	21	6.7	31	9.3	41	12.4
1	Kg.6	12	4.3	22	6.8	32	9.3	42	12.8
2	Gr.1.0	13	4.6	23	7.0	33	9.6	43	13.2
3	1.3	14	4.9	24	7.2	34	9.9	44	13.6
4	1.6	15	5.2	25	7.4	35	10.2	45	14.0
5	1.9	16	5.5	26	7.6	36	10.5	46	14.4
6	2.2	17	5.8	27	7.8	37	10.8	47	15.0
7	2.6	18	6.1	28	8.1	38	11.2	48	15.7
8	3.0	19	6.3	29	8.4	39	11.6	49	16.4
9	3.3	20	6.5	30	8.7	40	12.0	50	17.2
10	3.7							51	18.0

Level II

Test	Cumul Score
Copying	
4-9	1
10-17	2
18	3
Name	
1 letter	4
2 letters	5
Spelling	
1 point	6
per	to
word	51

Figure 11A.

Figures 13 and 14 provide an interesting contrast in the spelling of two nine-year-old boys who were being referred for special class placement. Both of these boys had difficulty in learning to read. Diagnostically there is a great deal of perceptual information in these two samples.

In Figure 13, the child shows a firm grip—even pressure is

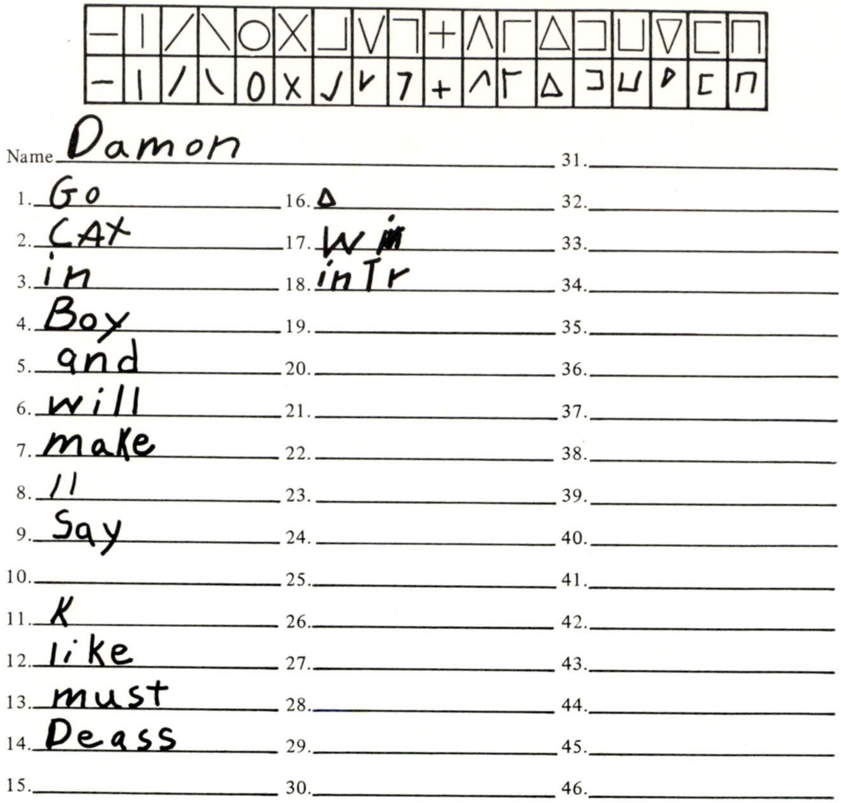

−	l	⁄	∖	O	X	⨆	V	⌐	+	∧	⌈	△	⊐	⨆	∇	⊏	⊓
−	l	⁄	∖	O	X	✓	⌵	7	+	∧	⌐	△	⊐	⨆	▸	⊏	⊓

Name **Damon**

1. **Go**
2. **CAt**
3. **in**
4. **Boy**
5. **and**
6. **will**
7. **make**
8. **ll**
9. **Say**
10.
11. **K**
12. **like**
13. **must**
14. **Deass**
15.

16. **△**
17. **W m**
18. **in Tr**
19.
20.
21.
22.
23.
24.
25.
26.
27.
28.
29.
30.

31.
32.
33.
34.
35.
36.
37.
38.
39.
40.
41.
42.
43.
44.
45.
46.

Figure 11B.

noted in the color of the line—but possibly an over-tight grip. There are some problems in spatial relations between letters and the writing looks cramped. There is no sense of flow, although the letters are clearly formed. The perceptual problems all relate to visual memory (*ake* for *ache, fest* for *feast, pece* for *piece, coca* for *cocoa, wimen* for *women,* and *women* for *woman*). As the words get more complicated at the end of the list, it is quite clear that the child is saying the words and spelling according to the sounds as he sequences them. As he does not read, it is entirely possible that he has not had much experience with the words on which to draw for stored visual associations. Some of the errors at the end of the list indicate mispronunciations or

WIDE RANGE ACHIEVEMENT TEST

Reading, Spelling, Arithmetic from Pre-School to College
By J. F. Jastak, S. W. Bijou, S. R. Jastak

Name __Joanne_____ Birthdate_____ M. F. Chron. Age __11_____

School_____ Grade __6th__ Reading Score_____ Grade_____ Stand-Sc___%ile_____

Referred by_____ Spelling Score_____ Grade_____ Stand-Sc___%ile_____

Date_____ Examiner_____ Arithmetic Score___ Grade_____ Stand-Sc___%ile_____

Percentiles and Standard Scores corresponding to grade ratings and age may be found in the Manual.

Level I–Spelling–Grade Norms.

Score	Grade	Score	Grade	Score	Grade	Score	Grade	Score	Grade	Score	Grade
1	N.5	12	Kg.4	23	1.5	34	3.0	45	5.7	56	10.3
2	N.8	13	Kg.5	24	1.6	35	3.2	46	6.0	57	10.9
3	Pk.1	14	Kg.6	25	1.7	36	3.5	47	6.3	58	11.5
4	Pk.2	15	Kg.7	26	1.8	37	3.7	48	6.5	59	12.2
5	Pk.3	16	Kg.8	27	2.0	38	3.9	49	6.8	60	13.0
6	Pk.5	17	Kg.9	28	2.2	39	4.2	50	7.2	61	13.8
7	Pk.7	18	Gr.1.0	29	2.3	40	4.5	51	7.7	62	14.5
8	Pk.9	19	1.1	30	2.5	41	4.7	52	8.2	63	15.2
9	Kg.1	20	1.2	31	2.6	42	5.0	53	8.7	64	15.9
10	Kg.2	21	1.3	32	2.7	43	5.3	54	9.2	65	16.7
11	Kg.3	22	1.4	33	2.9	44	5.5	55	9.7		

Level I

Test	Cumul Score
Copying	
1 point	1
per	to
mark	18
Name	
1 letter	19
2 letters	20
Spelling	
1 point	21
per	to
word	65

Level II–Spelling–Grade Norms.

Score	Grade	Score	Grade	Score	Grade	Score	Grade	Score	Grade
0	Kg.2	11	4.0	21	6.7	31	9.3	41	12.4
1	Kg.6	12	4.3	22	6.8	32	9.3	42	12.8
2	Gr.1.0	13	4.6	23	7.0	33	9.6	43	13.2
3	1.3	14	4.9	24	7.2	34	9.9	44	13.6
4	1.6	15	5.2	25	7.4	35	10.2	45	14.0
5	1.9	16	5.5	26	7.6	36	10.5	46	14.4
6	2.2	17	5.8	27	7.8	37	10.8	47	15.0
7	2.6	18	6.1	28	8.1	38	11.2	48	15.7
8	3.0	19	6.3	29	8.4	39	11.6	49	16.4
9	3.3	20	6.5	30	8.7	40	12.0	50	17.2
10	3.7							51	18.0

Level II

Test	Cumul Score
Copying	
4-9	1
10-17	2
18	3
Name	
1 letter	4
2 letters	5
Spelling	
1 point	6
per	to
word	51

Figure 12A.

auditory discrimination problems such as *asident* for *accident, prowseshoun* for *possession,* and *panthlit* for *pamphlet.* He may not have heard the word correctly as it was dictated and did not correct it as meaning added some information to help him in pronunciation. Perhaps this occurred because his attention was distracted by failure or because there wasn't any use in bothering; his uncertainty about the correct spelling was too great. Whatever

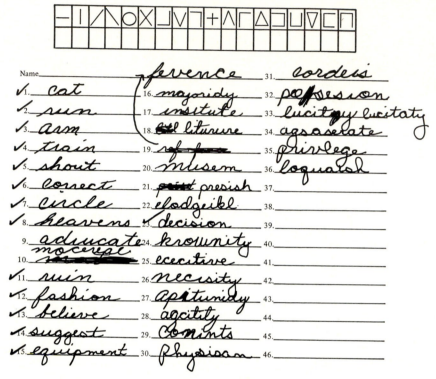

Figure 12B.

the reason, it is clear that he can sequence sounds in words and his difficulties are in visual memory for ambiguous spellings. The teaching should concentrate in this area and in the auditory area where emphasis is needed in teaching discrimination.

In Figure 14 there are many write-overs indicating as awareness of error and an attempt to correct. Uncertainty is one of the problems which needs to be considered, but obviously not the only one. There are auditory sequencing problems, and in spelling instruction these always need to be considered first. Visual memory problems are extreme and there are motor difficulties as well. These are seen in the uneven margins which indicate that he only uses the margin line as a spatial organizer sporadically and has visual problems. Pressure on the pencil is also light, except for the corrections. As the corrections indicate that he is aware that the words are incorrect, it is difficult to know if

1. about	31. arithmatic
2. brother	32. oughtthee
3. chair	33. delist
4. lion	34. inglsh
5. name	35. forteen
6. neat	36. loose
7. room	37. prowseshoun
8. were	38. prounouns
9. where	39. volention
10. youe	40. rap
11. ake	41. dsident
12. chapter	42. olthow
13. fest	43. consel
14. loose	44. corispondent
15. thought	45. differens
16. monkey	46. exkelent
17. picture	47. fraight
18. pece	48. labrctorie
19. stoies	49. panthlit
20. evomen	50. relef
21. cost	
22. coca	
23. doctor	
24. evrewhere	
25. fought	
26. gredy	
27. guide	
28. medison	
29. uach	
30. wimen	

Figure 13.

the problem lies in grip and pressure or in qualities of tentativeness and uncertainty. Probably a mixture of all of these is ouerating. Letter forms are imprecise, indicating both control difficulties and lack of memory for form (*m* is frequently written for *n* and *n* for *r*). The joining of letters is often broken and may be an indication of endurance problems. The instructional sequence for this child should be attention to auditory problems first, visual problems second, and motor difficulties last. If a

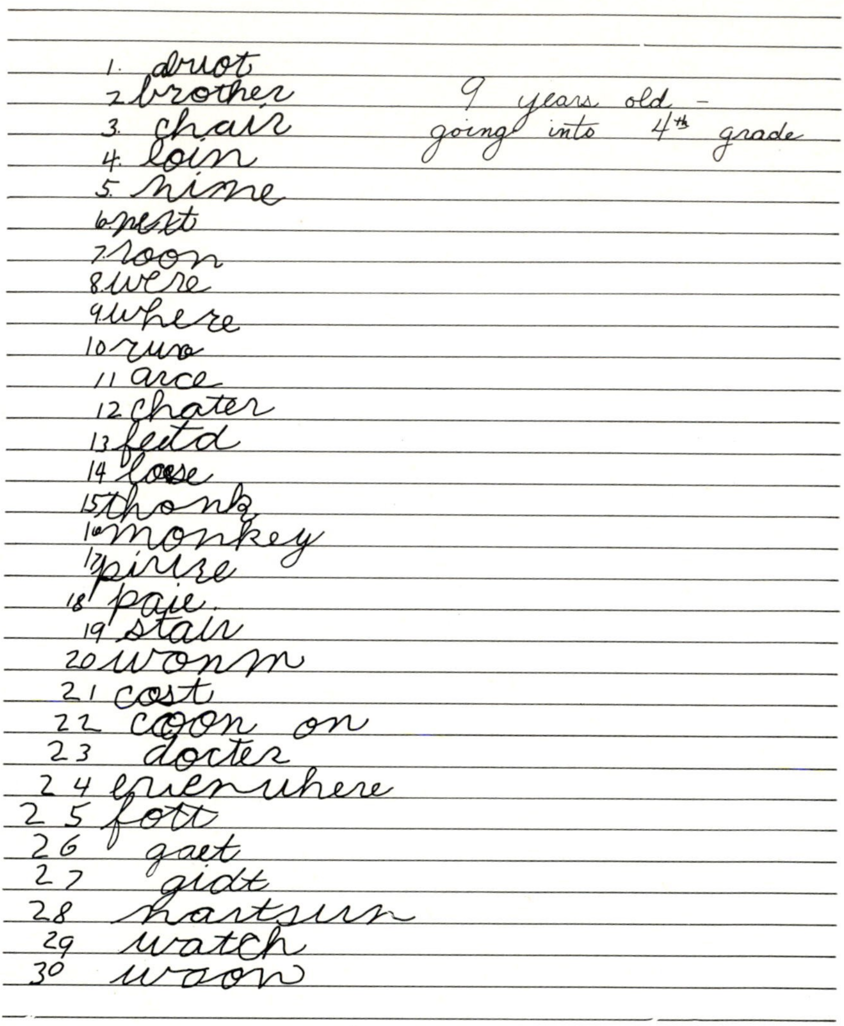

1. druot
2. brother
3. chair
4. loin
5. nime
6. nest
7. noon
8. were
9. where
10. ruo
11. arce
12. chater
13. feitd
14. loese
15. thonk
16. monkey
17. pirise
18. paie
19. stair
20. wonm
21. cost
22. cgon on
23. docter
24. evenuhere
25. fott
26. gaet
27. gidt
28. hartsun
29. watch
30. waon

9 years old —
going into 4th grade

Figure 14.

letter-form discrimination training program is indicated, motor problems might be tackled first.

The Importance of Auditory Sequencing

As spelling involves saying a word internally or responding to a word which is given (as a spelling test) by writing the letter correspondences in order, one of the main skills that may require observation and possible instruction is auditory sequencing. The child can frequently say the word as a unit without being able to say or think the parts in order. When it is evident from the error analysis that a child is not responding to the sequence of sounds irrespective of visual problems, training in this skill should be provided. A procedure for teaching this skill is delineated in *Sound Spelling* in the Appendix. In this technique, auditory sequencing is taught as an entirely separate skill with no visual or visual-motor involvement. The intent is to help children "think" sounds in order in words. Not all children need to have visual or visual-motor activities restricted. For some children "thinking and doing" presents a problem; the "doing" seems to distract from the thinking. For other children the "doing" or visual motor activities act as a support condition and increase the amount of information delivered to the central nervous system. This is the intent of what is termed the "VAKT Approach" (Visual, Auditory, Kinesthetic, Tactile Inputs). The only way to determine which approach is suitable for an individual child is to observe the function of the auditory and visual motor skills. If both skills require developmental or remediative teaching, or if the degree of dysfunction in either is extreme, then separating the skills for instruction is warranted. This will always be a matter for decisions based on diagnostic information gathered in error analysis.

The Place of Visual Memory

Auditory sequencing was chosen for prime emphasis in teaching because it is the initial perceptual act in the spelling process. Frequently, error analysis divulges information demonstrating that this skill is operating very well and that indeed the child is spelling all words according to the sound elements with great accuracy. In that case, the visual memory problems become the teaching target.

When children have perceptual problems which are extreme and visual in nature, the best bet as a teaching strategy is the use of tracing. Tracing or kinesthetic teaching, helps in processing all the visual information in the word (See Kinesthetic Teaching, Chapter 2). This can be a very effective learning strategy when used (1) with control of the number of words presented, (2) with greater emphasis on meaning, and (3) with careful restudy of the words missed. For older children the words can be dittoed so they are just large enough to provide some finger, hand and arm movement. This will allow for motor support, and the enlarged study model will make discriminations easier and will deemphasize the "babyish" qualities which many high school children object to in the word strips commonly used with this method. With a careful explanation of what their particular problem may be and why the tracing is helpful, most young adults accept the training procedures and quickly find them unnecessary. They learn to "see."

Configuration—To Teach or Not to Teach

Configuration in spelling refers to the shape of the word; it is commonly taught in two ways. The first way involves "boxing" the word:

This emphasizes the "general" shape, but as most of the children who have visual perceptual problems show more difficulty with detail, the second method may prove more suitable. It involves calling attention directly to the ascenders, descenders and unique features such as dotted *i*'s and crossed *t*'s, or any other line segments enhancing spatial perceptions.

While the research literature does not support the teaching of configuration in spelling as a valuable teaching strategy in general, there is some evidence which supports attention to salient visual cues in words, especially ascenders and descenders. The Simon model cited earlier theorizes that it is used. Probably the best teaching procedures is again to return to analyzing individual performance and emphasizing configuration if the child either is severely handicapped in both auditory and visual skill, or if it is evident that configuration is not used as a cue in the child's attempts to spell words.

Short- and Lon-term Memory

With children who have severe memory problems the number of words presented in any given year should be carefully predetermined. The number of words that can be remembered in one day, one week and one semester should be individually ascertained. The number of letters in the words should also be controlled as teaching commences and increased gradually. Retesting and restudy of missed words can become part of the teaching procedure. Daily and weekly tests can be combined with monthly reviews and the words to be restudied again included in the appropriate number. Overlearning of a limited number of words is a better procedure than a new list every week which is never committed to complete memory. This common practice acts as negative reinforcement and firmly establishes poor spelling performance.

Dealing with Complexity

In analyzing spelling performance it is not unusual to find that children can handle single-syllable words better than multisyllable words. While the research does not support syllabic presentations of words as fruitful teaching procedures, the reference is to visual divisions (in-ter-est-ing). Saying words in syllables as a teaching strategy may be quite a different matter. It can help stabilize auditory sequencing and may help with the visual equivalences when they are isomorphic or one-to-one. If there are elements in the word which require visual memory and this is an area of inadequate performance for an individual child—but one not severe enough for tracing—this strategy may be helpful. (See *The Syllable Sayer* in the Appendix for a teaching technique.)

Emphasizing the Difference Between Vision and Hearing

In mild visual memory problems it may be supportive to emphasize the difference between what is seen and heard in each word as it is presented. This is a case of not simply calling attention to the "hard spots," but seeing them in relation to their personal perceptual demands. In order to teach awareness of the difference, the child will have to rehearse the auditory sequence noting the spatial position in the word where visual memory will be needed as well as discriminating and possibly verbally mediating the memory demand.

Mnemonics are aids which entail the verbal association of ideas. Their use has a very legitimate place in the teaching of spelling and teachers should exploit them where suitable. Some children will use them more effectively than others. They do involve memory and some children will forget to use them. However, for most children if some personal, unusual or funny association is made, the chances of remembering the word will be greater. In the word "friend," which possesses the troublesome *ie,* the solution may be to say *fr-n-d* as the auditory elements, not the *ie* and its position in the word, and mediate it by saying *fri-end*—a deliberate mispronunciation—in order to emphasize the visual sequence. Children enjoy this and it serves its mediating and discriminating purpose well. Tracing the word would add a memory component and would insure that the visual discriminations are actually made as the fingers pick up "redundant" information available in the written form (Gibson, 1966). In using this technique in spelling, instructing the children to "Trace and Say, Write and Say, and Check" establishes the basic pattern. When children trace words, three tracings produce better retention if they occur before any writing occurs. Tracing the words should be accompanied by verbalization of the sounds; the child should be saying the word he traces softly to himself. The paper should be turned over and the word always written from memory. *Never alow copying in the study period in spelling.* The child should then check his own original and compare his work and restudy if errors occur. In this teaching activity the child is made aware of the perceptual demands of the stimuli in relation to his own perceptual strengths or weaknesses in an effort to develop compensatory behaviors. The teacher actually points out what the child does well and what he needs to attend to more carefully. The child is included in strategy planning and the teacher-learning situation is more meaningful to the child.

If the emphasis in the teaching is on auditory sequencing or hearing sounds in order in words, the teacher can guide the child's attention with instructions that emphasize saying the word and writing what is said: "Say and Listen, Write and Check." In mild sequencing problems, guiding the child through the word so that omissions do not occur can be sufficient. But if the problem is serious, then "Sound Spelling" is a good starting point for instruction. In this technique the writing is omitted and the child is helped to think and label sounds in order in phonetically-spelled words. The words are not simply organized in patterns on which children can rely, but also both visual memory and motor demands are restricted so that the emphasis can be placed on the simplest sound-symbol relationships, those that are one-to-one and in short words. No silent letters are presented and the teaching starts with three-letter sequences organized around short vowels and increases to five-letter sequences. The child usually gets the idea that there is some correspondence which he can master and writing is then introduced. Following that, visual memory problems can be introduced where words presented are organized around spelling patterns. (See *Sound Spelling* in the Appendix.) The Sound Spelling technique presumes that the child knows some sound-letter relationships.

Phonological and Morphological Elements—Some Problems in Teaching Word Structure

When words are presented to children in the manner suggested here, a great deal of emphasis is placed on awareness of parts of words. The teacher is directing the child's attention to many details. If attention is given to meaning, to the sound sequence, to the affixes to the root, to the visual memory demands, to the salient visual cues and the general configuration, the tendency is to break up the perceptual process. At present there is no way to determine which child would benefit from a synthetic method of teaching which "constructs" the child's perception of the words from attention to its elements or which child would benefit from an analytic method which deals with whole words in which the elements are learned implicitly through a particular organizational or structural emphasis. This is not likely to be soon determined and perhaps the best alternative at this time is for the teacher to be aware of the dilemma. Some cues can be picked up through error analysis. Some children may be distracted by all of the attention given to details during the scanning of the word and forget what the word is. As the child always starts with the whole word and its meaning, so should the teaching emphasize it in the opening and closing of any word study which emphasizes details.

Because familiarity with words is such an important aspect of adequate spelling performance, it too should be exploited in behalf of the child. Repetition is not the only strategy for dealing with the development of this skill, although it is probably the most commonly used teaching device. Motivation is a very important aspect in any teaching which is directed at helping a child compensate for inadequate performance. Words represent concepts, and the broader the child's experiences with aspects or details of the concept, the better his chances of remembering it. Besides the perceptual details or requirements of the word, a study of word origins should be intriguing; games can provide stimulation, various reinforcements can maintain and enhance improvement and, in the process, word concepts will be much broader than if simple repetition is the only strategy used. In a sense, perception, meaning and motivation interact, and teachers can consciously teach in all three areas to improve spelling performance.

LEARNING MANAGEMENT

15 SUGGESTIONS FOR TEACHING SPELLING TO DEVELOP PERCEPTUAL SKILL

1. *Meaning*
   Establish through use in sentences and discussion. Use dictionary for formal definitions. Use negative as well as

positive instances in developing concepts. Use graphs, pictures and models and direct experience whenever possible. Repeat definitions and elaborate concepts. Categorize words.

2. *Configuration*

   Have children draw the pattern of the word, calling attention to ascending and descending letters and unique features, such as dots or crosses, etc.

3. *Letter Span and List Length*

   Establish existing letter span and list length memory pattern for each child and help set goals for lengthening both.

4. *Direct Attention to the Middle Portion of Words and Syllables*

   Explain the discrimination problems with the middle vowel patterns auditorially and visually and help child develop the habit of noticing and verbalizing them to make them distinctive perceptually. Teach the use of memnomics.

5. *Phonological Elements*

   Call attention to the direct relationships of letters to sounds in the word or to the pattern used. (All *ai* words or *ou* words, etc.) Consonants, vowels, digraphs, or dipthongs. Direct attention to the stressed and unstressed syllables. Make child aware of a difference in his own pronunciation and graphic representation.

6. *Morphological Elements*

   Direct attention to roots, prefixes, suffixes, tense, plurals, capitals, possessives, etc. Teach word origins and word relationships.

7. *Make Child Aware of the Difference Between What Is Seen and Heard*

   Work on auditory sequencing—hearing sounds in order in words and visual memory—remembering what is not heard. Call child's attention to the difference. ("You can hear this and this and this, but you can't hear this" [saying and pointing]—"you're going to have to remember it.") Use mnemonics or verbal mediators and mispronunciations to highlight difficult spots. Use "Say and listen—write and check" approach with phonetic words when working on auditory sequencing. In extreme cases use "Sound Spelling." Use verbal direction and modeling to establish auditory sequencing. Use tracing for persistent visual memory problems—"Trace and say, write and say and check" (three tracings before writing). Use Forced Discrimination training with whole words to enhance awareness of correct form and heighten possibility of correct recall.

8. *Use Large Print or Script for Study Model*
   The necessary visual discriminations are more easily made.

9. *Recall the Word—Never Copy*
   Work on immediate and delayed recall as separate problems. Always have the child compare his performance to the study model upon completion of writing a word to provide immediate correction of error. Test on lists at predetermined levels to provide restudy of words forgotten.

10. *Teach Dictionary Use*
    Include practice in every spelling period so that a habit is established.

11. *Keep Records to Determine Learning Patterns*

12. *Reinforce for Effort as Well as Achievement*

13. *Control the Number of Words to Be Mastered in a Given Period of Time*

14. *Help Child Understand His Strengths and Needs and Set His Own Improvement Goals*

15. *Explain Teaching Strategy*

REMEDIAL SPELLING IN GROUPS

4 to 6 children
Pick 12 words
Prepare words on 3 x 10½ strips of paper—for older children, prepare dittoed copy large enough to allow for arm movement in the tracing. Use word boxes or folders for word pattern storage.

Monday
1. Present 3 words (Most children can start at this number.)
   a. Put words on board—say the word, have the child say the word.
   b. Direct attention to the details suggested in the "Suggestions."
   c. Conclude with "Trace and Say" (no attention directed to details as this is occurring). Have children trace and say 3 times before writing. Keep tracing and saying simultaneous. No attention to detail, write entirely from memory. *Never copy.* Have child check against model. Retrace immediately until word is written correctly from immediate memory.
2. Test on 3 words. Immediate restudy of words missed.

Tuesday
1. Test on Monday's 3 words and restudy.
2. Present 3 new words as on Monday.
3. Test on 6 words and restudy.

Wednesday
1. Test on Monday and Tuesday—6 words and restudy.
2. Present 3 new words.
3. Test on 9 words and restudy.

Thursday
1. Test on 9 words and restudy.
2. Present 3 new words, analyze and study.

Friday
1. Test on 12 words; carry any missed forward to next week.

Adjust number of words to group. Adjust days spent in this kind of study. Take words from regular spelling book (linguistic spellers are excellent), demon lists, or any special field: math, social studies, English, personal interest. Use rewards for effort (the amount of time spent in study) as well as achievement. Keep charts or graphs to determine learning rate (Precision Teaching is well suited to this activity) and to show progress.

SOUND SPELLING

This teaching technique is designed to help children hear sounds in words. It is an auditory exericse only, with no visual representation or writing involved. When there is an indication that children are unable to hear sounds in order in words, to sequence sounds or to blend them, the teacher begins to teach the listening skill in three-letter words which are those most likely to occur within the natural speaking vocabulary of the child. These are chosen so that problems related to word meaning will not interfere with the acquisition of this skill. Many teachers provide practice in this skill, but do so unsystematically and for periods of time which are too short to "fix" the skill and insure mastery. This exercise starts with a three-sound span and increases gradually to a five-sound span which allows the teacher to intorduce sound configuration, or syllabication, before dealing with the skills involving visual and motor perception. A limited number of words are provided, but teachers may add others where teaching indicates increased practice would be beneficial.

Teacher as Model-hearing Sounds

In initiating this activity, the teacher says: "These words have three sounds. Listen while I say the sounds of *man*. Man, m-ma-man. Now you say it with me." (Repeat, guiding the child through the sequence of sounds. Always start with the beginning sound and add successive sounds, maintaining the succession.) "Let's try *Pat*. Pat, p-pa-pat. Now, let's try *Red*. Red, r-re-red." As training begins, the teacher serves as model, withdrawing as the child gains in skill. Very little time is spent on this activity; as soon as the child indicates that he can follow the sequence, even though he cannot initiate it or maintain it alone, the teacher moves on to labelling sounds, always beginning and ending with saying the whole word.

Labelling Sounds

As soon as the child gains understanding, skill and confidence in manipulating sounds with the teacher as guide, the teacher shifts the emphasis in the teaching to include the knowledge that words have sounds and that those sounds have names. As the child thinks, isolating and sequencing the sounds, he is now taught to respond to the sound with the name of the letter.

The teacher says: "These words have three sounds each. Let's see if we can name each sound. *Man,* m, what letter, ma, what two letters, man, what three letters?" (Labelling of sounds cannot be taught until the child has some knowledge of the alphabet. If this is uncertain, the child should be taught the names and sounds, one for each letter, as quickly as possible.

If the child has difficulty, the teacher adds another cue. She indicates by using her fingers how many sounds are involved. If the child has unusual difficulty, tapping of sounds will increase their distinctiveness.

As the child moves into the four- and five-letter words, sounds containing two letters are taught and the teacher cues the child: "*Under,* U, right, u, Un, right, u-n, Und, right, u-n-d-, Under, two letters (er), right, er" (or sh or ch). If the child is uncertain, the teacher presents a correct model and gives the child another exercise with the same elements, or repeats the original one, until mastery.

All of the exericses are organized around discrimination of short vowel sounds which present greater difficulty than long vowel sounds for most children. As soon as the teacher becomes aware that the child has the idea of sequencing of sounds in words, writing of the letters can be included. Thinking and writing should be separated in the initial phase of learning.

The exercise does not attempt to exhaust the possibilities for presentation. The teacher may wish to add words from special readers or to include nonsense syllables. She may also wish to choose words based on a linguistic system. In this exercise, simplicity of perceptual input and repetition are very specific goals.

THREE-LETTER WORDS

A	E	I	O	U
bat	bed	big	rod	but
man	beg	did	dog	cut
tap	get	his	hot	sun
ran	let	pig	got	rub
pat	red	bit	top	run
sat	yes	fit	fox	nut
mad	hen	hid	hop	bud
and	leg	hit	log	pup
ask	pet	sit	not	gum
ant	set	six	pop	mud

FOUR-LETTER WORDS

A	E	I	O	U
fast	help	milk	long	jump
hand	nest	sing	stop	just
band	next	wind	song	hunt
bang	went	pink	drop	bump
glad	felt	wink	frog	junk
land	held	skin	pond	dump
last	kept	skip	soft	must
past	left	chin	stop	lump
sand	let's	rich	fond	sunk
chat	send	chip	prop	dust

FIVE-LETTER WORDS

A	E	I	O	U
catch	fresh	bring	slots	lunch
plant	blend	going	robin	trunk
stand	lends	robin	trots	crush
thank	helps	begin	shops	flush
camps	dents	river	clogs	shuts
grasp	crept	visit	shots	shuns
clasp	slept	sting	blots	slump
lamps	swept	blink	blobs	chump
stamp	belts	split	plops	clump
tramp	smelt	fling	clots	trump

THE SYLLABLE-SAYER

A similar strategy can be applied to teaching hearing syllables in words when an analysis of spelling errors shows this to be a problem. Omissions are one of the common categories of errors and words are frequently telescoped as they are written. Practicing saying the parts of the word in order, may help the student develop a compensatory technique for dealing with this difficulty.

As many of the syllables contain letters which are not heard individually, but are combinations which must be remembered, practicing verbalizing and recalling some of the combinations could be a first step in differentiation and discrimination. A good starting place for this exercise might be to increase familiarity with the common affixes.

Lists of practice words will not be presented, because it is a better teaching strategy for support, if syllabication is practiced on words the child is using in readers or spellers. Keeping lists of missed words, and using errors as the content of these lessons would provide the greatest opportunity for meaningful practice. Remember, the intent is to go from saying the sound or syllable to recalling and stating the letters, not necessarily writing them.

Rules

A very brief summary of some rules about syllables includes:
1. Every vowel sound indicates a syllable. (man-ner)
2. If the first vowel is followed by two consonants, divide the word between the two. (let-ter)
3. When the first vowel is followed by one consonant, it begins the second syllable. (be-gin)
4. When words end in -le, the consonant which precedes -le, begins the last syllable. (sta-ble)
5. Consonant digraphs and blends are not divided when words are separated into syllables. (teach-er)
6. Prefixes and suffixes are usually considered separate syllables. (un-less)
7. When the suffix-ed follows d or t, it forms a separate syllable and is pronounced "ed." If not, it is pronounced

"t," not forming a separate syllable. It also sounds like "t" when it follows an unvoiced consonant and "d" when it follows a voice one. (wished) (t); (rated) (d)

8. When syllables end with a consonant, they are called closed syllables and the vowel is short. If they end with a vowel, they are called open syllables and the vowel is long. (cat-tle); (ta-ble)

9. If "y" is the final sound in a one-syllable word, it usually has the sound of long "i" as in try; if it is the final sound in a multisyllabled word, it usually is sounded "e" as in sorry.

Accent or Stress

Because unstressed syllables obscure vowel sounds, directing attention to them as possible stumbling blocks can be used to help those children with visual memory problems. Children can learn to attend to the difference between what they hear and say, when unstressed syllables are detected in words. The place of accent in spelling is usually ignored or treated lightly. It can become a warning signal. A few helpful rules for the teacher are:

1. In two syllable words, accents usually fall on the first syllable. (kit-chen)

2. In inflected or derived word forms, the root word is usually accented. (un-eat-en)

3. If there are two vowels which occur together in the last syllable, it is usually accented. (a-gáin)

4. If repeated consonants occur in a word, the preceding syllable is usually accented. (mátter)

5. If the suffixes ion, ity, ic, ical, ian, ial, ion are employed, the preceding syllable is usually accented. (va-ca-tion)

The teacher will need to make decisions about whether to teach *any* rule. For some children, learning a rule will offer support. For others it will be a hinderance because the child cannot remember it or is not likely to apply it. For this group of children, categorizing and grouping words which exemplify a rule, and overlearning will have to suffice. It may be, that the teacher can lead the children in stating the rule from the categorized words. The teacher should not overlook this opportunity, but if the child has memory problems, he may not remember it. Remembering rules is only one way in which spelling proficiency is developed.

Multisyllabled Words for Younger Children

The teacher may select words from curricular areas or from standardized word lists as well as from individual error. The vocabulary in the reader or the speller would of course be a good choice for these exercises. The Dolch Basic Sight Vocabulary might also serve for primary children and the demon lists for intermediate students.

Multisyllabled Words for Older Children

For the junior high or senior high school student, greater difficulty and challenge may be reqiured. The Shaw (1965) list of One Hundred Demons is offered for use with this group. These can be used for exercises in syllabication, listening for stress or accent, meaning or spelling at the teacher's discretion.

SUGGESTED STEPS IN TEACHING SYLLABICATION

I. *If a child has difficulty with auditory omissions in spelling, begin by working at an auditory level only.*
   A. Pronounce the word as a whole and make certain the child knows the meaning of the word.
   B. Say the word in distinct syllables. Ask the child to say the word in syllables.
   C. Close by saying the whole word again and have the child do the same.
      (The child may state the number of syllables in the word as a review and support condition.)
II. *As soon as the child can sequence the syllables in a word correctly, shift strategy and include reading the word.*
   A. The child looks at the written word, says the whole word and reads it in syllables. Close this exercise by saying the whole word again.

1. The child may simultaneously
   a. move a clear plastic strip across the word, stopping briefly between each syllable
   b. use his finger to point to syllables or to move it beneath syllables, stopping briefly between each syllable
   c. underline the syllables
   d. fold the paper to note the divisions (when tracing is done on strips)

III. *As soon as the child has had sufficient practice on saying and reading the words, shift strategy and say the syllables and recall the letters verbally. (no writing)*

The main emphasis in this technique is on establishing the auditory sequence of syllables in words and recalling visual equivalents. It is useful, when students omit syllables or sounds in words as they spell. Its success will depend on how systematically it is used.

MULTIPLE-CHOICE SPELLING

This sample exercise is designed to provide practice for the student in choosing the correct spelling of a word from possible spellings that may relate to either auditory or visual clues in the word. Following the Simons (1970) model of the spelling process, which points out that spellers may make use of stored information about the whole word, this exercise provides practice in whole-word recognition, without writing. These words were taken from the Johnson (1950) list of *100 Most Frequently Misspelled Words by Children in the Elementary Grades;* however, any other group of words related to a particular child's academic efforts would provide suitable content.

Directions: Circle the word which is spelled correctly.

1. pretty   prity   pritty   prite
2. rning   runing   running   runng
3. butiful   butifl   beautifl   beautiful
4. stopd   stopt   stopped   stoped
5. somthing   something   sumthing   somthng
6. received   recieved   reseived   receivd
7. childern   cldren   children   childrin

8. again   agin   agen   agian
9. cours   cuorse   course   corse
10. cot   caught   cawt   coght
11. interesting   intresting   intersting   ntrstng
12. freingds   friends   frends   frends
13. every   evre   everee   evry
14. askt   asked   askd   asekd
15. happened   hapened   happend   hapnd

DIAGNOSTIC SPELLING TEST*

Dictate the following list of seventy words. They are listed by grade level, ten words to each level. The first level on which a student misspells two or more words is probably his instructional spelling level. For a more accurate diagnosis a larger sampling of words may be dictated. It is not likely that a student's instructional level will be above that determined by this test, but it may well be below it. The first group is for grade 2, the second for grade 3, etc.

1. about	11. ache	21. coast	31. arithmetic
2. brother	12. chapter	22. cocoa	32. author
3. chair	13. feast	23. doctor	33. dentist
4. lion	14. lose	24. everywhere	34. English
5. name	15. thought	24. fought	35. fourteen
6. next	16. monkey	26. greedy	36. loose
7. room	17. picture	27. guide	37. procession
8. were	18. piece	28. medicine	38. pronounce
9. where	19. stairs	29. watch	39. volunteer
10. your	20. woman	30. women	40. wrap

❖   ❖   ❖   ❖   ❖

41. accident	51. accommodation	61. abundant
42. although	52. acquaintance	62. appropriate
43. conceal	53. beginning	63. cafeteria
44. correspondent	54. brought	64. complexion
45. difference	55. character	65. congratulate
46. excellent	56. commercial	66. curiosity
47. freight	57. disappointment	67. prejudice
48. laboratory	58. government	68. privilege
49. pamphlet	59. principal	69. quarrel
50. relief	60. villain	70. restaurant

---

* From Strang and Bracken, 1957, p. 356.

To Determine Instructional Spelling Level:

MORE DIFFICULT HOMONYMS *

Accept—except
Advice—advise
Affect—effect
Air—heir
Aisle—isle
All ready—already
All together—altogether
Always—all ways
Aught—ought
Bear—bare
Beat—beet
Berth—birth
Blew—blue
Board—bored
Breadth—breath—breathe
Capital—capitol
Cent—scent
Cite—site
Clothes—cloths—close
Complement—compliment
Creak—creek
Dairy—diary
Days—daze
Dear—deer
Decease—disease
Decent—descent
Desert—desert—dessert
Die—dye
Due—do
Eminent—imminent
Fair—fare
Find—fined
Fir—fur
Flea—flee
Flour—flower
Fourth—forth
Gait—gate
Hair—hare
Heal—heel
Hear—here
Hole—whole
Hoping—hopping
Knew—new

Know—no
Later—latter
Lead—lead—led
Leaf—lief
Lean—lien
Least—lest
Lesson—lessen
Lie—lye
Loose—lose—loss
Mail—male
Main—mane
Of—off
On—one
Pain—pane
Pair—pare
Passed—past
Peace—piece
Plain—plane
Pray—prey
Principal—principle
Quiet—quit—quite
Raise—raze
Rain—reign—rein
Respectably—respectfully—respectively
Right—rite
Stair—stare
Stake—steak
Stationary—stationery
Straight—strait
Suite—suite
Tail—tale
Taught—taut
Their—there—they're
Threw—through
To—too—two
Waist—waste
Want—wont—won't
Weak—week
Weather—whether
Were—we're—where
While—wile
Whose—who's
Yore—your—you're

---

* Selected from Shaw, 1969.

THE DEMON LIST*

You are an above-average speller if you can score 75 or more on the following list of 100 words which range from "trouble makers" to outright "demons."

academy
accessory
accumulate
acoustics
alimentary
aloha
anonymity
apparatus
attendant
avoirdupois
baccalaureate
bullion
buoy
bureaucracy
cantankerous
catechism
collaborate
consensus
corollary
dahlia
defendant
desiccated
dilapidated
disastrous
eleemosynary
emphatically
eulogy
exaggerate
exercise
facile
fascinate
frantically
fulfilled
garage

Gesundheit
gnome
haughty
hearse
homogeneous
impromptu
innuendo
irreducible
irrelevant
jeopardize
knapsack
labyrinth
larynx
licorice
liqueur
mediocre
millennium
moratorium
naphtha
negotiable
notarize
octogenarian
orchid
overrun
paralysis
perennial
pharmaceutical
phosphorus
phrenology
phylactery
poinsettia
precinct
pseudo
psychiatry

queue
quinine
rarefied
rehearsal
rendezvous
reservoir
rheumatic
saxophone
schedule
seismograph
separation
sieve
silhouette
spontaneity
surveillance
thermometer
tonsillitis
tranquil
turgid
ultimatum
umbrella
uterus
vice versa
vitamin
vulnerable
wharf
wiener
wrestle
xylophone
yeast
zinnia
zoological

---

* Taken from Shaw, 1969, pp. 138-139.

MOST COMMON HOMONYMS ENCOUNTERED IN GRADES 3 TO 6 SPELLING LESSONS*

no	know	wood	would	sea	see
one	won	our	hour	right	write
red	read	line	lion	its	it's
too	to two	new	knew	your	you're
by	buy	roll	role	flower	flour
dear	deer	cent	sent	there	their
for	four	eight	ate	road	rode
here	hear	hole	whole		
week	weak	meet	meat		

100 WORDS MOST OFTEN MISSPELLED BY CHILDREN IN THE ELEMENTARY GRADES*

1. their	26. want	51. mother	76. February
2. too	27. where	52. another	77. once
3. there	28. stopped	53. threw	78. like
4. they	29. very	54. some	79. they're
5. then	30. morning	55. its	80. cousin
6. until	31. something	56. brought	81. all right
7. our	32. named	57. getting	82. happened
8. asked	33. came	58. going	83. didn't
9. off	34. name	59. course	84. always
10. through	35. tried	60. woman	85. surprise
11. you're	36. here	61. animals	86. before
12. clothes	37. many	62. started	87. caught
13. looked	38. knew	63. that's	88. every
14. people	39. with	64. would	89. different
15. pretty	40. together	65. again	90. interesting
16. running	41. swimming	66. heard	91. sometimes
17. believe	42. first	67. received	92. friends
18. little	43. were	68. coming	93. children
19. things	44. than	69. to	94. an
20. him	45. two	70. said	95. school
21. because	46. know	71. wanted	96. jumped
22. through	47. decided	72. hear	97. around
23. and	48. friend	73. from	98. dropped
24. beuatiful	49. when	74. frightened	99. babies
25. it's	50. let's	75. for	100. money

---

* Taken from Plessas, 1963.
* Taken from Johnson, 1950.

A BASIC INTEGRATING CORE VOCABULARY*

a	box	door	great	keep
about	boy	down	green	kind
after	bread	dress	ground	know
again	bring	drink	grow	leaves
all	brother	duck	guess	let
always	brown	eat	had	like
am	but	egg	hair	little
an	butter	every	hand	live
and	buy	face	hard	long
another	by	fall	has	look
any	cake	farm	hat	lunch
anything	call	fast	have	made
apple	came	father	he	make
are	can	feet	head	mamma
around	candy	fell	hear	man
as	car	find	help	many
ask	carry	fire	her	may
at	cat	first	here	me
ate	chair	fish	hill	milk
away	chicken	five	him	Miss
baby	children	flag	his	money
back	Christmas	floor	hold	morning
bait	clean	flower	hole	mother
barn	coat	fly	home	Mrs.
be	cold	for	horse	much
bear	color	found	hot	must
because	come	four	house	my
bed	corn	from	how	myself
been	could	funny	I	name
before	cow	game	ice	nest
bell	cut	garden	if	never
best	daddy	gave	I'll	new
better	day	get	I'm	next
big	did	girl	in	night
bird	do	give	into	no
birthday	does	go	is	not
black	dog	goes	it	now
blue	doll	going	its	of
boat	dolly	good	it's	off
book	done	got	jump	oh
both	don't	grass	just	old

* This list, taken from children's writing, is selected as a possible source of spelling words.

on	ride	squirrel	this	we
once	right	stand	those	went
one	robin	start	three	were
only	room	stay	tie	when
open	round	stick	time	where
or	said	stop	to	which
other	Santa Claus	store	today	white
our	saw	story	together	who
out	say	street	told	why
over	school	stammer	too	will
paint	scissors	sun	took	wind
paper	see	table	top	window
party	seven	take	town	winter
people	shall	teacher	train	wish
picture	she	tell	tree	with
pig	shoe	than	turn	wood
place	show	thank	two	work
plant	sing	thanksgiving	under	would
play	sister	that	up	write
please	sit	the	us	yellow
pretty	six	their	use	yes
pull	sky	them	very	you
put	sleep	then	walk	your
rabbit	snow	there	want	
rain	so	these	was	
ran	some	they	watch	
ready	song	thing	water	
red	soon	think	way	

364 ADDITIONAL WORDS OF AN INTEGRATING VOCABULARY*

across	balloon	board	butterfly	clock
afraid	bark	bought	can't	close
airplane	bath	bow	cape	clothes
almost	beat	bowl	catch	comes
alone	beautiful	bows	cent	coming
along	bee	break	chairs	cook
already	began	breakfast	chick	cooky
animal	begin	bridge	chickens	couldn't
answer	bigger	bright	child	count
apples	birdie	broke	chimney	country
apron	birds	broom	church	cows
arm	block	brought	city	cradle
asleep	bluebird	build	climb	crayon

* From Fitzgerald, J., and Fitzgerald, P. G.: *Teaching Reading and the Language Arts*, 1965, pp. 134-135. Milwaukee, Bruce. Used with permission.

cry	gets	lion	piece	tail
cup	getting	looked	pink	talk
danger	gingerbread	looks	played	ten
dear	glad	lost	playing	that's
didn't	goat	lot	pony	there's
dig	gold	lots	pumpkin	they're
dinner	good-by	love	pussy	things
dirty	grandfather	makes	rat	thought
dish	grandma	making	read	through
dishes	grandmother	maybe	real	tiny
doing	grandpa	mean	rest	tomorrow
draw	grew	meat	ring	toy
drum	half	men	road	toys
dry	handle	met	roll	trees
each	hands	mew	rooster	try
ear	hasn't	mice	rope	turkey
early	haven't	might	run	upon
earth	heard	mine	same	wagon
Easter	hen	miss	sand	wait
eggs	here's	monkey	Santa	wall
eight	he's	moon	sat	wanted
elephant	hey	more	says	wants
else	hid	mouse	sea	warm
end	hide	mouth	seat	wash
enough	hit	move	seed	wear
everybody	hop	Mr.	seen	wee
everything	horn	near	set	well
eye	horses	need	sheep	we'll
eyes	hungry	nice	she's	we're
fan	hurt	nine	ship	wet
far	ice cream	noise	shoes	what
farmer	I'd	nose	should	what's
feel	isn't	nothing	sick	wheat
fill	I've	nut	side	where's
fine	kid	O	sled	while
finish	kite	oak	small	whole
flowers	kitten	ones	soft	windows
food	kitty	orange	somebody	wolf
foot	lady	ought	something	woman
fork	last	outside	sometimes	won't
fox	late	own	star	wouldn't
friend	lay	pan	stocking	yard
front	leave	paste	straight	year
full	left	pet	string	yesterday
fun	leg	pick	sugar	yet
garage	let's	picnic	Sunday	your're
gate	letter	pictures	sunshine	yours
gee	light	pie	sure	

BIBLIOGRAPHY

1. Bloomer, R. H.: Some formulae for predicting spelling difficulty. *J Ed Resch, 57*:395-401, 1964.
2. Bock, Phillip K.: *Modern Cultural Anthropology.* New York, Knopf, 1969.
3. Brengelman, F. H.: Dialect and the teaching of spelling. *Research in Teaching of English, 3-4*:129-138, 1969-1970.
4. Brown, R. W. and Hildum, D. C.: Expectancy and the identification of syllables. *Language, 32*:411-419, 1956.
5. Cahen, L. S.; Craun, M. J., and Johnson, S. K.: Spelling difficulty—a survey of the research. *Rev Ed Resh, 41*:(4):281-301, 1971.
6. Carroll, J. B.: Words, meaning and concepts. *Harvard Ed Rev, 34*: 178-202, 1964.
7. Chomsky, C.: Reading, writing and phonology. *Harvard Ed Rev, 40*:287-309, 1970.
8. Crossland, H. R., and Johnson, G.: The range of apprehension as affected by inter-letter hair-spacing and by the characteristics of individual letters. *J Appl Psychol, 12*:82-124, 1928.
9. Dolch, E. W.: *The Dolch Basic Sight Word Tests.* Champaign, Garrard, 1942.
10. Fernald, G. M.: *Remedial Techniques in Basic School Subjects.* New York, McGraw, 1943.
11. Fitzgerald, J. A. and Fitzgerald, P. G.: *Teaching, Reading and the Language Arts.* Milwaukee, Bruce, 1965.
12. Fitzgerald, J. A.: *A Basic Life Spelling Vocabulary.* Milwaukee, Bruce, 1951.
13. Gibson, E.: *Principles of Perceptual Learning and Development.* New York, Appleton, 1969.
14. Gibson, J. J.: *The Senses Considered as Perceptual Systems.* Boston, Houghton Mifflin, 1966.
15. Gillingham, A. and Stillman, B.: *Remedial Training for Children with Specific Disability in Reading, Spelling and Penmanship.* Cambridge, Ed Pub Ser, 1960.
16. Hanna, P. R.: *Phoneme-Grapheme Correspondence as Clues to Spelling Improvement.* USOE Cooperative Research Project No. 1991. GPO, 1966.
17. Hodges, R. E. and Rudorf, E. H.: Searching linguistics for cues for the teaching of spelling. *Elem Engl, 42*:527-533, 1965.
18. Horn, T. D.: Spelling. In Gage, N. (Ed.): *Encyclopedia on Educational Research.* 4th ed. London, Macmillan, 1969.
19. Jastak, J. F.; Bijou, S. W., and Jastak, S. R.: *The Wide Range Achievement Test.* Wilmington, Guidance Assoc., 1965.

20. Johnson, L. M.: One hundred words most often misspelled by children in the elementary grades. *J Ed Resh, 44*:154-155, 1950.

21. Kohl, H.: *36 Children.* New York, NAL, 1967.

22. McLean, James: Language development and communication disorders. In Haring, N. (Ed.): *Behavior of Exceptional Children, An Introduction to Special Education.* Columbus, Merrill, 1974.

23. Miller, G. A.: The magical number seven, plus or minus two: Some limits on our capacity for processing information. *Psychol Rev, 63*:81-97, 1956.

24. Montessori, M. M.: *Discovery of the Child.* Adyar, India, Kalakshetra, 1958.

25. Personke, Carl: "A Comparison of the Spelling Achievement of Groups of Scottish and American Children." Unpublished Doctoral Dissertation, University of Michigan, 1963.

26. Plessas, G. P.: Children's errors in spelling homonyms. *Elem Sch J, 64*:163-168, 1963.

27. Plessas, G. P. and Ladley, D. M.: Some implications of spelling and reading research. *Elem Engl, 42*:142-145, 1965.

28. Russell, D. H.: Spelling ability in relation to reading and vocabulary achievement. *Elem Engl, 23*:32-37, 1946.

29. Schonell, F.: *Backwardness in the Basic Subjects.* London, Olivant, 1942.

30. Shaw, H.: *Spell It Right.* New York, Barnes and Noble, 1965.

31. Simon, D. P. and Simon, H. A.: Alternative uses of phonemic information in spelling. *Rev Ed Res, 43*(1):5-137, 1973.

32. Slingerland, Beth: *A Multi-Sensory Approach to Language Arts for Specific Language Disability Children.* Cambridge, Ed Pub Ser, 1971.

33. Strang, R. M. and Bracken, D. K.: *Making Better Readers.* Boston, Heath, 1957.

34. Thorndike, E. L. and Lorge, I.: *The Teacher's Word Book of 30,000 Words.* New York, Bureau of Publications, Teachers College, Columbia University, 1944.

35. Townsend, A.: An investigation of certain relationships of spelling with reading and academic aptitude. *J Ed Resch, 40*:465-471, 1947.

36. Venesky, R. L.: English orthography: its graphical structure and its relation to sound. *Read Resch Quart, 2*:75-105, 1967.

37. Weikert, David: *Perry Pre-School Project, Mimeographed Teaching Suggestions, Levels of Representation.* Ypsilanti, Michigan, 1968.

38. Yee, A. H.: The generalization controversy in spelling instruction. In Horn, T. D. (Ed.): *Research on Handwriting and Spelling.* National Conference on Research in English. Illinois, 1966, pp. 64-72.

CHAPTER 4

TEACHING HANDWRITING

$\mathbf{M}$ANY TEACHERS BEGRUDGE the time spent in teaching handwriting. They feel the time is better spent on other subject areas where content is emphasized or in teaching reading. While this may be argued for achieving children, for the low achiever teaching handwriting provides a means for integrating the teaching of visual motor skills in the language arts program and is directly related to proficiency in this area.

As a medium for developing perceptual awareness of individual letter form, handwriting is ideal. It is traditionally taught as a separate subject and expectations for improving form itself are already established. The problems encountered in the decoding-comprehension dichotomy and controversy—where emphasis on skill teaching may actually interfere with, compete with or supercede understanding—are not present. Instruction in composition and creative writing deals with other issues; no one is disturbed by the practice and repetition which are associated with perfecting what is commonly regarded as a "motor skill."

Even though children begin writing the letters in kindergarten as they learn them, using them as a base for the perceptual skill which is regarded as the foundation in all areas of graphic language is not at all exploited. Reading readiness programs usually focus on matching exercises or marking "x's" on correct forms, and the motor support and evidence of proficiency which writing can provide are largely ignored.

Many training programs have been developed in the last ten years which attempt to improve visual perception in low-

achieving children. Those most widely used depend upon geometric forms as the basic content of teaching materials (Hooper,
1962; Kephart, 1960, and Frostig, 1964). However, there has
been little evidence of any transfer of this training to improvement in reading, spelling or handwriting techniques (Keogh,
1974). The inadequacies of these programs suggest that as the
goal of all perceptual training is improved performance in
academic subjects, the symbolic content of any training program
should involve the letters or forms which are used in these three
areas. Some of the recent research indicates that the ability to
perceive the letters of the alphabet is a fundamental skill in the
reading process (E. Gibson, 1969; Pick, 1970). Obviously, it is
also a basic skill in hand writing. It may be even more critical
for this subject because reading is largely a recognition activity
and spontaneous handwriting is a recall one. Simon and Simon
(1973) have pointed out that recognition activities require less
information than those involving recall where complete information is necessary for successful performance. It seems reasonable
to use the alphabet as the content of any training program to
teach visual perception.

Starting Early

Many authorities have indicated that the early learning period
is an extremely active and important one (Hunt, 1961; Fowler,
1962; Bloom, 1964). Many preacademic motor skills are being
developed in the preschool period. Those involving language
and perceptual motor skills are critical for school success. It is
unrealistic to expect visual motor skills to be at the same level
of proficiency in all children at school entry. While we now
believe that a great deal of what is termed "perceptual behavior"
is learned and intrinsically involves motion (Hebb, 1949; Smith
and Smith, 1962), exact knowledge of what occurs in the sensory
system is still not completely known. Assumptions are made that
visual perception is achieved through fixations on the salient
visual cues in the stimulus and that this scanning procedure is
learned behavior which is developed very early. Almost any
kindergarten teacher can tell which children in the class are hav-

ing difficulty in remembering the letters or difficulty with drawing and writing. These children would benefit from the kind of teaching which will be suggested in this chapter.

Two Areas of Handwriting Proficiency

Handwriting can be divided, for teaching purposes, into two major areas: (1) visual perception and (2) motor performance. Both of these areas will be discused as well as the more conventional topics in the research literature. However, as the following summary indicates, very few studies in the research literature deal directly with the perceptual nature and demands of the handwriting task.

Research and the Teaching of Handwriting

In a survey of the literature related to issues in the teaching of handwriting, Askov, Otto and Askov (1970) summarize the studies in seven categories: (1) the nature of letter forms (here the discussions cover those which are most difficult, not their characteristics), (2) instructional techniques, (3) effects on writing performance of specific positions of the body, (4) effect of speed and stress, (5) effect of instructional sequences, (6) the nature of handwriting instruments and writing surfaces, and (7) the development of new handwriting scales. Very little discussion is allocated to the basic perceptual dimensions of the task in these categories. Since more recent research does look carefully at the letter forms from a perceptual point of view, this will be included in this discussion and serve as its starting point.

Recap of Differentiation Theory in Relation to Letter Forms

Gibson (1969), in analyzing the reading process, states that the child first learns to speak the language. Next, he learns to discriminate the letters of the alphabet visually. This occurs between the ages of five and six when he comes to school. As many kindergarten teachers know, children frequently have difficulty with this stage and can learn to name only a few letters and may have greater difficulty in writing them. Next, in Gibson's description, the reading process includes the decoding phase as the children learn the sound-symbol relationships and, finally, they learn to take in larger chunks of graphic language and deal with the more complex syntactical units of written language.

The very first task related to letter learning simply involves accurate perception. Distinguishing the letters is regarded as a basic reading skill and assumptions are made that most children can do this when they come to school. Usually, it is not taught as a separate skill. The child uses the act of writing the letters as part of the process of learning them, even at the kindergarten level. The children who are successful learn to distinguish the letters through repeated experiences in seeing and writing them. No one thinks of teaching children how to "look" at letters *systematically* when they do not learn them.

In discussing what is distinguished in the perception of letters, Pick (1970) concludes that as children improve in their form discrimination ability between four and eight, they may learn to attend to differences among forms. "They may learn to distinguish among letters primarily on the basis of learning the distinctive features rather than the shapes of the letters" (p. 173).

One of the factors which may affect letter perception is their distinguishing features. It takes longer to distinguish between letters which differ by only one or two features such as *b* and *d* where only orientation distinguishes the two, than it does to distinguish those which may have differing features such as *o* and *l*. There may be some systematic analysis of features involved in the process of discrimination among letters. If teachers had some inkling of what this might entail, they could more effectively teach those children who cannot seem to remember. "There is a great deal of evidence indicating that the process of form discrimination in the early stage of reading involves learning to distinguish among the letters of the alphabet by focusing on and utilizing the distinctive features of these previously unfamiliar two-dimensional forms" (p. 176).

Pick concludes by saying: "There are some clear implications for the classroom from the study of letter discrimination. One should focus the child's attention on the differences among the letters rather than on the shapes of individual letters, since it is the distinctive features which the child must learn in distinguishing among the letters" (p. 180).

What is not yet certain is whether one should begin with letters which differ by many features and are easy to discriminate or with those that differ by only one and are harder to discriminate. While this remains to be clarified by research, teachers working with low-achieving children are always interested in going from a successful experience to those which require supportive instruction, which is to say that for this group of children letters which are easy to discriminate should be taught first. Focusing on the shapes may still be a valuable teaching strategy as it can bring closure to the detail teaching done in highlighting individual features. As is usually done in practice, this is to present the letter to child and name it. What the child does perceptually is left entirely up to him. He may not be scanning form—noting a cross or a curve or an intersection—and as the teaching emphasis is on a shape and a label for the shape, he continues to be unable to remember. Pick, in suggesting that attention be paid to the differences in letter form and that the shape be largely ignored, is attempting to shift the teaching emphasis from whole to parts and get more "perceptual mileage" from instruction. The suggestions made in the discussion in this book always consider alternative ways of teaching the same information or skill. The group of children for whom this is written may benefit from teaching which is repetitive as part-whole relationships may require some structure in teaching if detail is emphasized. The teacher needs to be aware of this so that compensation can be made. When a great deal of emphasis is on details the child may not reconstruct the whole, and the teacher should direct attention to the total form as a safeguard.

Pick is arguing for this training for improvement in reading, not handwriting. But as the basic units—the letters—are the same, there may be greater chance for transfer of training if there is consistent teaching of this kind of perceptual skill in handwriting and spelling as well as in reading and if it is taught as soon as the letters are to be learned. Since the comprehension demands are more limited, this is more easily accomplished in handwriting and spelling than in reading.

The reader may ask, "Why put such emphasis on perception in an area which places such heavy demands on motor performance as does handwriting? Perhaps more emphasis could be placed on the motor aspects of writing." Theoretically, there are still unresolved arguments about which comes first, perception or performance. Traditionally, teaching precepts have placed heavy emphasis on copying and practice—or repetition—for improvement in handwriting. Actually the present emphasis on putting perceptual training first represents a shift in approach. Fernald and Montessori actually used movement in tracing to implicitly teach the perceptions through providing redundant information to other senses. Some research by Maccoby (1968) supports emphasis on the discriminations which need to be made in executing movements for effective performance in drawing triangles and diamonds. In this case geometric form is the content, limiting its application to the problem at hand. The important difference is the relationship between pointing out critical visual details or placing the emphasis on the writing of the letter, hoping that the movement of writing or drawing or the fact that the child successfully copied a letter will differentiate the details as part of the activity.

Another distinction needs to be made before this topic is closed; that is the place of memory. There is a great deal of difference in what occurs perceptually in copying and in writing spontaneously. Fernald understood this well, although it is not discussed in any detail, as her method requires writing words from memory, never copying. It is quite possible to construct a letter or a word from a copy without having any sense of the whole form, and many children can do this well. Spontaneous production requires an image and the quality of the image determines to a large extent what the quality of the letter or word will be. Of course, motor problems can interfere with good production and these will be discussed later in detail. The point being made is that execution depends first on a good image and the image depends on how successfully the letter or word has been distinguished.

In providing perceptual training in letter form, Gibson gives us three principles upon which to rely:

1. Emphasize distinctive features
2. Emphasize differences
3. Provide contrasts

Discriminations are easiest when there are lots of differences and hardest when there are few. Learning to note differences can be made easier if examples of graded contrasts along a particular dimension are provided so that a critical variable can be isolated. Small *n* and *h* might serve as a good example for contrast in letter learning. The critical variable is the length of the first vertical line. Exaggerating distinctive features can be helpful; familiarity with distinctive features will make a discrimination task easier.

What Are the Distinctive Features of Letters?

In the chart which folows, the distinctive features for the roman capital letters are set forth. Five major classifications are presented:

  straight
  curve
  intersection
  redundancy (repetition of form)
  discontinuity (line ends)

The features were not selected randomly by Gibson, but reflect the results from research which found that straight edges and curves as well as line orientation evoke neurophysiological responses in animals. It has been found that intersections and the closed-open distinction are perceived very early by children. Parallels act as units from some retinal image research which is used to support the redundancy classification; discontinuity or the end of a line provokes differential neural response, making it a likely distinguishing characteristic.

From research on the confusability of the letters, Gibson

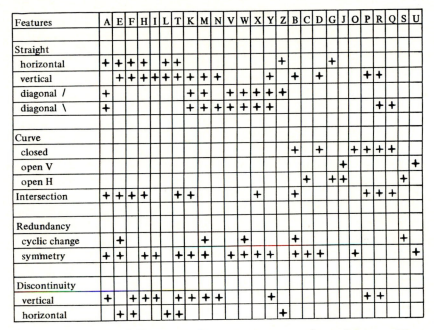

Figure 15. Chart of distinctive features for a set of graphemes. (From Gibson, E. J.: *Principles of Perceptual Learning and Development.* Appleton, 1969. Used with permission.)

found that the letters P and R were most often confused by adults and they also took the longest time in being able to discriminate them. E and F, N and M, C and G, and M and W followed in decreasing order of confusability. G and M, and G and N, were never confused. The results with children were quite similar but M and N and M and W took a longer time for them to discriminate. Diagonals were difficffiult for children to discriminate even at seven years. The curve-straight distinction is an easy one to make. P and F, which are rather similar in total shape, were almost never confused. Children took more time to make the discriminations, in general, than did adults. Gibson interprets this as demonstrating the effect of practice in discriminating the letters. The curve-straight and diagonality are important feature contrasts. There are indications from this research that some overall structure such as symmetry may be responded to when letters are seen simultaneously. The research on the perception of letter forms is far from complete, but even the foregoing discussion brings forth some guides for teachers to follow in planning instruction. The characteristics to emphasize are set forth and the easy contrasts—the curve-straight ones—might be a beginning point for differentiation training. The letters with diagonals might be given extra attention and practice in initial teaching.

In the research literature on handwriting only one set of studies reflects a stress on this aspect of differentiating letter form in teaching.

HANDWRITING AND PERCEPTUAL SKILLS

In three articles Furner (1969, 1969a, 1970) develops an approach which stresses perceptual skills rather than only motor skills in the teaching of handwriting as it is introduced in the first grade. In her approach, the child sees the letter as well as the formational process and specific instruction is provided in guiding the attention to perceiving visual cues through verbalization. While characteristics are not categorized in the Gibson matrix, they are starting point, direction of stroke, size, and stopping point. Furner's method provides that the child state these and attempts to use the auditory process ostensibly to mediate and reinforce the visualizations. The letters are introduced in terms of commonalities and implicitly provide experience with distinctive features, such as grouped straight-line or curved-line letters, or diagonals. Her method does not place as much emphasis on teaching differences and contrasts, although it occurs in the process. The verbalization that Furner uses is an important part of her method and the perceptual and motor processes are very consciously directed by it. Throughout the teaching the child is guided in the development of self-evaluation and correction.

Furner also makes use of peer models and asks the children to write the letter twice, thinking the description and trying to improve each time. In other words, they are asked to "think out loud," or verbalize, the instructions aloud for themselves as they write.

While Furner did not include kinesthetic teaching—tracing, positioning or manipulation—as learning supports, she did make use of child verbalization as a mediator of visual and motor inputs. She was interested in clarifying the perceptual aspects of the writing act and the teacher and child do verbalize in specifying the perceptual aspects of the task. No discussion of the modeling and imitation used is presented nor exploited significantly in her discussion, although it occurs regularly in her teaching description. The role of the adult in providing immediate feedback in the reinforcement process is not discussed, although this also occurs.

Her stated aims were for the internalization of a mental image from which spontaneous production of letters could occur. In the introduction, a good deal of time is spent discussing Hebb's (1949) work in relation to perceptual development. It is from his theory that perceptual development is a learned process involving movement and differentiated motor as well as perceptual actions that her procedures are derived. She translates this theoretical position into an attempt to specify visual cues while writing instead of leaving them to implicit learning. This approach makes her research and teaching method unique, since most teaching procedures only name the letter or attach a label to the total form accompanied by motor production. The child copies a model. As Furner, Gibson and Pick have all emphasized the perceptual aspects in their teaching, several of the implicit aspects of Furner's method are worth further exploration. These are modeling and imitation and the place of verbalization in the teaching of handwriting; the discussion will return to these topics shortly. However, as discrimination training in letter form is regarded as an important first step in proficiency with any aspect of graphic language, we should first look at some other groupings of letters and other perceptual issues.

Other Letter Groupings

Gibson has provided a matrix whose five salient cues encompass many of the characteristics of upper case manuscript letter form. Her matrix can be used for cursive as well as manuscript with some minor adjustments.

Furner (1969) has suggested that the letters be grouped by similar characteristics as they are introduced to children and she includes perceptual and motor directions for this activity. Sklar and Hanley (1972) provide a breakdown of the similar letters in the lower case roman alphabet. They group the letters in nine subsets:

1. a, c, e, o
2. b, d, g, h, p, q
3. f, t
4. i, j, l
5. m, n, u, v, w
6. s, z
7. x, y
8. k
9. r

It is obvious that there are a variety of ways that these letters could be grouped. In looking at the first group, two further groupings could be made, separating *a* and *e*, as they both require straight lines in their production although one is vertical and the other horizontal. In the second group it might be beneficial to separate the ascending letters from the descending ones and group them according to orientation. In the fourth group *j* could be considered a descender and included with group two. In group five, *m*, *n*, and *u* require rounded strokes and *v* and *w* require slanting strokes. While *s* and *z* have configurations which are the same, there are differences in orientation and in the roundness and angularity required in the strokes.

If grouped as suggested above, twelve subsets occur and others could be developed:

1. c, o
2. a, e
3. b, h, d
4. g, p, q, j
5. f, t
6. i, l

7. m, n, u
8. v, w
9. s, z
10. x, y
11. k
12. r

The Gibson categories of the matrix could be easily applied to the groupings presented as above. These groupings select according to some, but not all, of the characteristics which means that many of the letters will be taught in several groups to provide contrast or to emphasize either similarities or differences. Some children will have unique problems in relation to the orientation of letters or in their formation; others need greater attention to those letters requiring a slant line, or a change in direction of the stroke. This provides an excellent example of the intent of adaptive teaching. The teacher stands between a logical arrangement of the curriculum and the unique needs of the child. With this clearly in mind, an arbitrary grouping is presented, as a guide, for the upper case manuscript letters.

1. C, O, Q, G   (Circle)
2. E, F, H, I, L, T   (Straight Line)
3. A, K, M, N, V, W, X, Y, Z (Slant Line)
4. B, D, P, R   (Straight Line, Curve)
5. U, J   (Single Stroke Including Curve)

A great deal of emphasis is placed on the grouping of manuscript letters because many children prefer manuscript to cursive when given a choice, and because it is usually the first form introduced. Possible groupings for the cursive alphabet are also included. The suggestions being made here are focused on the introduction to writing, as training at this time is likely to prevent difficulties. However, the same teaching strategies are suggested for remedial teaching; therefore, both groupings are presented at this point.

Groupings of Cursive Alphabet*

b h l k e f

a d c p

i t

m n

u w

y z j g q

r s o

a o q c

m n w

h k x

f j

y z j

e l s y d

b p r

e q v

---

* These are purely arbitrary and subjective groupings. Letters can be grouped on the basis of more than one characteristic.

** Note difference in acceptable form of Q.

It is suggested that the teacher attend to the principle of grouping by common characteristics, distinctive features or contrast, and that *the child's performance be considered in providing the best presentation of letters for the individual child.*

The Extra-attention Letters

Difficult Letters—Manuscript

Lewis and Lewis (1964) identified those letters which are most difficult for first graders. They list them as *q, g, p, y* and *j*. They state that:

> In the descenders about one third of the errors were due to a failure to orient letters properly to the guidelines. Incorrect orientation to the guidelines occurred about ten times as often in the descenders as in other letters. . . . The letters *q* and *y* were more susceptible to reversal errors than were most letters. . . . Distortion of the shape of the letter . . . occurred most frequently in *j*. The error was usually due to difficulty in merging down stroke and the final upward curve. . . . Letter *m* was the most difficult of the non-descending letters. There were three main sources of error: size, relationship of letter parts and omission of letter parts. . . . Incorrect relationship of letter parts was greater in letter *k* than in any other letter (p. 856).

They state that boys were more prone to error than were girls; that age differences did not seem to matter in readiness for writing or in rate of progress. Pupils whose writing was of high quality made few errors and left-handed children made many errors at first related to reversals, inversions rotations, and omission or incorrect relationships of parts. After instruction, the left-handed child persisted in reversals and inversions.

Lewis and Lewis (1964) list the letters of the manuscript alphabet in order of difficulty.

It was particularly interesting to note that the reversal of *d* was more common than the reversal of *b* and that reversals occurred almost as frequently in the letter *N*. More attention in the initial teaching is warranted for the descending letters and for those letters which are inherently more difficult. Left-handed children need to be observed very carefully to determine

TABLE I

LETTERS OF THE MANUSCRIPT ALPHABET ARRANGED BY ORDER OF DIFFICULTY

Order of Difficulty	Letter	Order of Difficulty	Letter
1	q	27	K
2	g	28	W
3	p	29	A
4	y	30	N
5	j	31	C
6	m	32	f
7	k	33	J
8	U	34	w
9	a	35	h
10	G	36	T
11	R	37	x
12	d	38	c
13	Y	39	V
14	u	40	F
15	M	41	P
16	S	42	E
17	b	43	X
18	e	44	I
19	r	45	v
20	Z	46	i
21	n	47	D
22	s	48	H
23	Q	49	O
24	B	50	L
25	t	51	o
26	z	52	l

early if orientation is a particularly difficult distinction for them to maintain. If orientation training with letter form is started early, it will lessen the possibiilty of the reinforcement of error which accompanies the writing of the incorrect form.

Newland (1932) found that only four letters (*a, e, r, t*) contributed 45, 46 and 47 percent of the illegibilities to the elementary, high school and adult groups respectively. He also found that four types of difficulties caused over half of all the illegibilities in the formation of letters. These difficulties were the failure to close letters, closing looped strokes, looping nonlooped strokes and using straight-up strokes instead of rounded ones. In the capital letters, he found that *I* and *D* were particularly prone to malformation.

As he was looking at elementary, high school and adult writing, he discovered that illegibilities tended to increase with age. The effect of practice of the incorrect form becomes clearly evident. While nine forms of illegibilities accounted for 50 percent of all illegibilities at adult levels, six of those were common to all three levels. These were first, "e closed" as the most common, followed by "d" like "cl," "r" like "i," "i" not dotted, "h" like "li" and "n" like "u."

Newland suggests that corrective or preventive work should be directed to the different forms of illegibilities and adapted for the different age levels.

Simplified Form

Schell and Burns (1963) suggest that simplified letter forms should be taught initially to prevent the need for later modifications.

The Emerson (1954, pp. 44, 45) left- and right-hand alphabets present examples of simplified form, designed as it was to be used with children who had writing and reading problems. The first line of her alphabet is presented here.

When these letters are contrasted with the alphabet presented in the California State Series (1967), it is seen that Emerson has modified the loops and has used a simplified *F* and *T*. The *Q*-form is closer to printing and the *G* is an enlarged lower case letter.

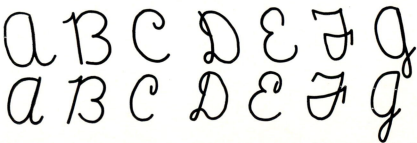

Structure 11. (From Emerson, Dorothy: *Help Yourself to Better Handwriting*. Cambridge, Educators Publishing Service, 1954. Used with permission.)

Aa Bb Cc Dd Ee Ff Gg

Again, without a body of research to guide us, the teacher's best strategy would be to observe the child and determine letter form based on an analysis of what may be easiest for each child. Our main goals in handwriting, for the child who has difficulty, are legibility and fluency.

Cursive or Manuscript

At the present time there seems to be no decisive answer to the question of which alphabet to use. For the child who is having problems with writing, it seems obvious that the one to use is that which is easiest for the child. Legibility is the main goal, fluency the next most important factor. These remain the guides which can direct the teacher when choices need to be made.

It is frequently a matter of school or district policy as to which form is introduced. It is common practice to introduce manuscript in the kindergarten, in a limited manner, and fully in the first grade and then shift to cursive in the third grade. Most children are able to handle the shift and master the two forms adequately, so it is not a critical matter as to which is introduced.

Currently, the research offers little aid in this decision making. Byers (1963) found that there were more transpositions and omissions of letters in manuscript and more substitutions of letters and omissions of whole words in cursive writing. Berry (1961) found that children who tend to write legibly in one style, do so in the other style also.

For the group of children with perceptual motor problems, the issues in remedial teaching are slightly different than those involved in the introduction of writing. Hampered by developmental, neurological or motivational differences, the major issue for this group rests on the length of time it will take for attaining proficiency in one system. It is not beneficial for these children to master a second writing system when they have not developed perceptual motor skill in the first one. It would be better for those children who are identified early as having perceptual motor problems to stay with one system.

The argument for introducing writing with the cursive alphabet rests on its continuity and rhythmic and integrative qualities. The argument for the use of manuscript is that it is simpler in form and closer to the print form that children read. These are both good arguments. As there is no longitudinal research with a group of children who have been identified early and presented with one or the other form, the decision at this point can be based on the system which is easiest for the child to master, child preference, teaching preference or the availability of teaching material.

The issues in remedial teaching rest on child preference, the system being used by the peer group, and the severity of the perceptual motor problem. If the child strongly prefers one system to another, that preference should be honored. Motivation will be greater if the child has choice. If the child is in a tutorial setting and spends most of the day in the regular classroom, then it may be beneficial to help him master the system being used by his peers. As handwriting is an area in which improvement can be effected relatively easily, the child can receive peer and teacher acknowledgement publicly. This can be very important as teachers move to enhance self-concept and develop achievement motivation. If the child spends the total day in the special class, the decision may be made on the basis of individual assessment. The system used would be the one that the child masters most easily. Again, ease and legibility are the major goals in handwriting. It is not essential that children use cursive writing. In fact, if the child has extraordinary difficulty, it may be advisable to spend a minimum amount of time on teaching handwriting and instead, teach him to type.

Maier (1973), in discussing remedial teaching, suggests use of a mixed form. She uses a manuscript capital letter with cursive small letters to circumvent the problem of the complexity of form and to utilize the benefits of rhythm and continuity in cursive writing. She relies on writing to music to develop speed and endurance. If the teacher is consistent and systematic in her teaching, this is probably a very good compromise solution for older children.

Perhaps one other issue should be discussed. Those who argue for cursive writing do so on the basis of the value of continuity, rhythm and its integrative function, even though the form is more complex. For some children, the discreteness of the manuscript form may be a facilitating factor. Time is allowed between letters and words for the cognitive activity necessary to guide the hand, or simply because they respond more slowly. This is probably more valid for the young child than the older one. As handwriting is a perceptual skill, it is probable that overlearning and practice in either form would develop the same amount of proficiency, given the same motivation and efficient teaching.

Consistent Form

It is not uncommon to find that the intermediate-age child having difficulties is mixing the manuscript and cursive forms indiscriminantly. It has been suggested that those children who have difficulty with cursive writing deliberately be taught to mix forms for simplicity and fluency, but this relates only to initial letters which require capitalization. However, the problem occurs when the child has been taught both forms and prefers manuscript and intersperses cursive letters randomly. He is "in between" and does not remember which to use. With a child who presents this problem, the first task would be to make a clear-cut decision as to which form to use. The child should be included in the planning so that he is aware of the goals. If cursive writing is the preferred form, then only the capital letters will be written in manuscript. If manuscript is the preferred form, then all letters will be written in manuscript form. Teacher-guided instruction should be given, and some provision should be made for checking spontaneous writing to see if the teaching has generalized. Diagnostically, not only does this behavior indicate memory problems, but it also means the child does not understand the function of capital letters.

The Basic Strokes

In manuscript writing, the basic strokes are clear and simple:

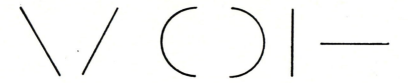

Because of the discreteness of this form of writing, practice in the basic strokes should be quite valuable. However, because of the continuity of cursive writing, practicing the basic strokes in isolation may have limited value. Practicing those basic strokes in the letters in which they present the greatest difficulty may be of greater benefit.

Peterson (1965) lists the basic strokes in this writing form as various curves, an under-curve and an over-curve as well as a combination-curve, ovals, rounded-top strokes, point-top strokes as well as short retraces. For our purposes here, it might be more helpful to distinguish these strokes in a slightly different manner.

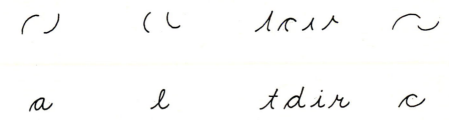

The strokes which present the greatest difficulty to children with what are diagnostically referred to as having "visual motor integration" difficulties in cursive writing are:

1. Reversing directions of strokes as in:

2. Retracing a stroke as in:

3. Slight retracings as in:

4. Loops as in:

5. Strokes requiring closure as in:

In a writing practice of basic strokes, these four areas should be given attention on an individualized basis. The practice should reflect an observation of difficulty with the stroke in the letter. Practice in writing these strokes and letters may serve as an aid to both the perception and production of letters.

Proportion of Letters

Furner (1969b) suggests a solution to the problem of letter proportion which is a common source of difficulty and error in writing.

> Children were guided, following a natural tendency, to make tall letters two thirds of a space high, small letters one third of a space high, and to make tails descend almost half a space below the baseline. These proportions were subsequently used in the introduction of the cursive form as they seemed more conducive to the development of rhythmical writing than the usual proportions in which small letters are over half the height of tall letters" (p. 1026).

This suggestion of maintaining the same proportions as the form changes may be helpful to many children. As cursive is more complex perceptually, than manuscript, this constancy reduces the number of dimension shifts with which children must cope. As difficulty with the relative size of letters shows up as a problem for children who write both manuscript and cursive, emphasis on this area is very important in both beginning teaching and remediation. Perceptually, this problem is one of visual judgments involving discrimination and memory for both spatial and form relationships. Again, it cannot be left to incidental learning; it must be brought to the level of awareness and taught specifically until the child can perform correctly and independently. Line awareness becomes an important visual cue in maintaining letter proportion.

Slant

Children can practice the correct slant by writing on prepared paper with the slant lines indicated.

In manuscript writing, *The California State Series,* Book 4, p. 45, supports a straight orientation.

Adventures in Handwriting, Book 5 (1965) supports a slant orientation, but states in the text that the child can choose to use a straight letter orientation. This seems reasonable and the teacher needs to observe preference and reinforce one or the other consistently. An example of a sentence written in slant orientation follows.

Emerson (1954, pp. 6-7), in her book on handwriting presents samples of slants appropriate for the left- and right-handed child in cursive writing.

We judge the quality

We judge the quality

As posture may be the most important factor affecting slant (Askov, Otto and Askov, 1970), attention should be given to this when slant problems are evident.

Spacing

When children are not aware of the consistency of the spatial relationships in writing, teachers can include it as an objective in a discrimination training program. Children who are beginning to write are frequently very erratic in spacing between letters, words or lines. Older students with visual motor problems may also ignore spacing as an important characteristic in writing. In helping them become aware of distance as a vital aspect of writing success, estimating distance is a good remedial technique. It can be done verbally, physically—using a child's fingers—or with a marker. The most important factor in helping children become consistent in spacing in writing will be the consistency with which the teacher directs their attention to it as an important detail. Verbalizing the spacing dimension, having the child write, and immediately evaluating and correcting should produce results with most children.

Line Discrimination

Frequently children behave as though the paper on which they were writing had no lines. They are so involved in the motor aspects of the handwriting act that they forget to attend to the perceptual ones. It is frequently helpful to darken the lines so that children cannot miss them. Bottom line, top line, mid-line or margin, can each be darkened, or one or another can be singled out for specific attention at one time. Color is also easily attached to visually meaningful cues; red and green can be used for starting and stopping guides. Broken lines are frequently used to cue the child to distinctions which are related to size. It is often helpful to place Scotch Tape® on the margin as it reflects the light and acts as a visual signal, and it also raises the surface so that the pencil can touch it as the child begins a line. Levine and Carter (1968, p. 38) suggest darkening or blocking out the spaces which are to be left empty. This is an excellent suggestion for beginning writers or children with great focusing difficulties. Lerner (1971) suggests using plastic template overlays to help develop spatial awareness.

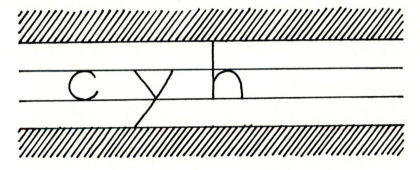

Whenever these supports are used, planning with the child should occur so that the transition to writing without them occurs gradually. It is very helpful to deliberately remove the support and help the child set the particular goal of line space or margin awareness without them. He actually practices *not* using them in the transition period.

Symmetry

Another aspect of handwriting is the result of awareness and use of all the perceptual characteristics discussed so far. When line relationship, relative size, spacing and slant are consistently discriminated, handwriting looks "even" or symmetrical. This quality should be called to the child's attention in the evaluation period so that it is included in the goals the child may set for himself.

While Quant (1946) found that the most important factor

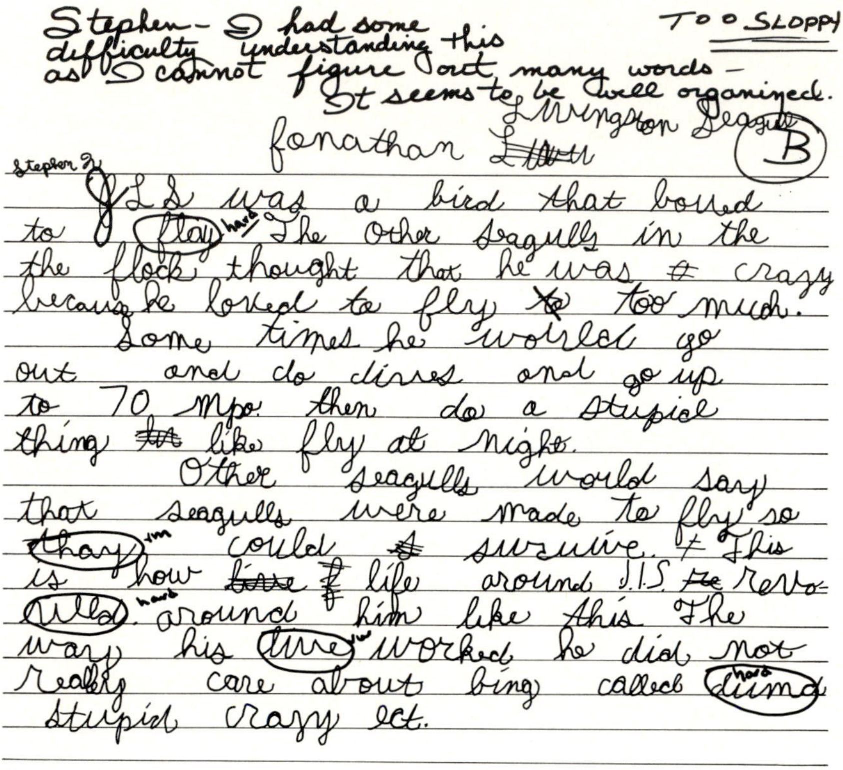

Figure 16.

determining legibility of handwriting was good letter formation, two other factors were also found to contribute significantly. One was *compactness* or the reduction of spacing between letters and words and the other was *regularity* of slant. In the example which follows (Figure 16) the handwriting is inconsistent in each of the dimensions discussed. It is not symmetrical and it looks "jumpy." The child uses the line as a guide sporadically, occasionally changes the spatial relationships, forms the same letter well sometimes and not others, varies the slant frequently and destroys the symmery of the writing. The teacher's comments evaluate the product but they do not direct the child's attention to the significant characteristics or details which might allow for change. They are: "Too sloppy. Stephen, I had some difficulty understanding this as I cannot figure out many words. It seems to be well organized."

Support Strategies

Verbalizing Salient Visual Cues

Earlier, Gibson (1966) stated the value of directing attention to distinguishing features of letters and Furner (1969) added another dimension in guiding the motor act of writing. In both cases this is done through verbalization. There is a great deal of support for the use of language to direct attention in the research literature.

Verbalization as a Mediator of Perceptual and Cognitive Behavior

All teachers instruct children by using language as their main means of communication. They tell children what and how to do things which are required of them in schools. They explain steps in processes. They point out details and elaborate verbally on skills the children are practicing and learning. For the group of children with visual motor problems, the verbalization which is commonly used in instruction may not be specific enough. Not only is it not specific enough, but as it requires only reception on the child's part it may be serving only half the function it could serve in developing visual motor proficiency. The child listens to language which is generated by an adult which directs his behavior. He does not receive instruction in using language to direct his own activities. Instruction might be more successful if the child were taught to use language to mediate his own perceptual motor behavior. The techniques suggested in this chapter will specify the child's use of language in handwriting to direct his own attention to the salient cues and characteristics of the forms.

Russian psychologists have long been involved in studying the role of language in the direction of behavior (Luria, 1957; Vygotsky, 1962). Many of the Russian studies have found that linguistic control increases with age. Vygotsky suggests that the ability of words to center attention and abstract and synthesize traits may be their chief role in guiding cognitive activities. American theorists involved in investigations in the same area have found an unclear relationship between language and action. While they feel that language assumes an important role in concept acquisition, they are resitant to assume that thought and action are directly correlated or that the relationships are simple (Amster, 1965). Stones (1970) feels that words provide cues to help focus attention and provide feedback not otherwise available. Amster also states that teachers' intentional instructions are important in concept learning. When concepts are formed without intention or deliberate attempts, associative proceses are dominant. Deductive processes are also involved in concept learning, and Amster suggests that younger children benefit more with practice and intention than incidental instruction. Older children tend to be cued to use deductive processes, perhaps because increased experience elaborates the information they have available—they have learned to direct their own attention.

Gibson (1969) specifically states:

> When words have been added to the cognitive repertory, perceptual learning can be facilitated by them. This can happen in two ways: one, by drawing attention to previously unnoticed features . . . and two, by increasing the efficiency of remembering, when an absent standard must be compared with a present stimulus (p. 155).

Concepts can be learned without language, but it serves a facilitating function when it is available. "It is unlikely that perceptual learning is appreciably distorted by language categories, though it is likely that it can be facilitated by calling attention, verbally, to distinctive features of things" (p. 160).

Research carried out by Jensen and Rohwer (1963) was specifically related to low-achieving children who had been taught to attach labels to tasks. They too found verbalization a facilitating procedure.

Both aspects of verbal mediation should be called upon to facilitate accurate perception and performance in handwriting, teacher verbal direction and child labeling and self-direction.

Establishing the Vocabulary

The first step in verbalizing the visual cues available in the graphic symbols of language is to establish a meaningful vocabulary. Terms for the lines on the paper should be clearly established. Bottom line, mid-line and top line are suggested as possibilities. The child should become familiar with these before writing instruction begins. He should also know the meaning of start and stop, of left and right—in relation to the paper—and of "turn" in relation to writing as the direction of the stroke will be emphasized. In the initial perceptual motor act, the child will verbalize starting point, direction, size, line intersections and stopping points. The verbalized act should always be initiated with the name of the letter and then move to the specifics of verbalized visual cues. These might include such terms as straight line, curve, slant line, size, intersection, open space, closed space, line end, parallels, and shift in direction. These words describe the five classifications that Gibson sets forth. Children and teachers may come up with others and should be encouraged to do so. The next step is verbalizing the motor act and such words as starting point, direction and stopping point are added. Closure is brought by again stating the name of the letter.

Who Verbalizes?

In the demonstration and modeling phase, the teacher verbalizes and the children observe. In the imitation phase, the children verbalize for themselves. This step is reemphasized as an important one in the initial teaching. If only the teacher verbalizes, the child will have missed the chance to use the language for self-direction. The intent of modeled verbal behavior is to focus attention and to offer greater possibilities for internalization and mediation for later self-directed perceptual motor activity. The children should have opportunities to perform not only the motor acts but the verbalized perceptual ones as well. For this reason, complete verbalization should be insisted on initially.

As a teaching strategy, greater emphasis has been placed on the use of modeling and imitation than on reinforcement in the discussion of these teaching suggestions. Both of these theories are part of the larger theory of social learning. As greater emphasis in teacher education has been placed on knowledge and use of reinforcement theory to facilitate learning than on the systematic exploitation of imitation and modeling as facilitators, they are stressed here. "Watch me. Do what I do and say what I say," should become a familiar introduction to each writing lesson. Immediate feedback and correction by the teacher in the imitation period which follows is essential so that incorrect forms are not fixed by repetition. Initially, the teacher directs the attention of the child, but the ultimate goal is to shift the attention direction to the child and to intensify attentional behavior by active rather than passive involvement in the teaching-learning process.

Modeling and Imitation as Support Strategies

One of the steps in the Furner (1969a, 1969b, 1970) teaching procedure involved having the children watch the teacher write the letter. While it was included as a step, its value and function was not discussed. Modeling or demonstrating a skill for children and then supervising performance, is a very common teaching practice. Teachers may not be aware of the value of using modeling and verbalizing together systematically for children who have perceptual or language problems. Teachers do both so casually it is difficult to view these two activities as "strategies." In teaching handwriting, the verbalization is intended to focus on the salient visual cues. As the writing act involves a process, a sequence involving intersensory integration, it may not be possible to verbalize every cue or all that is occurring. The child may also not process the language efficiently and have it cue appropriate motor responses. In viewing the act, the child may select those aspects not verbalized and include them in his own performance. In viewing a demonstration, the language can become meaningful as it is translated through the actions which are seen. Bandura (1969) has stated that "when a model is provided, patterns of behavior are rapidly acquired in large segments or in their entirety" (p. 187).

The point is also made by Bandura that nurturant behavior

on the part of the interacting adults facilitates imitative learning. He defines nurturant with the words warm, rewarding and affectionate. He found that children who had been exposed to a rewarding interaction displayed more imitative behavior, that precise imitative verbal response was elicited and the amount of nonimitative verbalization was increased. This was also established by Milner (1951) who found that children who had verbal and affectionately demonstrative mothers received higher reading readiness scores.

In using modeling and requiring imitation, the teacher is making certain that the behaviors necessary for successful visual motor performance have been rehearsed by the child and are possibly a part of his performance repertory. The positive effect in the response of the teacher as she directs or corrects the child has important consequences for learning outcomes. In the work of Hess and Shipman (1965) where the teaching strategies of middle- and lower-socio-economic class mothers were observed, it was clear that the middle-class mother verbalized instructions in detail and provided reexplanations and demonstrations when the child did not understand or perform.

Hewitt (1964) whose work is primarily directed toward children in special education, places great importance on nurturant adult behavior in his hierarchy of educational tasks. The first five task levels emphasize accepting teacher behavior with minimal independent performance demands related to academic achievement.

Because handwriting is introduced early in the child's academic career, and because the low-achieving child frequently has had inadequate adult-child relationships, this nurturant aspect in the modeling and imitation suggested as teaching strategy is underscored. "When the behavior in question has acquired positive properties, the child is likely to perform in the absence of socializing agents and externally administered awards" (Bandura, 1969 (p. 193). This is also applicable to older children in the low-achieving group who have failed repeatedly. These children tend to display more behavior problems and to attract less rather than more nurturant behavior from their teachers. Nurturance is an important adjunct to using imitation and modeling in teaching for this group of children.

Summary

Most of this section has been devoted to discussing perception of letter form and issues which are related to the perceptual aspects of handwriting. As far as teaching is concerned, the motor actions required are of equal importance. The next section will cover motor performance in handwriting and will emphasize teaching applications rather than theory.

MOTOR PERFORMANCE

In the research literature on handwriting, three strategies are described as most commonly employed as teaching aids: tracing, copying and manual guidance. Little research has been devoted to the role of these aids or their effectiveness in improving handwriting. The study of Birch and Lefford (1967) which deals with geometric form does approach these goals. They attempted to develop a model in which voluntary motor controls were viewed as a function of visual perceptual skill in improving associations between vision and other body sensations. This study demonstrated the value of tracing as an effective method of teaching. The "methods" of teaching which emphasize tracing are those of Fernald (1943) and Gillingham and Stillman (1940) which were designed for perceptually handicapped children. Slingerland (1969) who has adapted the Gillingham method, also places heavy emphasis on tracing as a teaching aid. In the Fernald method, the tracing is used to develop language form perception and developing writing skill is implicit but secondary to its main goal of reading. Gillingham actually uses tracing to develop handwriting skill as well.

In the Birch and Lefford study, the children were given geometric forms to draw and various support conditions in the training program. They used a tracing model, some connecting dot-and-line conditions, and freehand drawing. The results demonstrated that there were significant differences related to accuracy between tracing and freehand drawing and these differences persisted to age eleven, the oldest age group involved in the study. Tracing was the easiest task for the children and freehand drawing the most difficult. No discussion of why tracing may facilitate correct reproduction of the forms is given in the report on the study. Earlier it was suggested that in the act of tracing the eye and the hand pick up the redundant information in the stimuli and insure its reception. Pattern and detail may be learned through motor memory as well. The assumptions again are that motor improvement occurs with improved perception.

It is interesting to note, in the survey by Herrick and Okada (1963), that copying is the preferred teaching strategy throughout the country and tracing was listed as third preference. Even where manual guidance (which means the teacher actually guides the hand of the child) might be used, it is not used systematically, but sporadically, to help a child who has difficulty. In recent research on the Fernald method Berros (1972) found that the retention curve for children who were tracing words increased significantly if three tracings occurred before reproduction was attempted. This might prove valuable in teaching memory for letter form as well as word form.

Tracing

The child should view the teacher-model perform and trace a model before he is allowed to perform spontaneously. The teacher should go over her performance several times, verbalizing both the perceptual cues and the motor action of the moving hand. The child should then work from a tracing copy at his desk, "tracing and saying" three times before any spontaneous performance on paper is attempted. This rehearsal period allows for fixing the sequences of actions which will be required in performance. It also provides for motor memory of form and adds another dimension to the input of visual information. The child should then be encouraged to write the letter form from immediate short-term memory—*never copying*—so that short-term retention is encouraged. As soon as he finishes he should compare his copy with his model and make any corrections relating to form, line or size relationships.

Positioning

If a child continues to have difficulty after tracing letters and does not seem able to produce adequate letters, positioning should be tried as a support condition. The teacher guides the child's hand over the tracing model, making sure that he experiences the movements. If positioning is used, several important aspects of this technique need to be considered. The teacher needs to make certain that the guidance she provides by grasping the child's hand and moving it over the pattern directs exact motor performance, not approximate performance. Teacher and child verbalization of visual cues are intended, so much as the tracing, to develop skill. The tracing position may guide the eye and take in the visual information as well. The positioning guides the hand and motor memory is a primary goal; visual perception is secondary. The expectations in relation to performance should be delayed. As motor memory is being developed, it should be used initially without expectation for immediate improvement. It should be used as "throw-away" teaching, which means that its results will be noted with repetition, not immediately. As soon as we talk about repetition, it becomes necessary to talk about rote teaching and scheduling. It is more valuable in rote teaching where a skill may require many repetitions before mastery to plan for intermittent teaching, rather than continuous repetition. This means that the teacher watches the child for signs of boredom or inattentiveness in order to shift teaching strategy. It does not mean that repetition of the activity is abandoned, but rather that rest periods occur at planned intervals. This is very important where visual motor skill is involved, as consolidation of the learning seems to occur during the rest period and performance frequently improves after the rest.

Writing in the Air

This procedure is frequently used by teachers as a kinesthetic aid in developing an internal image of letters and facilitating memory of the motor patterns involved in producing letters.

Several points should be considered about the use and effectiveness of this technique. It is questionable whether a child can spontaneously write the letter form in the air if the internal image is not already present. The internal image is being developed in the receptive act as the child writes or copies to learn, and it serves as a model for direction in the expressive act. Many children who perform the air-writing may not actually have the image but will copy from their peer models or neighbors. They will watch the other children and do what they do. An observant teacher who is aware of this possible difference in performance can watch the children and pick out those who seem to be involved in a "directive" sense or just copying. However, copying is valuable if it results in an organized and recognizable form. Here again motivation may play a large part in the qualities of performance and the child may actually have the internal image but be uninvolved in the activity and be merely "going through the motions" to comply with the teacher's demands.

Suppose for a moment that this occurs: The child actually does not have the model but performs the motor act of moving his arm through the air in an approximation of the pattern of a letter. The effectiveness of this action may depend upon several factors—his motivational level or *intent to learn,* whether he verbalizes the letter name or sound at the same time, and whether the motor act is an exact but enlarged letter form or a sloppy general movement.

In tracing, the motor action actually is intended as a receptive support condition; in the writing in the air it is intended as an expressive support condition and what it may or may not be supporting is not directly observable by the teacher. Tracing has been researched and found to be an effective technique. Writing in the air awaits research effort but is worth trying to determine whether it may produce results with specific children.

Dot-to-Dot

Another support condition which can be helpful in learning the correct formation of letters is the dot-to-dot condition which allows the child to "construct" the letter perceptually. The letter is presented in a dot grid and the child draws lines from dot-to-dot, or the child finishes an incomplete form. (Presenting a com-

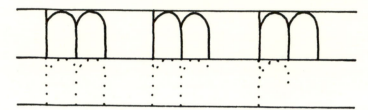

plete model just above the dot grid may circumvent some problems.) This has some advantages perceptually as the child's attention is directed to line segments of the letter, but it may not allow for or foster the continuity and flow of movement that characterizes motor memory. The teacher can decide about the use of this technique, basing it on child need in perceptual or motor terms. The fact that children usually enjoy it may be reason enough to include it.

Tactile Cues

Frequently a slight amount of resistance to the moving finger helps children perceive and execute forms. Drawing paper provides about the right amount of roughness. It is possible to use this surface repeatedly with children who are having extreme difficulties. It can be especially prepared by mimeographing lines on it for use in the introductory period.

Teachers often use sandpaper to increase tactile awareness. This is a questionable practice where form discrimination is intended, since sandpaper becomes an aversive stimuli with repetition. It may distract the child's attention from form perception and focus it instead on the discomfort in the finger itself or on surface qualities. When letter form discrimination and memory are main goals, tactile cues serve as a support condition in processing visual information. In letter form perception, tactile awareness or surface features are not goals in themselves. *Form* is the main goal. In a general perceptual stimulation program, tactile awareness of all surfaces might be an end objective. The teacher should understand this difference and be clear about why tactile perception is being used.

Manipulation

An added support condition can be given by using letters made of rubber, plastic or cardboard. The child can be encouraged to manipulate the letters with a moving hand and verbalize in order to enhance perception of the form . This will not automatically be transformed to the writing act; writing requires pencil guidance and awareness of line relationships. However, manipulation will assist in providing an internal image which may aid the child in becoming self-guiding. With small model letters, the child holds them in the palm of his hand, moving his fingers over the surface. With larger ones, he holds the letter with one hand and explores the surfaces with the fingers of the other hand.

Resistance

If children seem to have great difficulty in the control of the pencil, resistance can be introduced in order to develop skill. A clay pan can be prepared, with regular ceramic clay covering a baking pan large enough to provide a writing surface. The child writes in the clay with a pencil. This forces control in order to produce a legible letter. Children enjoy this activity and for those who have great difficulties this is a valuable teaching aid. The clay can be kept moist with wet towels and covered with plastic; a tongue depresser can be used to "erase" depressions from the clay. A sand pan can be prepared in the same manner. Since sand provides less resistance, as the child improves he can finally be shifted to writing on paper towels which provide even less resistance.

Developing Muscle Strength

Frequently the child will have a problem in writing because his fingers, arm and hand do not possess enough strength to control the writing instrument. If this seems to be the case, the following exercises are suggested to develop muscle strength. They are selected because they can be performed at a desk. It would also be helpful to include other exercises involving larger manipulative movements. These exercises can be practiced regularly for short periods preceding writing instruction. Each of the exercises is performed with the preferred hand.

1. Finger, wrist, elbow, and shoulder circling. Reverse direction each five times.
2. Finger tapping, one finger at a time, the others held immobilized each five times.
3. Finger figure eights with each finger five times.
4. Squeezing (modeling clay, a ball or pretense) five times.
5. Finger and hand waving—fingers held rigid, bend from first knuckle, second knuckle, third knuckle, and wrist five times.
6. Finger stretching—extend all fingers rigidly five times.
7. Fingers out and in with increasing tempo.
8. Separating fingers one at a time.
9. Individual fingers, waving from third knuckle five times each.
10. Opposing each finger to thumb five times.

Fluency

It is helpful to practice the basic strokes of either alphabet separately as fluency drills. The "push-pull" and the moving

(Repetitive Movements, Top Curve)

(Repetitive Movements, Bottom Curve)

(Ascending Loops)

(Reverse Direction, Curve)

(Reverse Direction, Straight Crossing of T's, or dotting of i's at the end of sequence in order to maintain continuity)

"ovals" can be very good exercise for cursive writing. The same kind of exercise can be given in manuscript by grouping down-strokes, slants, circles and curves. The continuity in cursive writing may requrie more endurance on the child's part and the following may prove helpful:

King (1968, p. 9) provides some distinctive exercises for cursive warmups:

Easy Exercises

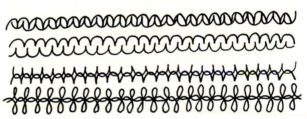

Difficult Exercises

Difficult exercises

Structure 28. (From King, D. H.: Some practical considerations in the teaching of handwriting. *Academic Therapy*, 4:7-12, 1968. Used with permission.)

These exercises are particularly good because they actually provide practice in the strokes which are used in cursive writing. These can be prepared on plastic-covered cards for tracing, using grease pencils which allow for erasures. The closer the exercise is to the form of the difficult strokes, the more useful it will be.

Developing Endurance

In this chapter a great deal of emphasis has been placed on knowledge of the formation of the individual letters. However, writing usually involves writing letters in words in sentences and this aspect should receive direct teaching attention.

Quite often children write for short periods and then the quality of their writing deteriorates. It may be helpful to the child with this problem to time and record the results of the writing periods, lengthening them slowly. It is very helpful for the child to be aware of the amount of writing that he produces before deterioration occurs. His awareness and intent to increase the amount alone can produce change. Teacher assistance in setting some expectations and keeping records about the amount and quality of the writing can provide a systematic rather than casual approach to the problem.

Rhythm

Music or a metronome can help the child maintain the writing flow. If the amount of writing produced before fatigue sets in is small, then these two supports are valuable. Rhythm and sequence are involved in all writing acts. Frequently the child cannot pace himself, but can be paced. Either the metronome or music can set the tempo and the child can be prepared to carry on alone when the pacing stops. This is an enjoyable and challenging activity and almost all children find it helpful.

Speed and Stress

Rarick and Harris (1963) looked at the writing of sixth graders under four different writing conditions: normal, fast, best, and relaxed. They classified the children as bright, average and slow. In general, they found that high legibility tended to occur with a slow rate, that the superior writers tended to produce legible writing under all conditions, and that legibility was a function of the condition of writing. They also measured galvanic skin response, muscular tension and fine motor control. They found that for the bright and average groups the greatest stress relations tended to occur in the fast writing condition and were accompanied by lower legibility. The least stress was observed during relaxed writing, but legibility was not always improved. Optimum speed can be determined on an individual basis.

Speed, however, may not be the only factor that should be observed. Rarick and Dobbins (1972) found several physical differences in children in special classes, and attention to physical strength and endurance should be included in any developmental or remedial teaching program for children with severe visual motor problems.

EVALUATION

Herrick and Okada (1963) also stressed the need for helping children evaluate their writing. They felt that children should be taught goal setting in relation to their performance. They called this kind of evaluation normative and aspirational perception. *Normative perception* relates to the child's ability to identify a sample of handwriting as like his own. It involves matching skills. *Aspirational perception* relates to the child's ability to choose and set a model as a goal for himself. This involves achievement motivation. In making this distinction, the researchers felt that more emphasis should be placed here than on letter formation drills. They felt that if a child does not possess a clear perception of his own handwriting, the use of an aspirational model—or a scale—would be ineffective in producing change. Teaching both aspirational and normative perception would involve analysis of form and errors with individual children and would provide excellent perceptual training as well as developing achievement motivation in a group of children in whom it is frequently weak or nonexistent.

Evaluation as Perceptual Training

In group or individualized teaching, the development of goals and standards or, stated more formally, of aspirational and normative perception is valuable. Most teachers can easily collect samples of an individual child's writing repeatedly as teaching proceeds. Using the child's own samples is an excellent method of developing self-evaluation of progress.

The child also needs to know what a "good" sample of handwriting looks like. He needs this in order to know what to emulate and to set a goal toward which he strives.

While a variety of handwriting scales are available commercially (Ayers, 1912; Freeman, 1958), they require training for effective use. "Scales that are developed for research purposes must permit fine discriminations among samples, thus, many quality levels must be provided" (Askov, Otto and Askov, 1970, p. 109). They go on to state that in the classroom these tend to have low reliability and are cumbersome in application. They suggest that an internalized scale developed through training and experience will probably be the most useful and point out the need for further research in this area.

In the meantime, the classroom or remedial teacher who is faced with finding a solution to the problem immediately can select some samples of handwriting from children within the school and rank them to use as comparison models. The teacher then helps the child compare his handwriting to the sample designated as "best, better, good, fair, or poor" and helps him visualize the difference in his performance in relation to the models in respect to:

1. letter form and characteristics,
2. line relationships,
3. spatial relationships,
4. relative size of letters,
5. slant,
6. pressure (line quality), and
7. fluency.

In this way, normative perception or comparison to a standard is being developed and internalized and specifics are set forth so that the child knows what qualities are causing a poor rating. At the same time, the teacher can help the child set goals which will make his own writing closer to the next step up on the scale, and aspirational perception is also being developed; these perceptions will not occur automatically, but they serve an important function in developing handwriting skill. As children go through the procedure of self- and normed-evaluation with teacher guidance, the amount of time spent in boring repetition and practice should be reduced. The process involves discrimination training which is at least half of the handwriting problem. If this were the only teaching done consistently with self- and normed-evaluations, including attention directed to the seven factors in the list given above, many children would probably improve because of the implicit perceptual training involved.

Using Other Writing Instruments and Tools

If the problem of control is severe, the child should be exposed to diversified experience with other tools. The use of hoes, rakes, brooms, hammers, saws, needles, eating utensils, and any other tool that requires eye-hand coordination can be valuable developmental experiences.

When diversified activities are included in any teaching program, expectations about their effectiveness should be *clarified*. Handwriting is a set of specific skills which can be trained directly. Diversified activities using other skills and tools involving eye-hand coordination—but not involving pencils, pens or letter forms—will not automatically produce improvement in handwriting. These activities should be used for relief activities in the academic program, for suggestions given to parents to help develop general manipulative skills in children where the problem is a severe one and involves other areas besides handwriting. For most children, direct training is sufficient.

Writing instruments may also be diversified and used in an "easy-to-more-difficult" order. Paintbrushes as writing instruments can be helpful because of the ease of movement. Chalkboard writing can be useful because of the large arm movements involved. Flow-pens are also easy to control and can be included as well as crayons; but finally, training should focus on the pencil which may not be easy but difficult to control.

Posture

The child should be sitting in his chair with his feet flat on the floor. His body should be comfortably straight and leaning slightly forward, not touching the desk. The child should assume the responsibility for maintaining this posture, based on his understanding of its importance. Teachers can help with this problem by setting it as one of the conditions in the evaluation period.

Arm Position

The forearm should rest on the largest part of the arm muscle and be able to move freely. The hand should rest on the fleshly side of the palm and should slide easily. The wrist should be turned *somewhat* to the right.

Arm Movement and Relaxation

Practicing that involves movement of the arm will be helpful in developing a more relaxed grip on the writing tool and will also help the child learn to maintain the quality of the writing for longer periods of time.

In order to make certain that the child grasps the pencil without undue tension may require direct verbal instruction, supervision and extrinsic motivators. As the teacher suggests and demonstrates a loose rather than a tense grasp, the quality of the writing may deteriorate. The teacher and the child should persist until the "feeling" of loose control becomes familiar to the child. The attention is directed only to the feeling of "easy" direction of the pencil, not to the quality or amount of writing. The child may resist and maintain the old grip because the looseness at first generates a feeling of loss of control and panic. If this is verbalized, it will help the child overcome such fear and gradually attend to the perceptual motor aspects involved.

Paper Position

For manuscript writing, the paper should be placed on the desk so that the lower edge of the paper is parallel to the front edge without a slant. For cursive writing the lower edge of the paper should be at right angles to the writing arm. This means tilted about 30° for the right-handed writer. While this is the Peterson-suggested correct position for the left- and right-handed writers, Enstrom's study shows that children prefer a tilt of about 45°. Lerner suggests that "the paper is tilted at an angle approximately sixty degrees from vertical . . . (p. 192)." This divergence of opinion allows the teacher some leeway. Again, observation of the optimum performance of the individual child in relationship to the degree of tilt will provide the guide which is necessary.

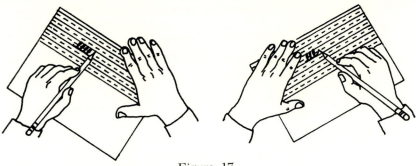

Figure 17.

Grip

The pencil should be held *lightly* and firmly. It should be held by the thumb and the first two fingers. The index finger should rest on top of the pencil and the second finger should be at the side and the same distance from the point, about an inch. The thumb should be slightly above the first or index finger. The end of the pencil should point over the writing shoulder. This means the wrist is flat on the table rather than tilted on the fleshy outer edge of the palm.

Commercial grips are available if the child has persistent problems. These are small one-inch sleeves which slip over the pencil and insure proper grip. A rubber band can be placed on the pencil to insure that the pencil is griped the proper distance from the point, or a piece of adhesive tape can be applied. Grip is very important in control and extra attention should be given to it in the initial teaching to prevent difficulty.

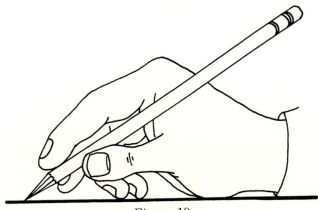

Figure 18.

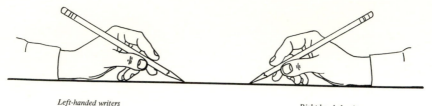

Left-handed writers   *Right-handed writers*

Figure 19.

Changing an Awkward Grip

Teachers frequently ask about suggestions for changing a grip which is too tense, improperly placed and often very unusual as far as finger positions are concerned. This is not easy to accomplish but neither is it impossible. Two suggestions are offered.

1. Use a plastic grip (a sleeve which fits over the pencil and insures correct finger position). Reinforce the use systematically.

2. Precision teaching (Lindsley, 1971) is a useful technique for this problem.

3. Provide teacher-guided instruction on a daily basis, in ten to fifteen minute sessions, with verbalization of correct position and reinforcement of effort as well as achievement. When this strategy is used, six weeks should be the *least* amount of time provided to make the change. The teacher's expectations of change should be realistic so that the child can be supported in practice periods, which at first seem to be useless. With persistence, the correct position will be assumed by the child and can be reinforced by the teacher. After the six weeks of regular training sessions, a *regular intermittent* schedule of practice is suggested; the child should be encouraged and reinforced by the teacher for use of the correct position, outside the training periods. This will take planning with the child in order to set goals and observation by the teacher in order to reinforce and support the correct position when it is assumed by the child without teacher guidance.

Writing Instruments

In the study of writing instruments, Herrick (1961) reported that children prefer adult pencils over beginning pencils and that no objective evidence is available for supporting the use of beginning pencils.

Pencil Size

Any pencil that is comfortable for the child is adequate at any age. However, the teacher should observe the children with perceptual motor difficulties to see if, on an individual basis, the factor of size does facilitate performance.

The Left-handed Writer

The single most important factor in success for the left-handed writer is *correct paper position*. If the child has difficulty remembering the correct paper position, it should be permanently indicated on his desk with tape. No slant is indicated for manuscript.

Enstrom (1962, p. 577) has indicated the positions that left-handed children prefer for cursive writing. Hand below the line, or the "hook" position is the most common. However, the following illustrations (redrawn from Enstrom) show frequent positions preferred by left-handed children.

Children with orientation problems frequently shift their papers. By indicating the position on the desk, this can be avoided.

Most experts agree that "pencil below the line" is preferable to the "hook." The question of changing a child who uses the "hook" will depend upon his proficiency with this grip and position. It is very difficult to change if the child does not indicate a desire to do so. If resistance is too great for change, the teacher should insist on legibility.

Emerson (1954) has suggested that before a child begins a practice session, he should be in proper position and practice swinging an arc with his pencil in his hand so that he gets the "feel" of relaxed movement across the page. She also suggests warm up drills with groups of downstrokes all at the same slant.

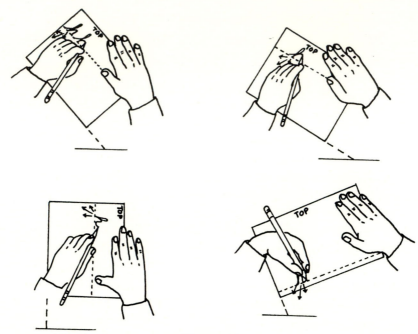

Figure 20.

The important aspect of this drill is that the strokes are grouped and keep moving across the page, and that relaxation is emphasized. The same would be true for right-handed children.

The Ambi-Nondextrous Child

If a young child (kindergarten, first grade) seems to pick up writing tools alternating hands and seems to write equally well (or poorly) with either hand, the teacher should begin to record preferences at a regular time during the day. This should be done for a long enough period of time to begin to see a pattern of preference. If no pattern appears, the product of the writing should be examined to determine whether right or left hand is producing better performance. The teacher can then safely reinforce the use of either the preferred hand or the superior performance.

The same procedure would be carried out with an older child, but he also could be asked about his preference.

SOME SPECIAL PROBLEMS

Reversals in Manuscript Writing

All teachers are familiar with this problem. The *b-d* orientation is very difficult for some young children and often continues as a problem for some low achievers. Many authorities favor cursive writing for this reason. Frequently children also have difficulty with the joining of letters in cursive writing and in the reversal of direction in movements. Thus, each form presents some difficulties which will provide stumbling blocks for children with directionality problems. While the *b-d* confusion is the most common and often asked about by teachers, other letters are also confused, *p-q*, *u-n*, *m-w*, and so forth. Directionality problems are the most common, but other discrimination difficulties are also frequent. These involve *h-n*, *m-n*, *f-t* as common examples and all of the vowels also present arduous discriminations. The following steps are suggested when there are directionality or discrimination problems related to manuscript writing.

Primarily, this technique involves prevention. The teacher analyzes the handwriting sample of the child and picks out the confusions which are to be eradicated. The teacher then presents the child with a sentence containing the problem letters or they make up one together. The confusing letters are presented separately. If perception of the letter *b* is being taught, the sentence will not contain the *d*. The teacher then makes certain the *child works from a model and not from imagery*. As the child is projecting an incorrect orientation onto the letter, the first step is to interfere and make certain the letter is correctly written a sufficient number of times to "set" the orientation internally. What usually occurs is uncertainty or confusion on the part of the child in orientation of the letter, and uncertainty on the part of the teacher as to what to do about it. No systematic approach is used. In working on the orientation of the letter *b*, the teacher would work with the child on a sentence containing the letter *b*, possibly "The baby bit big bananas." Seeing this as a rote teaching exercise, a little humor in the sentence might lighten the drudgery of the task. The child should also be made aware of the teaching goal so that he understands that he is confusing the letters and that the teaching strategy is going to correct the confusion.

As the child writes and comes to the *b*, the teacher presents a correct model from which the child copies. This is placed immediately above his writing sample so that visual shift problems are not introduced. The child always works with the teacher and from a correctly oriented model in the initial stage of the teaching. The teacher says, "This letter is a *b* and is made like this." As orientation is the prime visual cue on which the teaching is focusing, the verbalization is directed to that problem. "The line comes first and the half-circle comes next." Closure is brought by then saying the name of the letter. Each time the letter needs to be written, the teacher places a correct model just above the line on which it is to be written and the child copies it under teacher supervision, verbalizing visual cues. The model can be a lightly written letter or a printed one on a small card which is placed above the line during the writing act. *The child always works from a model, not from memory.* As the teaching progresses, the child will begin to indicate that he remembers the orientation. He will say, "I can do it," or a similar phrase to indicate that he thinks he has mastered the problem. The teacher continues the individual teaching but shifts strategy. The problem-oriented sentences are still presented but instead of interfering and presenting the model the teacher reminds the child, "This is a *b*, so think about which way it goes." "How do you write this letter?" "What comes first?" The direction, through hand movements without writing, may even be indicated. As the teaching progresses and the child makes fewer and fewer errors in spontaneous writing, the teaching strategy again shifts and the teacher presents the "problem-oriented sentence" but allows the child to perform and evaluates after the sentence is finished with immediate corrections if errors occur.

To summarize these three steps:

Interfere: present the correct model, do not work from memory;

Remind: have the child think about the orientation as the problem letter arises. Verbalize the orientation;

Evaluate: allow the child to perform without direction.

Correct mistakes immediately.

This technique was designed to deal with orientation problems, but could also be used with problems relating to line, size, or spatial relationships. It takes approximately six weeks of teaching to make certain the child has had sufficient practice in the correct orientation to be able to perform in spontaneous writing without error.

Another technique which might be faster is one which involves systematic discrimination training with the two letters that are presenting the problem. This is a "forced discrimination" technique. The teacher must also be working directly with the child to make certain that the child verbalizes correctly. The child says *b*'s and *d*'s at first in alternation and after he performs correctly, in random sequence. Again the child must be working with teacher or peer guidance. The aims are to fix the correct associations and to establish automatic performance. The size of the letters should be quite large to begin with and reduced in size as the training proceeds.

> *Alternating*: The teacher says: "This is a *b* and this is a *d*. (Points to each.) Put your finger under each letter and say them as fast as you can."
>
> *Random*: Random sequence after the alternating sequence is performed correctly.

Following the theory that improved motor performance occurs as the result of improved perception, the child is then asked to write the letters on teacher demand. (Mnemomics and unusual associations are also helpful.)

The Problem of Reversing Direction in Cursive Writing

Many intermediate grade children have difficulty with letters which require a change of direction in writing. Particular letters which seem to pose the greatest difficulties are *o*, *a* and *d*. However, any letter which requires a return sweep on an already written line will present the same difficulty.

All present this problem.

The first remedial strategy is to make the child aware of the problem so that he can participate in an active attempt at solution. Tracing and verbalization will help many children. However, when language does not effectively direct motor performance, the best strategy involves positioning the hand through the movements with verbalization, five or six times on a regular basis at a certain time during the writing period. The teacher guides the child's hand through the movements with verbalization, has the child practice doing the same, and then watches the spontaneous writing in regular assignments to indicate when guidance is no longer necessary. In this case, motor memory is being developed at an automatic level. It may be very helpful for some children to start with large muscle movements at the board and then systematically reduce the size of the movement to writing large on paper, perhaps using primary paper for this task, and shifting to smaller lines until the child can perform on paper that is regularly used at his grade level. In this case, perception and motor performance are being improved simultaneously and verbalization of the cue that the child has not attended to is very important in this activity. Something like, "Over and back on the same line, around and up and touch, down and touch the line around and up and finish," might accompany the writing of the letter *a*. The teacher adapts the verbalization for each letter.

Following a form, the teacher systematically analyzes handwriting samples and writes in the lessons for the next day. The letter or letter connections are presented in a correct model with lines left for practice. The letters or connections are also presented in various positions in words with lines for practice. Spatial relationships rather than connections are important in manuscript writing. Finally, a sentence is given which provides for practice in writing the problem letters in movement across a page. This is done very systematically until the change is reflected in spontaneous writing. The practice page might look like this (Figure 21). Lines are left between each exercise for the child's work.

Practice in isolation:	g g g g g g g g g
Practice in words:	good beg engine
Practice in a sentence:	The grey bag is big.
General control and fluency—strokes (The descender with a curve)	J J J J J J J J J
(The curve)	C C C C C C C C C

Figure 21. Practice form for manuscript writing.

SUMMARY

Teaching handwriting has been proposed as the ideal vehicle for a visual motor training program because it deals directly with the symbols which are used in the language arts. Briefly, the suggestions are summarized as follow:

1. *Start training early*—begin in kindergarten for those children who have difficulty remembering the alphabet or excessive difficulty with writing and drawing.
2. *Group the letters* using the Gibson classification of straight curve, intersection, redundancy and discontinuity or any of the others suggested. Emphasize distinctive features, differences and contrasts.

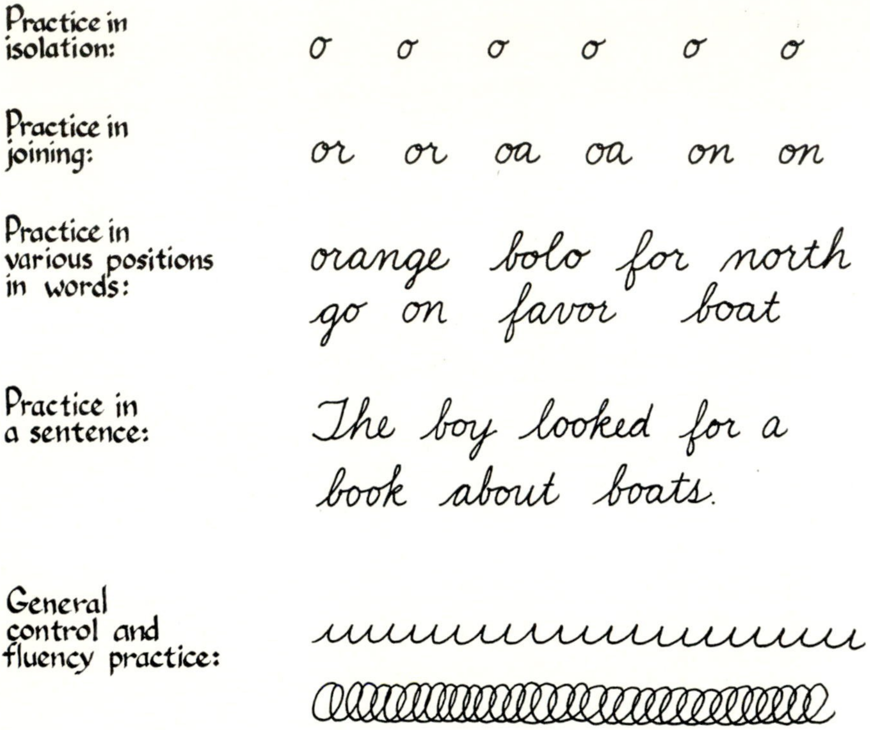

Practice in
isolation:

o   o   o   o   o   o

Practice in
joining:

or   or   oa   oa   on   on

Practice in
various positions
in words:

*orange   bolo   for   north
go   on   favor   boat*

Practice in
a sentence:

*The boy looked for a
book about boats.*

General
control and
fluency practice:

Figure 22.   Practice form for cursive writing.

3. *Verbalize salient visual cues and the motor act* using the
   Gibson classification as a guide for verbalizing visual cues
   and the Furner suggestions for verbalizing the motor act
   itself.

4. *Model and require imitation.* This strategy is intended to
   provide visual cues in the modeling phase which cannot
   be easily verbalized or may have been missed. It provides
   an opportunity for immediate correction of error and is
   likely to be more successful if the teacher is "nururant"—
   warm and accepting.

5. *Reinforcement.* This variable involves motivation and the
   strengthening of appropriate successful performance. It
   is most effective when the reinforcement is immediate and
   is positive.

6. *Tracing.* The intent of this support condition is to develop visual perception. The finger and arm movements pick up all of the visual information available in the letter. It does not involve spontaneous or self-directed performance and the motor act is being used in behalf of the visual one.

7. *Writing in the air* is intended as a kinesthetic or motor support for visual perception.

8. *Dot-to-dot or broken line.* In this strategy it is assumed that the child will "construct" the letter. The intent is to develop an awareness of the total form through a process of assembling its parts. It is a "synthetic" technique and destroys the continuous motor patterning involved in making the "strokes" as the letter is being written. It is a technique which may not be equally valuable for all children.

9. *Positioning.* The intent of this technique is to develop motor memory patterns; visual cues are secondary.

10. *Manipulation* is intended to focus on visual cues and to strengthen the visual input by actually touching in three dimensions what is usually perceived in only two. The motor involvement does not include pencil guidance but coordination of eye-hand movements. *Tactile cues* use differences in surface textures, again to heighten awareness of visual form and focus more perceptual attention on the finger which is guiding the eye. Again, no pencil direction is involved but eye-hand coordination is implicit.

11. *Resistance.* The intent of this technique is to strengthen motor control; no visual cues are available but are projected from the cognitive image. (Use wet clay or wet sand in this exercise.)

12. *Developing muscle strength.* This strategy is employed to make certain the finger, hand and arm muscles can support the visual-motor skills. The child may possess a clear visual image and know the motor pattern involved and yet not have the strength necessary to guide the pencil through the writing act.

13. *Endurance.* Attention to this variable is intended to help a child with intact visual perceptual skills whose performance deteriorates in relation to the amount of writing required; motor skills are primarily involved here.
14. *Evaluation.* Both normative evaluation where a child compares his writing to a standard, and aspirational evaluation where a child decides how much better he wants to make his handwriting, can be valable in developing perceptual skills. Both evaluations demand that comparison and differences be made and noted; they involve perceptual judgment.

It should be quite clear, in summary, that the emphasis in this discussion has been on developing visual and visual-motor skills in a discrimination training program involving language symbols. The main point made has been that learning the alphabet for writing provides excellent content for learning to discriminate the forms which need to be read.

While a training program based on the variables which have been suggested will be of benefit to children who have discrimination problems, *it will not remediate associational problems which may also be present.* In other words, teaching a child to recognize and correctly produce the letters will not deal with the symbol-sound (reading) or the sound-symbol (spelling) relationships or sequencing problems he may also have. The associational and sequencing problems involve another set of teaching strategies and will be dealt with in the discussion on the *Reading Spelling Inversion* and *Teaching Spelling to Develop Perceptual Skill.*

A SAMPLE TEACHING SEQUENCE

MODEL	1. Model the correct writing of the letter.
VERBALIZE VISUAL CUES AND SET EXPECTATIONS FOR IMITATION	2. Guide the children in verbalizing visual cues and exact steps in each letter writing process. *Tell the children you are going to expect them to do and say exactly what you are doing.* (Do this at the board—use lines.)
Use Consistent Terminology	(a) Use consistent terminology for strokes and direction (clockwise turn, or counter-clock-

wise, or "left and right" for direction of turn, and straight line and circle for strokes).

Children Verbalize Exactly What Is Done

(b) Help them say precisely what is done. "In the letter *b*, the straight line begins at the head line, goes straight down, and crosses the center-line and ends right on the base line. The circle starts on the right side of the straight line, just below the center line and goes up the center-line to make the circle around to the right. It touches the base-line and turns up and touches the straight-line." The teacher is writing and saying at the board; the children are watching and saying (murmuring).

Children Verbalize Starting and Stopping Points

(c) Help them observe and say starting and stopping points on all letters.

Children Verbalize Directions

(d) Help them observe and say the direction of the stroke. "In the letter small *o*, the circle begins on the center-line, curves left, touches the base-line, curves up to the right and ends, where it began, on the center-line."

Children Verbalize Size

(e) Demonstrate (model) again using the *O* and this time emphasize size. Make the letter too large for the lines on the board. Help the children say, "It is too large." Make it smaller.
Help the children say, "It is too small." Help the children verbalize the exact description of the lines that the letter touches and the direction in which it must go.

Children Verbalize Peer Modeling Performance

(f) Use a child to model the letter at the board and have other children verbalize the exact process. (The children verbalize together, aloud.)

Child Imitates Exactly

(g) Establish by teacher model and child verbalization and imitation: sitting posture, hand position, pencil grip, paper position, and verbal behavior.

Child Writes and Verbalizes for Self

(h) Ask the children to write each letter three times and to try to improve each time—verbalizing the process softly to himself. ("Say, what you are doing (to yourself), just as I did. Do and say what I did and said.")

Children Verbalize Likeness and Differences in Groups

(i) As letters in the various groups are introduced, call attention to similarities and differences i.e., *o, c, e,* and *a.* Have the children verbalize these.

Child Verbalizes Practice in Letters and in Words and Sentences

(j) Practice the letter in isolation and later in words to develop spatial awareness. Have the child verbalize how much space is required between letters. Later, use simple sentences.

POSITIONING

3. Difficulties in Form Perception.

(a) If the child has difficulty in forming the letters, the teacher can guide the child's hand and help with the exact verbalization. This involves "positioning" the child's hand so that he learns the correct motor pattern. This technique requires consistent use to be maximally effective i.e., five "positionings" each day on each letter being studied.

Tracing

(b) For some children it may be helpful to provide a graphic tracing model. (Straight line or dot-to-dot.)

Tactile and Kinesthetic Cues

(c) Some children may be helped by including tactile cues. (These should not be aversive i.e., sandpaper.) Drawing paper, because of its *slightly* rough surface, may increase the awareness of form.

Manipulation

(d) Some children may be helped by feeling, *with a moving hand,* all of the verbalized visual cues in the letter. "Here is a straight, long stick with a curve on the right near the end. It goes around the bottom of the stick and stops. There is an empty space in the middle of the circle."

ESTABLISH GRIP

4. Difficulties in Motor Performance.

(a) If a child has difficulty in controlling the writing instrument, make certain pencil grip is comfortable and clearly understood. (Use a groove or a commercial grip aid if necessary to establish correct distance from the point—about one inch.)

Develop Finger Dexterity

(b) Use the suggested exercises to develop manipulative control and dexterity, if fingers seem weak.

Vary Writing Instruments

(c) Practice letter formations with a variety of writing instruments (paintbrush, chalk, felt pen, crayon, pencil).

Use Resistant Materials

(d) Practice letter formation in or on resistant materials: a clay pan, a wet sand pan, sandpaper, paper towels.

5. Grip, posture, and position.

    (a) The writer should face the desk, rest both arms upon it. For manuscript writing, the paper should be placed on the desk so that the lower edge of the paper is parallel to the front edge of the desk. For cursive writing, the lower edge of the paper should be at right angles to the writing arm. This means tilted about 30 degrees for the right-handed writer.

    (b) The forearm should rest on the muscle pad at its largest part and should be able to move freely from left to right to carry the hand across the page or up and down.

    (c) The hand should rest on the last joint of the last two fingers and should slide easily. The wrist should be turned a little to the right.

    (d) The pencil should be held lightly by the thumb and first two fingers, the index finger on top and the second finger at the side and the same distance from the point. The thumb should be above the first or index finger. The pencil would be held not less than an inch from the point.

    (e) For the left-handed writer, the following positions are suggested, as described in the given order to insure quality, rate, freedom from smearing, posture. The suggested position is the writing hand held below the line rather than the writing hand above the line which is known as the "hook." (The hook has inherent probelms in the difficulty of sliding the side of the hand forward in carrying the writing across the page and in the smearing tendencies.

Left-handed positions:
Writing hand below the line:

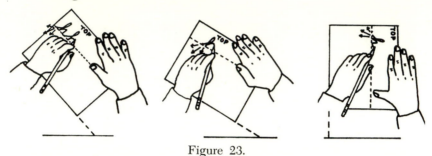

Figure 23.

Writing hand above the line (the "hook"):

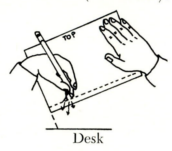

Desk

Figure 24.

EVALUATION

6. Help the child compare his performance with previous (aspirational) samples and with standard (normative) models and set expectations for improved performance.

MATCHING EXERCISES

Teachers frequently use matching exercises in initial alphabet instruction. These exercises are very common in reading and writing readiness materials. Based on the rationale that improved perception means improved production, there is justification for including matching exercises in handwriting instruction as well. Using some of the ideas from Gibson Matrix (1969), reproduced on p. 217, distinctive features can be selected for providing contrasts. Paired with verbalization to direct the scanning behavior which is presumed to occur in visual reception and kinesthetic teaching with systematic tracing and manipulation of letter form, an excellent training program could be developed in the primary grades for any child who evidenced difficulty.

In order to provide systematic matching exercises, Pick's Matrix (1970, p. 171) for matching artificial letter form could be adapted for this task. The chart (Fig. 25) presents a stimulus figure and systematically varies it in categories such as straight line changed to curve; 45, 90 and 180 degree rotations; right-left and up-down reversals; changes in perspective such as size and line slant, and topological changes such as breaks and closures.

In the chart (Fig. 26) which follows, the left-hand vertical column contains the stimulus letter and the horizontal categories are: (1) straight to curve or curve to straight, (2) stimulus figure, (3) a 45 degree rotation, (4) a 90 degree rotation, (5) stimulus figure, (6) right-left reversal, (7) stimulus figure, (8) up-down reversal, (9) stimulus figure, (10) perspective transformation, (11) break, (12) stimulus figure, and (13) open-close. The child is asked to mark all of the letters that look like the first letter.

The following chart presents the categories of letters for comparison purposes to the child and specifies the characteristics which are being isolated. When children make mistakes, the errors can be analyzed by the teacher and speical exercises devised to clarify the child's perceptual confusion. Reversals are very common during the primary period and special emphasis should be placed on orientation awareness in instruction. Most of the terms in the chart are self-explanatory; discontinuity refers to line ends; "redundant" indicates a repetition, and "symmetry" indicates balance and regularity in form.

The previous activities can provide for the perception of the letters without performance. However, when children write the letters support can be given for perception and production by verbalizing and touching, tracing, and manipulating the letters. In order to establish the fact that the child has had systematic training in individual letter perception, teachers can easily provide a chart of the letters and go over the five characteristics and

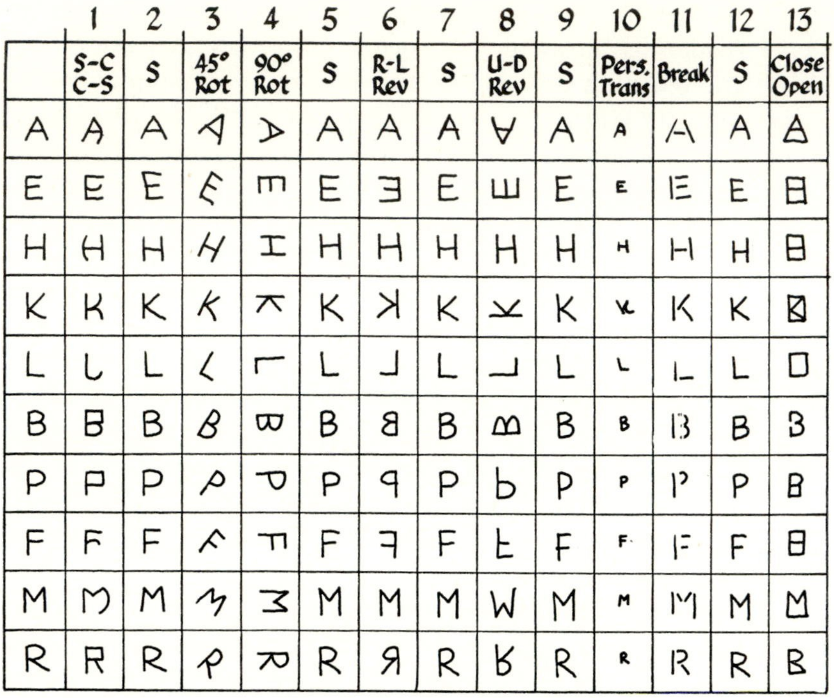

	1	2	3	4	5	6	7	8	9	10	11	12	13
	S-C C-S	S	45° Rot	90° Rot	S	R-L Rev	S	U-D Rev	S	Pers. Trans	Break	S	Close Open
A	A	A	A	◁	▷	A	A	A	∀	A	ʌ	/\	A	A
E	E	E	E	Ɛ	m	E	Ǝ	E	Ш	E	ᴇ	Ⅼ	E	⊟
H	H	H	H	Ƶ	I	H	H	H	H	H	ʜ	H	H	⊟
K	K	ʀ	K	∢	ㅈ	K	⋋	K	⋎	K	ᴋ	K	K	⊠
L	L	∪	L	⟨	Γ	L	⌐	L	⌐	L	ʟ	∟	L	☐
B	B	�ʙ	B	ß	⅏	B	ꓭ	B	⋒	B	ʙ	⅃ʒ	B	ʒ
P	P	ꟼ	P	⍴	℧	P	ꟼ	P	b	P	ᴘ	ᒋ	P	ꓔ
F	F	ꜰ	F	⋏	⊓	F	ꓞ	F	Ł	F	ꜰ	⊧	F	⊟
M	M	ᴍ	M	⅄	Ʒ	M	M	M	W	M	ᴹ	ᴍ	M	⊔
R	R	ʀ	R	℘	⋊	R	ꓤ	R	ʁ	R	ʀ	⅁	R	ꓐ

Figure 25. Matching letter form.

their subskills with each letter with each child who needs this training. If the child had difficulty with the letter after the verbalized teaching, the child could trace the letter and, if difficulties persisted, could manipulate the letter. The materials required (Fig. 27) would be a chart of the letters, a tracing form and a set of manipulable letters, some paper for writing the letters or a small chalkboard. Children should begin the writing in kindergarten at a chalkboard or at least on unlined paper.

Straights	H	I	L	H	F	E	T
Straight + Curve	R	B	D	G	P	R	Q
Straights + Redundants	E	F	H	T	E	F	H
Straights + Slant	K	M	N	K	Y	Z	K
Curves + Intersections	B	D	P	R	B	Q	B
Discontinuity + Vertical	A	F	H	I	T	K	A
Redundancy Symmetry	N	A	E	H	K	M	N
Curve Open	J	C	G	S	U	J	C
Closed	D	B	O	D	R	Q	P

Figure 26.

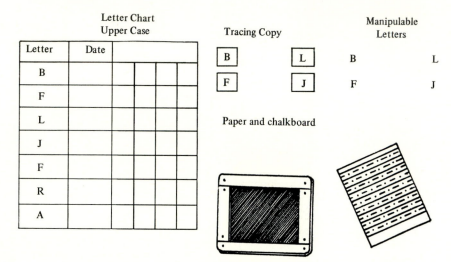

Letter Chart
Upper Case

Letter	Date				
B					
F					
L					
J					
F					
R					
A					

Tracing Copy

B   L

F   J

Paper and chalkboard

Manipulable
Letters

B   L

F   J

Figure 27.

Figure 28. (From Noble, J. K.: *Better Handwriting for You.* Book 1. California State Series, California State Department of Education, 1967.)

Aa Bb Cc Dd Ee Ff Gg
Hh Ii Jj Kk Ll Mm
Nn Oo Pp Qq Rr Ss
Tt Uu Vv Ww Xx Yy Zz
1 2 3 4 5 6 7 8 9 10 ? . :

Figure 29. (*Ibid.*, Book 5.)

BIBLIOGRAPHY

1. Amster, H.: Concept formation in children. *Elem Engl,* 42:543-551, 1965.
2. Askov, E.; Otto, W., and Askov, W.: A decade of research in handwriting: progress and prospect. *J Ed Resh, 64,* #3, 1970.
3. Ayers, L. P.: *A Scale for Measuring the Quality of Handwriting.* New York, Russell Sage Foundation, 1920.
4. Bandura, Albert: The role of modeling processes in personality development. In Gelfand, D. M. (Ed.): *Social Learning in Childhood, Readings in Theory and Application.* Belmont, 1969.
5. Berros, M.: Personal communication. June, 1972.
6. Berry, W.: Italic writing. *Edt Digest,* April, 50-51, 1961.
7. Birch, H. G., and Lefford, A.: Visual differentiation, inter-sensory integration and voluntary motor control. *Monographs of the Society for Research in Child Development 32,* 110, #2, 1967.
8. Bloom, B. S.: *Stability and Change in Human Characteristics.* New York, Wiley, 1964.
9. Byers, L.: The relationship of manuscript and cursive handwriting to accuracy in spelling. *J Ed Resh,* 57:87-89, 1963.
10. Duncan, A. D.: Precision teaching in perspective: an interview with O. R. Lindsley. *Teaching Excep Children,* 3, #3, 1971.
11. Emerson, Dorothy: *Help Yourself to Better Handwriting.* Cambridge, Ed Pub Ser, 1954.
12. Enstrom, E. A.: The relative efficiency of the various approaches to writing with the left hand. *J Ed Resh,* 55:573-577, 1962.
13. Fernald, G. M.: *Remedial Techniques in Basic School Subjects.* New York ,McGraw, 1943.
14. Fowler, W.: Cognitive learning in infancy and early childhood. *Psychol Bull,* 59(2):116-152, 1962.
15. Freeman, Frank N.: *Evaluation Scale for Guiding Growth in Handwriting.* Columbus, Zaner Bloser, 1958.
16. Freeman, Frank N.: What research says to the teacher, No. 4 *Teaching Handwriting.* Washington, Am Ed Resh Assoc., NEA, 1962.
17. Frostig, M., and Horne, D.: *The Frostig Program for the Development of Visual Perception.* Chicago, Follett ,1964.
18. Furner, B. A.: An analysis of the effectiveness of a program of instruction emphasizing the perceptual motor nature of learning in handwriting. *Elem Engl,* 47:61-69, 1970.
19. Furner, B. A.: The perceptual motor nature of learning in handwriting. *Elem Engl,* 46:886-894, 1969 (a).
20. Furner, B. A.: Recommended instructional procedures in a method emphasizing the perceptual motor nature of learning in handwriting. *Elem Engl,* 46:1021-1030, 1969 (b).

21. Gibson, E. J.: *Principles of Perceptual Learning and Development.* New York, Appleton, 1969.
22. Gibson, J. J.: *The Senses Considered as Perceptual Systems.* Boston, Houghton, 1966.
23. Gillingham, A., and Stillman, B.: *Remedial Training for Children with Specific Disability in Reading, Spelling and Penmanship.* New York, Sackett and Wilhelms, 1940.
24. Hebb, D. O.: *The Organization of Behavior.* New York, Wiley, 1949.
25. Herrick, V. E., and Okada, N.: The present scene: practices in the teaching of handwriting in the United States. In Herrick, V. E. (Ed.): *New Horizons for Research in Handwriting.* Madison, U of Wis Pr, 1963.
26. Hess, R. D., and Shipman, V.: Early experience and the socialization of cognitive modes in children. *Child Develop, 36*:869-886, 1965.
27. Hewitt, F. M.: A hierarchy of educational tasks for children with learning disorders. *Except Children, 31*(4):207-214, 1964.
28. Hooper, J. E.: *Analysis of Winterhaven Project; in a Preliminary Report.* Winterhaven Study of Perceptual Learning. Winter Haven, Fla., Winter Haven Lions Res. Found. 1962.
29. Hunt, V. McV.: *Intelligence and Experience.* New York, Ronald, 1961.
30. Jensen, A. R., and Rohwer, W. D., Jr.: Verbal mediation in paired associate and serial learning. *J Verbal Learn and Verbal Behav, 1*:346-353, 1963.
31. Kephart, N. C.: *The Slow Learner in the Classroom.* Columbus, Merrill, 1960.
32. Keogh, B .K.: Optometric vision training programs for children with learning disabilities. Review of issues and research. *J Learn Disabil, 7*(4), 1974.
33. King, Diana Hanbury: Some practical considerations in the teaching of handwriting. *Acad Therapy, 4*(1):7-12, 1968.
34. Lerner, J.: *Children with Learning Disabilities.* Boston, Houghton, 1971.
35. Lewis, E., and Lewis, H.: Which manuscript letters are hard for first graders? *Elem Engl, 41*:855-858, 1964.
36. Levine, Norman, and Carter, Joan: Handwriting for the learning disabled. *Acad Therapy, 4*(1):35-38, 1968.
37. Luria, A. R.: The role of language in the formation of temporary connections. In Simon, B. (Ed.): *Psychology in the Soviet Union.* Stanford, Stanford U Pr, 1957.
38. Maccoby, E. E.: What copying requires. *Ontario J Ed Resh, 10*:163-170, 1968.
39. Maier, Arlee: Personal communication, 1973.

40. Milner, Esther: A study of the relationship between reading readiness and patterns of parent child interaction. *Child Develop, 22*:95-112, 1951.

41. Montessori, M.: *Spontaneous Activity in Education.* New York, Schocken, 1965.

42. Newland, T. E.: An analytical sutdy of the development of illegibilities in handwriting from the lower grades to adulthood. *J Ed Resh, 26*:249-258, 1932.

43. Noble, J. Kendrick: *Better Handwriting for You.* California State Series, Book 4. Sacramento, Calif State Dept of Education, 1967.

44. Peterson, P.: *Adventures in Handwriting, Peterson Directed Handwriting, Teacher's Edition,* Book 5. New York, Macmillan, 1965.

45. Pick, A. D.: Some basic perceptual processes in reading. *Young Children, 25*:162-181, 1970.

46. Quant, L.: Factors affecting the legibility of handwriting. *J Ex Child, 14*:297-316, 1946.

47. Rarick, G. L., and Dobbins, D. A.: *Basic Components in the Motor Performance of Educable Mentally Retarded Children: Implications for Curriculum Development.* Final Report, Dept HEW. Berkeley, Dept Physical Education, 1972.

48. Rarick, G. L., and Harris, T. L.: Physiological and motor correlates of handwriting legibility. In Herrick, N. E. (Ed.): *New Horizons for Research in Handwriting.* Madison, U of Wisconsin Pr, 1963.

49. Schell, L. M., and Burns, P. C.: Retention and changes by college students of certain upper-case cursive letter forms. *Elem Engl, 40*:513-517, 1963.

50. Simon, D. P., and Simon, H. A.: Alternative uses of phonemic information in spelling. *Rev Ed Resh, 43*(1), 1973.

51. Sklar, B., and Hanley, J., M.D.: A multi-fontal alphabet for Dyslectic children. *J Learn Disab, 5*(3):160-164, 1972.

52. Slingerland, B. II.: Early identification of preschool children who might fail. *Acad Therapy,* No. 4(Summer), 1969.

53. Smith, K. U., and Smith, W. M.: *Perception and Motion.* Philadelphia, Saunders, 1962.

54. Stones, E.: Verbal labelling and concept formation in primary school children. *Br J Ed Psychol, 40*:245-252, 1970.

55. Vygotsky, L. S.: *Thought and Language.* New York, Wiley, 1962.

NAME INDEX

SUBJECT INDEX

A

Abstraction, 19-20
  see also Reading-spelling inversion,
    perceptual theory
Air-writing, 242-243
  see also Handwriting, motor
    performance
Alphabet, California State Series
    alphabet, 225
  cursive, 219, 221, 226-228, 229-230
  Emerson left- and right-hand, 225
  Initial Teaching Alphabet, 46
  manuscript, 219, 221, 223-225, 226-
    228, 229
  see also Handwriting, perceptual
    skills
Arm position, 252
  see also Handwriting, evaluation
Association, 7, 17
  see also Reading-spelling inversion
Attention behavior, 19
  abstraction, 19-20
    filtering, 20
  attention span or duration, 22-23
  impulsivity vs. reflectivity, 20-21
  scanning, 21-22
  see also Reading-spelling inversion,
    perceptual theory
Auditory Conceptualization Test, 44
Auditory perceptual skills,
    developmental importance of, 33
  see also Reading-spelling inversion,
    Communication System
    Hierarchy

B

Basic Integrating Core Vocabulary, 73,
  205-206
  additional words, 206-207

Basic Sight Vocabulary, 83, 199
Boehm Basic Concept Test, 87

C

Categorization, 7, 17-18
  see also Reading-spelling inversion
Communication System Hierarchy, *see*
    Reading-spelling inversion
Comparison, 16
  see also Reading-spelling inversion
Comprehension, basic types of, 107
  definition of, 14-16
  elements determining successful,
    107
  skills for reading and listening, 106-
    107
  word knowledge, 38
  see also Reading
  see also Reading-spelling inversion
Configuration, 186-187
  analysis of individual performance,
    187
  boxing, 186
  salient visual cues, 186
Cross-modal integration, 26-27, 30-31
  see also Reading-spelling inversion,
    perceptual theory
Cue training, 18, 27
  basis of, 18-19
  definition of, 15
  time factor, 53
Cursive writing, reversals in, 259-261
  see also Handwriting

D

Deaf children, 12
  good-speller/poor-reader, 12
  visual skills, 14
Decoding, 4, 7, 14-15

I